*Betty Crocker*

# the big book of slow cooker, casseroles & more

WILEY

Wiley Publishing, Inc.

Copyright © 2011 by General Mills, Minneapolis, Minnesota. All rights reserved.

Published by Wiley Publishing, Inc., Hoboken, New Jersey

Published simultaneously in Canada

For general information on our other products and services or for technical support, please contact our Customer Care Department within the United States at (877) 762-2974, outside the United States at (317) 572-3993 or fax (317) 572-4002.

Wiley also publishes its books in a variety of electronic formats. Some content that appears in print may not be available in electronic books. For more information about Wiley products, visit our web site at www.wiley.com.

Library of Congress Cataloging-in-Publication Data

Crocker, Betty.
  Betty Crocker the big book of slow cooker, casseroles & more / Betty Crocker.
    p. cm.
  Includes index.
   ISBN 978-0-470-87840-8 (pbk.); ISBN 9780470943632 (ebk); ISBN
   9780470943649 (ebk.); ISBN 9780470946824 (ebk.)
  1. Electric cooking, Slow. 2. Cookbooks. I. Title. II. Title: the big book of slow cooker.
   TX827.C7295 2010
   641.5'884—dc22
                             2010025451

Manufactured in the United States of America

10 9 8 7 6 5 4 3 2 1

Cover photos: (clockwise) Greek Lentils with Pita Wedges (page 186), Maple-Butternut Squash Soup (page 56), Thai Orange Pork Lo Mein (page 156), Caramel Maple Pears (page 320), Slow-Cooked Korean Beef Stew (page 42), Spicy Chipotle-Orange Squash (page 288)

## General Mills

*Editorial Director:* Jeff Nowak

*Publishing Manager:* Christine Gray

*Editor:* Grace Wells

*Recipe Development and Testing:* Betty Crocker Kitchens

*Photography:* General Mills Photography Studios and Image Library

*Photographer:* Chuck Nields

*Food Stylists:* Amy Peterson, Karen Linden


## Wiley Publishing, Inc.

*Publisher:* Natalie Chapman

*Associate Publisher:* Jessica Goodman

*Executive Editor:* Anne Ficklen

*Editor:* Charleen Barila

*Production Editor:* Abby Saul

*Cover Design:* Suzanne Sunwoo

*Interior Design and Layout:* Holly Wittenberg

*Manufacturing Manager:* Kevin Watt

The Betty Crocker Kitchens seal guarantees success in your kitchen. Every recipe has been tested in America's Most Trusted Kitchens™ to meet our high standards of reliability, easy preparation and great taste.

Find more great ideas at *BettyCrocker*.com

# Dear Friends,

Mmm . . . comfort food. Just the thought of it stirs the soul and conjures up homey images of steaming hot dishes brimming with the finest, freshest ingredients. In this fast-paced age, you might think it's impossible to offer your family down-home dinners. But with *The Big Book of Slow Cooker, Casseroles & More,* you can make it happen!

A hot, bubbling casserole has the incredible ability to warm the body and soothe the spirit. Plus, the one-dish-dinner convenience can't be beat! From Cheesy Chicken Pot Pie and Layered Mexican Casserole to Seven-Layer Rigatoni and Salmon Paella Bake, you'll have a hard time deciding which oven-baked entree to try first.

On particularly busy days when dinner needs to be done as soon as you walk in the door, take a few minutes in the morning to prep a recipe and then flip the switch of your slow cooker. Chicken Stroganoff, Pork Chops with Apple-Cherry Stuffing and Santa Fe Turkey Breast are a few of the from-scratch suppers to welcome you home.

Sometimes 30 minutes is all you can spare to get dinner on the table. Don't panic! "Fast food" can be fast, flavorful *and* from your own kitchen. In fact, Ginger Asian Beef, Super-Quick Salsa Chicken and Sausage with Fettuccine are all ready in just half an hour.

And because dessert is the king of comfort food, we've included tasty treats like Caramel-Apple Crisp, Raspberry Bread Pudding and Triple-Ginger Pound Cake. They're sure to end your dinners on a sweet note.

## Happy Cooking!

*Grace Wells*

**Grace Wells**

# contents

# classic comfort foods at your fingertips

Do you remember when Mom would spend hours in the kitchen creating a fabulous feast? It didn't matter if it was a holiday or a regular weeknight supper. Every bite was brimming with the love and care she put towards turning out a hearty, home-spun dinner for the family.

These days, from-scratch suppers may seem like a thing of the past. But thanks to *The Big Book of Slow Cooker, Casseroles & More*, it's possible to provide your family with the same kind of comfort foods that your mom made for you . . . all with present-day convenience.

You don't need to slave over a hot stove to prepare classics like Beef Roast with Onions and Potatoes or Provençal Pot Roast. These favorites rely on the fix-and-forget ease of a slow cooker. When you need down-home dinner ideas in a hurry, you can't beat 30-minute prep time for meals such as Chicken Cacciatore, Curried Turkey Stir-Fry, Couscous-Stuffed Peppers or Beef and Barley Soup. There are even easy dishes for sides, appetizers and desserts that deliciously round out any dinner.

Simple, speedy and satisfying, all 214 of the recipes in *The Big Book of Slow Cooker, Casseroles & More* go back to the basics of comfort-food cooking but with an updated time twist for today's home cook.

# Secrets to Slow Cooker Success

## BUYING A SLOW COOKER

Head to any department or discount store and you'll find slow cookers for sale in a variety of shapes and sizes. Here are some things to consider before buying.

- The size of the slow cooker should suit your family. A 3- to 4-quart slow cooker works well for a household of two adults. Purchase a 5- to 6-quart if you have a family of four or more or if you like to prepare large cuts of meat. A small slow cooker (about 1⅓ quarts) is ideal to have on hand for keeping hot appetizer dips and spreads at the right temperature.

- If you have to decide between a round or oval slow cooker, go with the oval option. The design is better suited to hold whole chickens and roasts.

- Make sure the slow cooker has a heating element around the side as well as on the bottom. Plus, there should be options for low and high heating.

- Many slow cookers have timer and warming functions. You can set the timer for a certain number of hours, and then it will switch to a warming setting. This will ensure that your slow cooker dinner won't be overcooked if you're late getting home. For food safety reasons, make sure the temperature at the warm setting is at least 140°F.

- Sometimes while cooking, the contents in the slow cooker will bubble. A deep rim (about 1 inch wide) on the top of the slow cooker will prevent any moisture from running down the side of the appliance.

- There's nothing more frustrating than a kitchen appliance that's hard to clean. For a slow cooker, a removable insert is a must.

- Look for a model with a glass lid, which tends to sit more securely on the rim and to be more durable than a plastic or metal lid.

## TIPS FOR USING SLOW COOKERS

Following any of the recipes in this book guarantees you great results and these tips will aid in your success.

- To aid in cleanup, coat the slow cooker insert with nonstick cooking spray before adding the recipe ingredients.
- Slow cookers should be filled between one-half and two-thirds full. If filled any more or less, the cooking time will be affected and the food may be over- or undercooked.
- If you want to prepare a slow cooker recipe the night before, place the mixture in a different covered container and transfer to the slow cooker insert in the morning. If possible, cook on the high setting for one hour and then switch to the low setting to help the contents reach a food-safe temperature.
- Preparing recipes in a slow cooker is different from cooking on the stovetop or in the oven—there's no need to check on the contents. Every time you lift the lid, you add at least 20 minutes to the cooking time and rob the slow cooker of the moisture it's creating to produce fork-tender foods.

- When making large pieces of meat in a slow cooker, you may want to brown them first in a skillet on the stovetop to add a richer flavor.
- Slow cooking can dilute flavors. When possible, use fresh herbs and whole spices, which provide a more intense taste. If using dried herbs and spices, add them during the last hour of cooking.

## SLOW COOKER CONVERSIONS

Want to enjoy a family-favorite soup tonight but would like the convenience of preparing it in the slow cooker? Or do you have a wonderful slow cooker recipe that calls for low heat—and many hours—and you need it faster?

Many of your family-favorite recipes, especially those that call for long simmering or roasting, can be prepared in the slow cooker. Keep in mind that because a slow cooker creates its own moisture, the liquid in the recipe should be reduced by one-third or one-half. Use the table below to convert traditional cooking times to slow cooker times:

| TRADITIONAL OVEN OR STOVETOP TIME | LOW SLOW COOKER SETTING (ABOUT 200°F) |
| --- | --- |
| 15 to 30 minutes | 4 to 6 hours |
| 35 to 45 minutes | 6 to 8 hours |
| 50 minutes to 3 hours | 8 to 10 hours |

# Fabulous Feasts in a Flash: The Beauty of Batch Cooking

The idea of serving your family comforting, made-at-home meals during the week may seem like a dream. But it can be a reality! By taking the time on a weekend, you can prepare a bounty of foods for your family and have them ready to go in the freezer for "fast-food" dinners during the week. Roasted meats, soups, stews, chiles, spaghetti sauces and casseroles lend themselves beautifully to freezing.

## BASICS OF BATCH COOKING

- A few days before cooking, pick out three to four recipes you'd like to prepare. Maybe select one soup, a sauce, one casserole and a roasted meat.
- Create your grocery list and shop two days in advance. Be sure to stock up on freezer bags and containers.
- The day before your cooking session, do prep work like chopping veggies and cooking pasta. Assemble the dry ingredients on the counter.
- Make a plan of what recipe you'll prepare first. For example, get the roast in the oven or the sauce simmering on the stove and then start another recipe.
- Brown several pounds of ground beef along with chopped onions. Divide into 1-pound portions and freeze to use in a variety of casseroles. You can also flavor some of the meat with taco seasoning for a fast, Mexican fiesta.
- Employ your slow cooker to prepare a whole chicken or beef roast. Shred the meat and freeze in 2-cup portions.

## FACTS FOR FREEZING FOODS

- After making a recipe, cool it down quickly for food safety issues. To do this, place the cooking pot in a sink filled with ice-cold water or transfer the hot food to small, shallow containers. Don't let foods stand at room temperature longer than 30 minutes before freezing.
- Label and date containers and packages with a permanent marker to identify their contents.
- Soups and other liquids expand when frozen, so allow a little room in the bag or container for expansion. For all other foods, seal the bag or container with as little air as possible. Consider investing in a vacuum-sealer.
- Don't stack bags or containers during freezing. Spread them out in a single layer until frozen and then stack.
- It's important that your freezer temperature be at a constant 0°F.
- Create a system in your freezer where the item that went in first is the first to be removed.
- Make sure you don't pack your freezer too full. There should be room for air to circulate.
- Thaw foods overnight in the refrigerator. Thoroughly reheat to at least 165°F before serving. Consume within one day.
- It's best to eat prepared frozen foods within two to three months.

# The Frugal Family Table

During tough economic times, families more often find themselves gathered around their home dinner table enjoying tasty meals. You can provide your family nutritious, wholesome dinners without breaking the bank.

## SUPERMARKET SAVVY—AND SAVINGS!

Unfortunately for families, groceries aren't immune from rising prices. Try these tips for trimming your grocery bill.

- **Shop the sales.** Prepare your grocery list—and your weekly menus—based on what's on sale at the store. If an item is on special (like usually pricey meats), stock up on as much as you can and then store in the freezer.

- **Clip coupons.** Start keeping a file of coupons for products you use and organize them according to food category, such as convenience items, frozen foods and canned goods. Most importantly, remember to take the coupons with you to the store!

- **Do double coupon days.** Many supermarkets offer double discounts on manufacturer coupons at least one day a week. Those are the times to shop and save even more.

- **Shop around.** It pays to look over ads from all the grocery stores in your area in search of the best deals. Save money on gas by combining errands.

- **Make a list.** Go to the grocery store with your shopping list in hand and stick to it by avoiding impulse purchases.

- **Play the perimeter.** Substantial foods (like fresh produce, meat, dairy and frozen vegetables) are typically placed around the outline of the store. Stock up on those items first, making a quick calculation along way. If you still have money to spend, then you can head into the aisles to check out the deals.

- **Look at labels.** Compare prices between name-brand and generic items. No-name products are usually less expensive and taste just as good.

- **Buy in bulk.** Supermarkets usually charge a little less for larger packages of an item, like apples, nuts and meat. As long as you eat it, it's a deal.

- **Don't shop when hungry.** You've heard it before, but it's true. When your stomach is grumbling, all foods look fantastic and you may as well throw your list away! Why tempt fate?

## BUDGET COOKING POINTERS

You can also reduce your grocery bill by being more practical in the kitchen.

- It's easy to rely on pre-cut produce from your grocer, but you'll feel the impact at the checkout. When time allows, slice and dice fruits and veggies at home.

- By having an assortment of foods in your freezer, you won't be inclined to make an unscheduled stop at the supermarket or drive-thru.

- Bottled water may be convenient, but it isn't cheap—and it's certainly not "green." Also keep in mind that ready-to-drink beverages (like juice and drink mixes) and foods (such as oatmeal and pudding) are more costly than concentrates or packets that you have to make yourself.

- Tossing uneaten foods in the trash is the same as throwing away money. Keep track of the food that's in your fridge and eat up cooked items before making something new. If your family isn't a fan of leftovers, disguise them in second-time-around sensations.

- Whether you live on many acres or a small lot, there's a way to grow some of your own produce. Check out books on creating gardens in the ground or in containers on the patio.

## CASSEROLE COOKING

Bubbling, steaming, cheesy, pleasing. Nothing says "comfort food" quite like a casserole. These one-dish wonders are great ways to fill up a famished family or crowd.

- Enhance the flavor of your favorite casserole by sprinkling it with a tasty topping before baking. Ideas include buttered bread crumbs, French fried onions, crushed potato chips, shredded cheese or cooked, crumbled bacon.

- If you're preparing a casserole to take to a potluck or to share with a neighbor, use a disposable foil pan. Then there's no need to worry about getting your pan back.

- To keep a casserole hot on the way to a potluck, place two kitchen towels in the bottom of a basket; set the hot casserole dish inside. Tuck additional hand towels around and over the top of the dish. Dishes can stay at room temperature for 2 hours (an hour if the outside temperature is hot).

- Many casseroles can be assembled ahead and chilled until baking. Remove the dish from the refrigerator 20 to 30 minutes before putting it in the oven. You also may need to add a few minutes to the baking time.

- When making a casserole to freeze, line the dish with foil, allowing 3 inches of foil to hang over each side. Assemble the casserole as directed; cover and freeze. When frozen, use the foil to lift the casserole out of the dish. Peel off the foil, wrap the casserole in freezer paper and return it to the freezer. When ready to bake, unwrap and place the casserole back in the pan.

# moment's notice menu planner

From weeknight dinners with family to weekend gatherings with friends, meal planning is a common task for every cook. Take the worry out of what to make by following one of these ready-made menus.

## italian-style supper

Take your taste buds on a delectable trip to the Tuscan countryside!

- ○ **minestrone with italian sausage (p. 38)**
- ● **roasted vegetable lasagna with goat cheese (p. 178)**
- ○ gelato

## asian inspiration

Make any weeknight meal one to remember with a menu infused with flavors of the Orient.

- ● **simple teriyaki steak dinner (p. 80)**
- ○ **spicy stir-fried green beans (p. 266)**
- ○ fortune or almond cookies

Betty Crocker The Big Book of Slow Cooker, Casseroles & More

## easy elegant entertaining

Even time-crunched cooks can host a casual dinner for friends with little fuss.

- ○ **salmon paella bake (p. 162)**
- ○ garlic bread
- ● **bittersweet chocolate cheesecake with white truffle sauce (p. 310)**

## country-style special

A down-home dinner will delight your clan after a long day at school and work.

- ● **barbecued baby back ribs (p. 238)**
- ○ **apricot-glazed carrots (p. 254)**
- ○ **baked corn pudding (p. 261)**
- ○ brownies

## fall favorites

Surprise your loved ones with a meal that will warm both body and soul.

- ● **wild mushroom–stuffed pork roast (p. 226)**
- ○ **roasted autumn vegetables (p. 270)**
- ○ **toffee apple turnover pie (p. 318)**

## game day dinner

Whether you're having the team over for a season-ending celebration or inviting friends to watch the big game on TV, this simple supper is sure to please.

- ○ **southwest chicken nachos (p. 299)**
- ● **three-chile chunky beef chili (p. 40)**
- ○ crusty rolls and a tossed green salad
- ○ **country apple streusel cake (p. 312)**

As the sun sinks lower in the sky and cooler winds begin to blow, steaming bowls of homemade soup, stew or chili are guaranteed to warm you up.

From Grandma's Slow Cooker Chicken Noodle Soup, Minestrone with Italian Sausage and Seafood Bisque to Fire-Roasted Tomato Basil Soup, Cheesy Potato Soup and Chipotle-Pork Chili, these soul-stirring selections will create mouthwatering memories.

# 1

# hearty soups, stews & chilies

¾ lb boneless skinless chicken thighs, cut into 1-inch pieces

2 medium stalks celery, sliced (1 cup)

1 large carrot, chopped (¾ cup)

1 medium onion, chopped (½ cup)

1 can (14.5 oz) diced tomatoes, undrained

1 can (14 oz) chicken broth

1 teaspoon dried thyme leaves

2 cups frozen sweet peas, thawed

1 cup frozen home-style egg noodles (from 12-oz bag)

# grandma's slow cooker chicken noodle soup

**prep time:** 20 minutes    **start to finish:** 7 hours 20 minutes    **4 servings** (1½ cups each)

**1** Spray 10-inch skillet with cooking spray; heat over medium heat. Place chicken in skillet; cook about 5 minutes, stirring frequently, until brown.

**2** In 3- to 4-quart slow cooker, mix chicken and remaining ingredients except peas and noodles.

**3** Cover; cook on Low heat setting 6 hours 30 minutes to 7 hours.

**4** Stir in peas and noodles. Increase heat setting to High; cover and cook about 30 minutes longer or until noodles are tender.

## time-saver

If you have a food processor, chop the fresh vegetables quickly by cutting them into chunks and then pulsing in the food processor. Process each vegetable separately because they don't all require the same processing time.

**1 SERVING:** Calories 330; Total Fat 9g (Saturated Fat 2.5g; Trans Fat 0g); Cholesterol 90mg; Sodium 730mg; Total Carbohydrate 35g (Dietary Fiber 5g); Protein 27g **EXCHANGES:** 1½ Starch, ½ Other Carbohydrate, 1 Vegetable, 3 Lean Meat **CARBOHYDRATE CHOICES:** 2

# creamy herbed chicken stew

**prep time:** 30 minutes    **start to finish:** 7 hours 40 minutes    **12 servings** (1½ cups each)

1 In 5- to 6-quart slow cooker, place carrots, potatoes, onion and celery. Sprinkle with 1 teaspoon of the thyme and the salt and pepper. Top with chicken and broth.

2 Cover; cook on Low heat setting 7 to 8 hours, adding sugar snap peas for last 5 to 10 minutes of cooking.

3 Using slotted spoon, remove chicken and vegetables from cooker; place in serving bowl. Cover to keep warm. Increase heat setting to High. In small bowl, mix whipping cream, flour and remaining 1 teaspoon thyme; stir into liquid in cooker. Cover; cook on High heat setting about 10 minutes longer or until thickened. Pour sauce over chicken and vegetables.

## easy variation

Don't have any baby-cut carrots? You can use regular carrots cut into 2-inch lengths instead. Also, frozen, slightly thawed sugar snap peas can be used instead of the fresh.

## quick prep

4 cups ready-to-eat baby-cut carrots

4 medium Yukon gold potatoes, cut into 1½-inch pieces

1 large onion, chopped (1 cup)

2 medium stalks celery, sliced (1 cup)

2 teaspoons dried thyme leaves

½ teaspoon salt

½ teaspoon pepper

2 lb boneless skinless chicken thighs

3 cups chicken broth

2 cups fresh sugar snap peas

1 cup whipping cream

½ cup all-purpose flour

**1 SERVING:** Calories 270; Total Fat 13g (Saturated Fat 6g; Trans Fat 0g); Cholesterol 70mg; Sodium 430mg; Total Carbohydrate 19g (Dietary Fiber 3g); Protein 20g **EXCHANGES:** 1 Starch, 1 Vegetable, 2 Medium-Fat Meat, ½ Fat **CARBOHYDRATE CHOICES:** 1

**1¼ lb boneless skinless chicken thighs, cubed**

**1 can (14.5 oz) diced tomatoes, undrained**

**1¾ cups chicken broth**

**1 cup water**

**½ teaspoon red pepper sauce**

**½ lb cooked kielbasa, sliced**

**1 cup frozen bell pepper and onion stir-fry (from 1-lb bag), thawed**

**½ cup uncooked instant white rice**

# spicy chicken and sausage soup

**prep time:** 20 minutes    **start to finish:** 8 hours 35 minutes    **6 servings** (1⅓ cups each)

**1** In 3- to 3½-quart slow cooker, mix chicken, tomatoes, broth, water and red pepper sauce.

**2** Cover; cook on Low heat setting 8 to 10 hours.

**3** Stir in kielbasa, stir-fry vegetables and rice. Increase heat setting to High; cover and cook 10 to 15 minutes longer or until rice is tender.

## easy variation

Season this soup to suit your family. For a spicier flavor, increase the amount of red pepper sauce. Also, any cooked spicy sausage can be used—why not try turkey kielbasa or smoked sausage for a change of flavor?

**1 SERVING:** Calories 330; Total Fat 19g (Saturated Fat 6g; Trans Fat 0g); Cholesterol 80mg; Sodium 810mg; Total Carbohydrate 14g (Dietary Fiber 1g); Protein 27g **EXCHANGES:** ½ Starch, 1 Vegetable, 3½ Lean Meat, 1½ Fat **CARBOHYDRATE CHOICES:** 1

¼ cup packed brown sugar

2 teaspoons dried oregano leaves

1 teaspoon salt

¼ teaspoon pepper

3 cloves garlic, finely chopped

⅓ cup white wine or chicken broth

2 tablespoons red wine vinegar

2 dried bay leaves

2½ lb boneless skinless chicken thighs

½ cup pimiento-stuffed green olives

½ cup pitted bite-size prunes (from 12-oz package)

½ cup roasted red bell pepper, coarsely chopped

2 tablespoons capers, drained

1 box (10 oz) couscous

¼ cup chopped fresh parsley

# mediterranean chicken marbella

**prep time:** 30 minutes    **start to finish:** 9 hours 30 minutes    **8 servings**

**1** In large bowl, mix brown sugar, oregano, salt, pepper, garlic, wine, vinegar and bay leaves. Add chicken; turn to coat well. Cover; refrigerate at least 4 hours or overnight to marinate.

**2** Spray 3- to 4-quart slow cooker with cooking spray. In cooker, place chicken and marinade mixture.

**3** Cover; cook on Low heat setting 5 to 6 hours.

**4** Stir olives, prunes, bell pepper and capers into chicken mixture. Cover; cook on Low heat setting about 15 minutes longer or until hot. Remove bay leaves.

**5** Meanwhile, cook couscous as directed on package.

**6** Transfer chicken with juices to large serving bowl or deep platter; sprinkle with parsley. Serve couscous with chicken.

## time-saver

You can skip the marinating step if you're short on time. Just mix all the ingredients from step one right in your slow cooker. The flavor will be a bit milder, but it's still delicious!

**1 SERVING:** Calories 430; Total Fat 13g (Saturated Fat 4g, Trans Fat 0g); Cholesterol 85mg; Sodium 640mg; Total Carbohydrate 43g (Dietary Fiber 3g); Protein 35g **EXCHANGES:** 2 Starch, 1 Other Carbohydrate, 4 Lean Meat **CARBOHYDRATE CHOICES:** 3

## ingredients

6 boneless skinless chicken thighs (about 1 lb)

3 boneless skinless chicken breasts (about ¾ lb)

1 medium onion, chopped (1 cup)

1 can (28 oz) diced tomatoes, undrained

1¾ cups chicken broth

2 tablespoons grated gingerroot

2 tablespoons tomato paste

2 teaspoons curry powder

1 teaspoon crushed red pepper flakes

½ teaspoon salt

1½ lb dark-orange sweet potatoes (3 medium), peeled, cubed (about 4 cups)

1 lb small red potatoes (about 12), cut into eighths (about 2½ cups)

¾ cup peanut butter

# african groundnut stew with chicken

**prep time:** 30 minutes    **start to finish:** 8 hours 30 minutes    **8 servings** (1½ cups each)

**1** Spray 5- to 6-quart slow cooker with cooking spray. In cooker, layer all ingredients, spooning peanut butter in dollops.

**2** Cover; cook on Low heat setting 8 to 10 hours. Before serving, break up chicken.

## easy variation

The combination of chicken thighs and breasts works well in this recipe but you can choose to use all chicken thighs instead.

**1 SERVING:** Calories 420; Total Fat 19g (Saturated Fat 4.5g; Trans Fat 0g); Cholesterol 60mg; Sodium 710mg; Total Carbohydrate 32g (Dietary Fiber 6g); Protein 31g **EXCHANGES:** 1½ Starch, ½ Other Carbohydrate, 1 Vegetable, 3½ Lean Meat, 1 Fat **CARBOHYDRATE CHOICES:** 2

- 1 carton (32 oz) chicken broth
- 1 cup chunky-style salsa
- 2 cups shredded deli rotisserie chicken (from 2- to 2½-lb chicken)
- ¾ cup crushed tortilla chips
- 1 medium avocado, pitted, peeled and chopped
- 1½ cups shredded Monterey Jack cheese (6 oz)
- 2 tablespoons chopped fresh cilantro
- Lime wedges, if desired

# chicken tortilla soup

**prep time:** 35 minutes   **start to finish:** 35 minutes   **6 servings** (1 cup each)

**1** In 3-quart saucepan, heat broth, salsa and chicken to boiling over medium-high heat, stirring occasionally.

**2** Meanwhile, divide crushed chips among 6 serving bowls. Spoon hot soup over chips. Top with avocado, cheese and cilantro. Serve with lime wedges.

## time-saver

When you pick up the rotisserie chicken for this recipe, get an extra one. It's easy to keep shredding the chicken when you can do a bunch all at once. Then freeze what you're not using now for another meal or two.

**1 SERVING:** Calories 330; Total Fat 20g (Saturated Fat 8g; Trans Fat 0g); Cholesterol 65mg; Sodium 1390mg; Total Carbohydrate 13g (Dietary Fiber 2g); Protein 24g **EXCHANGES:** 1 Starch, 3 Lean Meat, 2 Fat **CARBOHYDRATE CHOICES:** 1

- 1 lb lean (at least 80%) ground beef
- 1 medium onion, chopped (½ cup)
- 1 package (1.25 oz) Tex-Mex chili seasoning mix
- 1 can (28 oz) diced tomatoes, undrained
- 1 can (28 oz) crushed tomatoes, undrained
- 1 can (15 oz) spicy chili beans, undrained
- 1 oz unsweetened baking chocolate, coarsely chopped

# chili mole

**prep time:** 15 minutes    **start to finish:** 4 hours 15 minutes    **6 servings** (1½ cups each)

**1** In 10-inch skillet, cook beef and onion over medium heat 8 to 10 minutes, stirring occasionally, until beef is thoroughly cooked; drain.

**2** Spray 4- to 5-quart slow cooker with cooking spray. In cooker, mix beef mixture and remaining ingredients.

**3** Cover; cook on Low heat setting 4 to 6 hours. Stir well before serving.

## healthy twist

Mole (pronounced "MOH-lay") refers to a Mexican sauce that is characterized by the addition of chocolate. You can reduce calories and fat in this version just by using extra-lean ground beef.

**1 SERVING:** Calories 310; Total Fat 12g (Saturated Fat 5g; Trans Fat 0.5g); Cholesterol 45mg; Sodium 1100mg; Total Carbohydrate 29g (Dietary Fiber 8g); Protein 20g **EXCHANGES:** 1½ Starch, 1 Vegetable, 2 Medium-Fat Meat **CARBOHYDRATE CHOICES:** 2

# chicken enchilada chili

prep time: 15 minutes   start to finish: 7 hours 15 minutes   **6 servings** (1⅔ cups each)

**1** Spray 4- to 5-quart slow cooker with cooking spray. In cooker, mix all ingredients except sour cream and cilantro.

**2** Cover; cook on Low heat setting 7 to 8 hours.

**3** Stir mixture to break up chicken. Top each serving with sour cream and cilantro.

- 1¼ lb boneless skinless chicken thighs
- 1 medium onion, chopped (½ cup)
- 1 medium yellow or green bell pepper, chopped (1 cup)
- 2 cans (14.5 oz each) stewed tomatoes with garlic and onion, undrained
- 2 cans (15 to 16 oz each) chili beans in sauce, undrained
- 1 can (10 oz) enchilada sauce
- ⅓ cup sour cream
- 2 tablespoons chopped fresh cilantro

## easy variation

Instead of the flavored stewed tomatoes, use regular stewed tomatoes and add some chopped onion and a dash of garlic powder or finely chopped fresh garlic.

**1 SERVING**: Calories 370; Total Fat 11g (Saturated Fat 4g; Trans Fat 0g); Cholesterol 65mg; Sodium 1690mg; Total Carbohydrate 38g (Dietary Fiber 8g); Protein 30g **EXCHANGES**: 2 Starch, 2 Vegetable, 3 Very Lean Meat, ½ Fat **CARBOHYDRATE CHOICES**: 2½

1¾ lb boneless skinless
chicken thighs

1 medium onion, chopped
(½ cup)

2 medium stalks celery,
sliced (¾ cup)

2 cans (14.5 oz each)
stewed tomatoes
with garlic and onion,
undrained

2 cans (15 to 16 oz each)
pinto beans, undrained

1 can (10 oz) enchilada
sauce

2 teaspoons chili powder

1 teaspoon ground cumin

⅓ cup sour cream

2 tablespoons chopped
fresh cilantro, if desired

Scoop-shaped corn chips,
if desired

# mexican chicken chili

**prep time:** 25 minutes    **start to finish:** 7 hours 25 minutes    **6 servings** (1⅔ cups each)

**1** Spray 4- to 5-quart slow cooker with cooking spray. In cooker, mix all ingredients except sour cream, cilantro and corn chips.

**2** Cover; cook on Low heat setting 7 to 8 hours.

**3** Stir mixture to break up chicken. Top each serving with sour cream and cilantro. Serve with corn chips.

## easy variation

In place of the stewed tomatoes with garlic and onion, use regular stewed tomatoes and add a teaspoon of finely chopped garlic.

**1 SERVING:** Calories 410; Total Fat 11g (Saturated Fat 4g; Trans Fat 0g); Cholesterol 60mg; Sodium 860mg; Total Carbohydrate 47g (Dietary Fiber 13g); Protein 31g **EXCHANGES:** 2 Starch, 1 Other Carbohydrate, 3½ Lean Meat **CARBOHYDRATE CHOICES:** 3

# enchilada chili

prep time: 35 minutes    start to finish: 35 minutes    **4 servings** (1½ cups each)

**1** In 4-quart saucepan, cook beef and onion over medium-high heat 5 to 7 minutes, stirring frequently, until beef is brown; drain.

**2** Stir in tomatoes, enchilada sauce and corn. Heat to boiling. Reduce heat to medium-low; cook 10 minutes, stirring occasionally.

**3** Stir in beans. Cook 5 to 8 minutes, stirring occasionally, until thoroughly heated. Sprinkle individual servings with corn chips.

1 lb lean (at least 80%) ground beef

1 medium onion, chopped (½ cup)

1 can (14.5 oz) diced tomatoes with green chiles, undrained

1 can (10 oz) enchilada sauce

1½ cups frozen corn

1 can (15 to 16 oz) spicy chili beans in sauce, undrained

1 cup chili cheese-flavored corn chips, if desired

## healthy twist

Save a little on calories and fat by substituting lean ground turkey for the ground beef in this recipe. Then top servings with chopped fresh tomato and cilantro instead of the chips.

**1 SERVING:** Calories 380; Total Fat 15g (Saturated Fat 5g; Trans Fat 1g); Cholesterol 70mg; Sodium 1440mg; Total Carbohydrate 38g (Dietary Fiber 8g); Protein 29g **EXCHANGES:** 2½ Starch, 3 Lean Meat, 1 Fat **CARBOHYDRATE CHOICES:** 2

10 oz uncooked spaghetti

1 tablespoon vegetable oil

1 lb ground turkey breast

1 medium onion, chopped (½ cup)

1 clove garlic, finely chopped

1 jar (26 oz) chunky vegetable-style tomato pasta sauce

1 can (15 oz) dark red kidney beans, drained, rinsed

2 tablespoons chili powder

# cincinnati chili

**prep time:** 30 minutes   **start to finish:** 30 minutes   **5 servings** (2 cups each)

**1** Cook and drain spaghetti as directed on package.

**2** Meanwhile, in 10-inch skillet, heat oil over medium heat. Add turkey, onion and garlic; cook 5 to 6 minutes, stirring occasionally, until turkey is no longer pink.

**3** Stir in pasta sauce, beans and chili powder. Reduce heat to low; simmer uncovered 10 minutes, stirring occasionally. Serve sauce over spaghetti.

## healthy twist

Have you ever tried one of the new whole grain pastas? There are many varieties available from partly whole grain to completely whole grain. Why not experiment with one when you make this recipe?

**1 SERVING:** Calories 625; Total Fat 15g (Saturated Fat 3g; Trans Fat 0g); Cholesterol 60mg; Sodium 1020mg; Total Carbohydrate 96g (Dietary Fiber 11g); Protein 37g **EXCHANGES:** 6 Starch, 1 Vegetable **CARBOHYDRATE CHOICES:** 6½

# red and white turkey chili

**prep time:** 30 minutes    **start to finish:** 9 hours    **6 servings** (1½ cups each)

**1** In 4- to 5-quart slow cooker, mix all ingredients except turkey, corn, flour, water and lime. Place turkey on bean mixture.

**2** Cover; cook on Low heat setting 8 to 10 hours.

**3** Remove turkey from cooker; place on cutting board. Remove meat from bones; discard bones. Cut turkey into bite-size pieces. Add turkey and corn to cooker. In small bowl, mix flour and water; stir into turkey mixture. Increase heat setting to High; cover and cook 20 to 30 minutes longer or until thoroughly heated and slightly thickened.

## healthy twist

Here's a great lower fat option for dinner. Keep the meal on the right track by topping the chili with chopped fresh tomatoes, green onions and bell peppers. Then serve the chili with your favorite fresh fruit.

**quick prep**

- 1 medium onion, chopped (½ cup)
- 1 clove garlic, finely chopped
- 2 teaspoons ground cumin
- ⅛ teaspoon ground red pepper (cayenne)
- 1 can (15.5 oz) great northern beans, drained
- 1 can (15 oz) dark red kidney beans, drained
- 2 cans (4.5 oz each) chopped green chiles, undrained
- 3½ cups chicken broth
- 2 lb turkey thighs, skin removed
- 1 cup frozen white shoepeg corn, thawed
- 2 tablespoons all-purpose flour
- ¼ cup water
- 1 lime, cut into wedges, if desired

**1 SERVING:** Calories 370; Total Fat 5g (Saturated Fat 1.5g; Trans Fat 0g); Cholesterol 95mg; Sodium 970mg; Total Carbohydrate 40g (Dietary Fiber 9g); Protein 40g **EXCHANGES:** 2½ Starch, 4½ Very Lean Meat, ½ Fat **CARBOHYDRATE CHOICES:** 2½

1½ lb beef stew meat

3 medium carrots, sliced
(1½ cups)

1 large onion, chopped
(1 cup)

2 cloves garlic, finely
chopped

⅔ cup frozen corn, thawed

⅔ cup uncooked medium
pearl barley

½ teaspoon salt

½ teaspoon pepper

1 can (14.5 oz) diced
tomatoes, undrained

5¼ cups beef broth

1 cup frozen sweet peas,
thawed

# beef and barley soup

**prep time:** 20 minutes   **start to finish:** 9 hours 50 minutes   **8 servings** (about 1½ cups each)

**1** Spray 5- to 6-quart slow cooker with cooking spray. Cut beef into bite-size pieces, if desired. In cooker, mix beef and remaining ingredients except peas.

**2** Cover; cook on Low heat setting 9 to 10 hours.

**3** Stir in peas. Increase heat setting to High; cover and cook 20 to 30 minutes longer or until peas are tender.

## healthy twist

There's lots of healthful goodness in this hearty soup. Keep it low in fat by selecting lean beef at the meat counter. Then remove any visible fat before making the soup.

**1 SERVING:** Calories 280; Total Fat 11g (Saturated Fat 4g; Trans Fat 0g); Cholesterol 50mg; Sodium 930mg; Total Carbohydrate 25g (Dietary Fiber 5g); Protein 21g **EXCHANGES:** 1 Starch, ½ Other Carbohydrate, 1 Vegetable, 2 Medium-Fat Meat **CARBOHYDRATE CHOICES:** 1½

1 bag (16 oz) frozen cooked Italian meatballs, thawed

1¾ cups beef broth

1 cup water

1 can (14.5 oz) diced tomatoes with basil, garlic and oregano, undrained

1 can (19 oz) cannellini beans, drained

⅓ cup shredded Parmesan cheese (1⅓ oz)

# italian meatball soup

**prep time:** 10 minutes    **start to finish:** 8 hours 10 minutes    **5 servings** (1½ cups each)

**1** In 3- to 4-quart slow cooker, mix all ingredients except cheese.

**2** Cover; cook on Low heat setting 8 to 10 hours. Sprinkle individual servings with cheese.

## easy variation

Cannellini beans are also called white kidney beans. If you prefer, red kidney beans or pinto beans could be used instead.

**1 SERVING:** Calories 410; Total Fat 15g (Saturated Fat 6g; Trans Fat 1g); Cholesterol 100mg; Sodium 1540mg; Total Carbohydrate 38g (Dietary Fiber 6g); Protein 31g **EXCHANGES:** 2 Starch, ½ Other Carbohydrate, 3½ Lean Meat, ½ Fat **CARBOHYDRATE CHOICES:** 2½

# hungarian beef stew

**prep time:** 20 minutes    **start to finish:** 7 hours 35 minutes    **6 servings** (1⅓ cups each)

**1** Spray 3- to 4-quart slow cooker with cooking spray. In cooker, toss beef, potatoes, onions, flour, paprika, peppered seasoned salt and caraway seed until well mixed. Stir in broth.

**2** Cover; cook on Low heat setting 7 to 8 hours.

**3** Stir in peas and sour cream. Cover; cook on Low heat setting about 15 minutes longer or until peas are tender.

### easy variation

If you don't have the frozen onions on hand, you can use ½ cup chopped onion instead.

2 lb beef stew meat

6 unpeeled small red potatoes, cut into ¾-inch pieces (3 cups)

1 cup frozen small whole onions (from 1-lb bag), thawed

¼ cup all-purpose flour

1 tablespoon paprika

½ teaspoon peppered seasoned salt

¼ teaspoon caraway seed

1 can (14 oz) beef broth

1½ cups frozen sweet peas, thawed

½ cup sour cream

**1 SERVING:** Calories 460; Total Fat 22g (Saturated Fat 9g; Trans Fat 1g); Cholesterol 105mg; Sodium 530mg; Total Carbohydrate 31g (Dietary Fiber 5g); Protein 37g **EXCHANGES:** 2 Starch, 4 Medium-Fat Meat **CARBOHYDRATE CHOICES:** 2

# creamy beef, mushroom and noodle soup

- 2 tablespoons butter or margarine
- 1 medium onion, coarsely chopped (½ cup)
- 2 teaspoons finely chopped garlic
- 1 package (8 oz) sliced fresh mushrooms (3 cups)
- 1½ lb boneless beef top sirloin steak, cut into 2 × ¾ × ¼-inch pieces
- 6 cups beef broth
- ½ cup dry sherry or beef broth
- ¼ cup ketchup
- ¾ teaspoon salt
- ⅛ teaspoon pepper
- 2 cups uncooked medium egg noodles
- 1 container (8 oz) sour cream

**prep time:** 1 hour    **start to finish:** 1 hour    **7 servings** (1½ cups each)

**1** In 5- to 6-quart Dutch oven, melt butter over medium-high heat. Add onion, garlic and mushrooms; cook 5 to 6 minutes, stirring frequently, until mushrooms are softened.

**2** Stir in beef. Cook 5 to 6 minutes, stirring frequently, until beef is no longer pink. Stir in remaining ingredients except noodles and sour cream. Heat to boiling. Reduce heat to medium-low; cover and cook 10 minutes, stirring occasionally.

**3** Stir in noodles. Cover; cook 5 to 7 minutes, stirring occasionally, until noodles are tender. Stir in sour cream. Cook 3 to 5 minutes, stirring frequently, until well blended.

## healthy twist

Be sure to trim the visible fat from the beef. Then, if you want to reduce the fat a bit, you can choose to use low-fat or fat-free sour cream.

**1 SERVING:** Calories 290; Total Fat 14g (Saturated Fat 7g; Trans Fat 0g); Cholesterol 90mg; Sodium 1100mg; Total Carbohydrate 15g (Dietary Fiber 1g); Protein 26g **EXCHANGES:** 1 Starch **CARBOHYDRATE CHOICES:** 1

# minestrone with italian sausage

- 1 tablespoon olive or vegetable oil
- 1 lb bulk sweet Italian pork sausage
- 1 medium onion, chopped (½ cup)
- 2 medium carrots, coarsely chopped (1 cup)
- 2 teaspoons dried basil leaves
- 2 teaspoons finely chopped garlic
- 3 cans (14 oz each) beef broth
- 2 cups diced tomatoes (from 28-oz can), undrained
- 1 can (15 to 16 oz) great northern beans, drained, rinsed
- 1 cup uncooked small elbow macaroni (3½ oz)
- 1 medium zucchini, cut lengthwise in half, then cut into ¼-inch slices (1 cup)
- 1 cup frozen cut green beans

**prep time:** 45 minutes    **start to finish:** 45 minutes    **7 servings** (1½ cups each)

**1** In 5-quart Dutch oven, heat oil over medium-high heat. Add sausage, onion, carrots, basil and garlic; cook 5 to 7 minutes, stirring frequently, until sausage is no longer pink. Drain.

**2** Stir in broth, tomatoes and great northern beans. Heat to boiling. Reduce heat to medium-low; cover and cook 7 to 8 minutes, stirring occasionally.

**3** Stir in macaroni, zucchini and frozen green beans. Increase heat to medium-high; heat to boiling. Cook 5 to 6 minutes, stirring occasionally, until vegetables are hot and macaroni is tender.

## easy variation

It's easy to make this soup meatless. Just substitute an additional can of great northern beans or other favorite canned beans for the sausage and use vegetable broth instead of beef broth.

**1 SERVING:** Calories 380; Total Fat 16g (Saturated Fat 5g; Trans Fat 0g); Cholesterol 25mg; Sodium 1400mg; Total Carbohydrate 38g (Dietary Fiber 6g); Protein 20g **EXCHANGES:** 2 Starch, 1 Vegetable, 1½ Medium-Fat Meat, 1½ Fat **CARBOHYDRATE CHOICES:** 2½

# chunky beef ragu

**prep time:** 35 minutes    **start to finish:** 8 hours 35 minutes    **6 servings** (1⅓ cups each)

**1** In 10-inch nonstick skillet, cook prosciutto over medium-high heat about 5 minutes, stirring frequently, until crisp. Drain on paper towels.

**2** Spray 5- to 6-quart slow cooker with cooking spray. In cooker, mix all ingredients.

**3** Cover; cook on Low heat setting 8 to 9 hours (or on High heat setting 4 hours to 4 hours 30 minutes).

3 oz thinly sliced prosciutto or pancetta, chopped

1½ lb beef stew meat, cut into 1-inch pieces

2 jars (7 oz each) sun-dried tomatoes in oil, drained, chopped (1¼ cups)

2 medium carrots, sliced (1 cup)

1 cup chopped celery

1 medium onion, chopped (½ cup)

2 cloves garlic, finely chopped

1 can (14.5 oz) diced tomatoes, undrained

½ cup dry red wine

1½ teaspoons dried basil leaves

1½ teaspoons dried oregano leaves

½ teaspoon salt

¼ teaspoon crushed red pepper flakes

**1 SERVING:** Calories 300; Total Fat 16g (Saturated Fat 6g; Trans Fat 0.5g); Cholesterol 70mg; Sodium 640mg; Total Carbohydrate 13g (Dietary Fiber 3g); Protein 26g **EXCHANGES:** ½ Other Carbohydrate, 1 Vegetable, 3½ Lean Meat, 1 Fat **CARBOHYDRATE CHOICES:** 1

- 2 lb boneless beef chuck roast, cut into 1-inch cubes
- 1 large onion, chopped (1 cup)
- 1 to 2 chipotle chiles in adobo sauce (from 7-oz can), chopped
- 1 ancho chile, cut into small pieces
- 1 tablespoon chili powder
- 1 teaspoon ground cumin
- ½ teaspoon salt
- ½ teaspoon garlic powder
- 2 cans (14.5 oz each) diced tomatoes with green chiles, undrained
- 1 can (15 oz) black beans, drained, rinsed

# three-chile chunky beef chili

**prep time:** 20 minutes **start to finish:** 8 hours 20 minutes **6 servings** (1⅓ cups each)

**1** In 3- to 4-quart slow cooker, mix all ingredients.

**2** Cover; cook on Low heat setting 8 to 10 hours (or on High setting 4 to 5 hours).

## time-saver

Spray the cooker with cooking spray before adding ingredients for easy cleanup.

**1 SERVING:** Calories 420; Total Fat 17g (Saturated Fat 6g; Trans Fat 0.5g); Cholesterol 80mg; Sodium 1010mg; Total Carbohydrate 30g (Dietary Fiber 11g); Protein 37g **EXCHANGES:** 1½ Starch, ½ Other Carbohydrate, ½ Vegetable, 4½ Lean Meat, ½ Fat **CARBOHYDRATE CHOICES:** 2

**Betty Crocker The Big Book of Slow Cooker, Casseroles & More**

- 2 lb beef stew meat, cut into 1-inch pieces
- 1 bag (16 oz) ready-to-eat baby-cut carrots
- 6 green onions, cut into 1-inch pieces
- 2 cloves garlic, chopped
- ½ cup tomato juice
- ¼ cup soy sauce
- 3 tablespoons sugar
- 2 tablespoons sesame or vegetable oil
- ¼ teaspoon pepper
- 2 teaspoons cornstarch
- 4 teaspoons cold water
- 3 cups hot cooked rice

# slow-cooked korean beef stew

**prep time:** 5 minutes    **start to finish:** 9 hours 25 minutes    **6 servings** (1 cup each)

**1** In 3- to 4-quart slow cooker, mix beef, carrots, green onions, garlic, tomato juice, soy sauce, sugar, oil and pepper.

**2** Cover; cook on Low heat setting 9 to 11 hours (or on High setting 4 hours 30 minutes to 5 hours 30 minutes).

**3** In small bowl, mix cornstarch and cold water until blended; stir into beef mixture. If needed, increase heat setting to High; cover and cook about 20 minutes longer or until mixture is slightly thickened. Serve with rice.

## healthy twist

Serve with brown rice instead of white rice for additional nutrients and fiber. Sprinkle servings with chopped green onions.

**1 SERVING:** Calories 470; Total Fat 21g (Saturated Fat 7g; Trans Fat 0.5g); Cholesterol 80mg; Sodium 1070mg; Total Carbohydrate 39g (Dietary Fiber 3g); Protein 31g **EXCHANGES:** 1½ Starch, 1 Other Carbohydrate, ½ Vegetable, 3½ Medium-Fat Meat, ½ Fat **CARBOHYDRATE CHOICES:** 2½

- 1 tablespoon olive or vegetable oil
- 2 medium onions, cut in half, then cut into ¼-inch slices and slices separated
- 2 teaspoons finely chopped garlic
- 2 lb boneless pork loin roast, cut into 1-inch pieces
- 1 tablespoon ground cumin
- 1 teaspoon salt
- ⅛ teaspoon pepper
- 1 chipotle chile in adobo sauce, finely chopped, plus 1 teaspoon adobo sauce (from 7- to 11-oz can)
- 3 cans (14.5 oz each) diced tomatoes with green chiles, undrained

# chipotle-pork chili

**prep time:** 30 minutes    **start to finish:** 1 hour 10 minutes    **5 servings** (1½ cups each)

**1** In 4½- to 5-quart Dutch oven, heat oil over medium-high heat. Add onions and garlic; cook 4 to 5 minutes, stirring occasionally, until onions are softened.

**2** Stir in pork, cumin, salt and pepper. Cook 6 to 8 minutes, stirring frequently, until pork is lightly browned.

**3** Stir in chipotle chile, adobo sauce and tomatoes. Heat to boiling. Reduce heat to medium-low; cover and cook 35 to 40 minutes, stirring occasionally, until pork is no longer pink in center.

## easy variation

An easy substitute for the 3 cans of tomatoes with green chiles is to use 3 cans of regular diced tomatoes and 1 can of diced green chiles.

**1 SERVING:** Calories 400; Total Fat 18g (Saturated Fat 5g; Trans Fat 0g); Cholesterol 115mg; Sodium 1300mg; Total Carbohydrate 16g (Dietary Fiber 4g); Protein 43g **EXCHANGES:** 1 Starch, 6 Lean Meat **CARBOHYDRATE CHOICES:** 1

# golden pea and ham soup

**prep time:** 10 minutes    **start to finish:** 8 hours 40 minutes    **5 servings** (1½ cups each)

**1** In 3- to 4-quart slow cooker, mix all ingredients.

**2** Cover; cook on Low heat setting 8 to 10 hours.

**3** Increase heat setting to High; stir well. Cover; cook 30 minutes longer.

## easy variation

You can substitute 1 cup thinly sliced carrots if you don't have julienne-cut carrots.

**1 SERVING:** Calories 390; Total Fat 6g (Saturated Fat 2g; Trans Fat 0g); Cholesterol 25mg; Sodium 1410mg; Total Carbohydrate 51g (Dietary Fiber 25g); Protein 33g **EXCHANGES:** 3½ Starch, 3 Very Lean Meat, ½ Fat **CARBOHYDRATE CHOICES:** 3½

---

## quick prep

1 bag (1 lb) yellow split peas, rinsed, sorted

1 cup julienne-cut carrots (from 10-oz bag)

½ lb cooked ham, chopped (1⅓ cups)

½ teaspoon dried thyme leaves

½ teaspoon dried marjoram leaves

¼ teaspoon pepper

2 cans (14 oz each) chicken broth

1½ cups water

2 cups diced cooked ham

1 cup julienne-cut carrots (from 10-oz bag)

¾ cup uncooked wild rice

1 medium onion, chopped (½ cup)

1¾ cups chicken broth

1 can (10¾ oz) reduced-sodium cream of celery soup

¼ teaspoon pepper

3 cups water

1 cup half-and-half

¼ cup sliced almonds

2 tablespoons dry sherry, if desired

¼ cup chopped fresh parsley

# ham and wild rice soup

**prep time:** 15 minutes    **start to finish:** 7 hours 30 minutes    **6 servings** (1½ cups each)

**1** In 3- to 4-quart slow cooker, mix all ingredients except half-and-half, almonds, sherry and parsley.

**2** Cover; cook on Low heat setting 7 to 8 hours.

**3** Stir in remaining ingredients. Increase heat setting to High; cover and cook 10 to 15 minutes longer or until hot.

## healthy twist

You can reduce the fat in this recipe by using whole milk instead of the half-and-half.

**1 SERVING:** Calories 290; Total Fat 12g (Saturated Fat 5g; Trans Fat 0g); Cholesterol 40mg; Sodium 1190mg; Total Carbohydrate 28g (Dietary Fiber 3g); Protein 17g **EXCHANGES:** 1½ Starch, ½ Other Carbohydrate, 2 Lean Meat, 1 Fat **CARBOHYDRATE CHOICES:** 2

## Ingredients

⅓ cup butter or margarine

⅓ cup all-purpose flour

2 cans (14 oz each) chicken broth

4 cups (1 qt) half-and-half

½ cup dry white wine or water

½ cup chopped drained roasted red bell peppers (from 7-oz jar)

12 oz cod fillet, cut into 1-inch pieces

12 oz uncooked deveined peeled medium shrimp, thawed if frozen, tail shells removed

½ cup basil pesto

¼ teaspoon salt

⅛ teaspoon freshly ground pepper

# seafood bisque

**prep time:** 25 minutes   **start to finish:** 25 minutes   **8 servings**

**1** In 4-quart Dutch oven, melt butter over medium-high heat. Stir in flour. Gradually stir in broth, half-and-half and wine. Stir in bell peppers and cod. Heat to boiling, stirring occasionally.

**2** Stir in shrimp. Simmer uncovered 2 to 3 minutes or until shrimp are pink. Stir in pesto, salt and pepper.

## easy variation

Cooked shrimp works great in this recipe, too. Just add the shrimp to the bisque and simmer until heated through.

**1 SERVING:** Calories 420; Total Fat 31g (Saturated Fat 15g; Trans Fat 1g); Cholesterol 150mg; Sodium 860mg; Total Carbohydrate 11g (Dietary Fiber 0g); Protein 22g **EXCHANGES:** ½ Starch, 3 Very Lean Meat, 6 Fat **CARBOHYDRATE CHOICES:** 1

# fire-roasted tomato basil soup

prep time: 30 minutes   start to finish: 30 minutes   **5 servings** (1½ cups each)

**1** In 4-quart saucepan, heat oil over medium heat. Add onion and carrots; cook 2 to 3 minutes, stirring occasionally, until softened.

**2** Stir in tomatoes, broth, water and pepper sauce. Heat to boiling. Stir in pasta. Return to boiling. Reduce heat to medium; cook uncovered 10 to 15 minutes, stirring occasionally, until pasta and carrots are tender.

**3** Stir in basil. Cook about 1 minute, stirring constantly.

## easy variation

Use any very small pasta you like in place of the orzo. Then serve the soup with your favorite grilled cheese sandwiches.

**1 tablespoon olive or vegetable oil**

**1 large onion, chopped (1 cup)**

**2 medium carrots, chopped (1 cup)**

**2 cans (14.5 oz each) fire-roasted diced tomatoes, undrained**

**2 cans (14 oz each) chicken broth**

**1 cup water**

**1 teaspoon red pepper sauce**

**½ cup uncooked orzo pasta (3 oz)**

**1 teaspoon dried basil leaves**

**1 SERVING**: Calories 160; Total Fat 4g (Saturated Fat 0.5g; Trans Fat 0g); Cholesterol 0mg; Sodium 990mg; Total Carbohydrate 23g (Dietary Fiber 4g); Protein 7g **EXCHANGES**: 1½ Starch, 1 Vegetable, ½ Fat **CARBOHYDRATE CHOICES**: 1½

1 bag (32 oz) frozen southern-style diced hash brown potatoes, thawed

½ cup frozen chopped onion (from 12-oz bag), thawed

1 medium stalk celery, diced (½ cup)

3½ cups chicken broth

1 cup water

3 tablespoons all-purpose flour

1 cup milk

1 bag (8 oz) shredded American-Cheddar cheese blend (2 cups)

¼ cup real bacon pieces (from 2.8-oz package)

4 medium green onions, sliced (¼ cup)

# cheesy potato soup

**prep time:** 15 minutes   **start to finish:** 6 hours 45 minutes   **6 servings** (1½ cups each)

**1** Spray 3- to 4-quart slow cooker with cooking spray. In cooker, mix potatoes, onion, celery, broth and water.

**2** Cover; cook on Low heat setting 6 to 8 hours.

**3** In small bowl, mix flour and milk; stir into potato mixture. Increase heat setting to High; cover and cook 20 to 30 minutes longer or until mixture thickens. Stir in cheese until melted. Garnish servings of soup with bacon and green onions. Sprinkle with pepper.

## easy variation

Make this an easy meatless choice—just omit the bacon pieces and use vegetable broth instead of the chicken broth.

**1 SERVING:** Calories 410; Total Fat 15g (Saturated Fat 9g; Trans Fat 0g); Cholesterol 45mg; Sodium 1210mg; Total Carbohydrate 50g (Dietary Fiber 5g); Protein 19g **EXCHANGES:** 3½ Starch, 1 High-Fat Meat, 1 Fat **CARBOHYDRATE CHOICES:** 3

**2 large dark-orange sweet potatoes (1½ lb), peeled, cut into ½-inch cubes (about 5 cups)**

**3 cups chopped onions (3 large)**

**3 cloves garlic, finely chopped**

**1 tablespoon ground cumin**

**2 tablespoons chili powder**

**1 can (28 oz) diced tomatoes, undrained**

**1 can (16 oz) refried black beans**

**1 can (15 oz) black beans, drained, rinsed**

**2 cups chicken broth**

**2 teaspoons red wine vinegar**

**Shredded cheese**

**Sour cream**

# black bean–
# sweet potato chili

**prep time:** 35 minutes    **start to finish:** 7 hours 35 minutes    **8 servings** (1½ cups each)

**1** Spray 5- to 6-quart slow cooker with cooking spray. In cooker, mix sweet potatoes, onions, garlic, cumin, chili powder, tomatoes, refried beans, black beans and broth.

**2** Cover; cook on Low heat setting 7 to 8 hours (or on High heat setting 3 hours 30 minutes to 4 hours).

**3** Before serving, stir in vinegar. Serve chili topped with cheese and sour cream.

## time-saver

Make quick work of chopping the garlic and onions by enlisting the help of your food processor. Start by chopping the garlic first, then add the onions and continue chopping. Depending on the size of your food processor, you may need to do the onions in batches.

**1 SERVING:** Calories 260; Total Fat 2g (Saturated Fat 0.5g, Trans Fat 0g); Cholesterol 0mg; Sodium 900mg; Total Carbohydrate 48g (Dietary Fiber 13g); Protein 12g **EXCHANGES:** 2½ Other Carbohydrate, 2 Vegetable, 1 Lean Meat **CARBOHYDRATE CHOICES:** 3

6 mini pattypan squash, cut into quarters, or 1 yellow summer squash, sliced

4 medium tomatoes, chopped (3 cups)

1 orange bell pepper, cut into bite-size strips

1 medium onion, sliced

2 cloves garlic, finely chopped

¼ cup chopped fresh parsley

1 teaspoon salt

¼ teaspoon pepper

4 cans (14 oz each) chicken broth

1 zucchini, cut lengthwise in half, then cut crosswise into slices

1 baby eggplant, cut lengthwise into quarters, then cut crosswise into slices

Chopped fresh basil leaves, if desired

# summer vegetable ratatouille soup

**prep time:** 25 minutes    **start to finish:** 6 hours 55 minutes    **9 servings** (1½ cups each)

**1** In 5- to 6-quart slow cooker, mix squash, tomatoes, bell pepper, onion, garlic, parsley, salt, pepper and broth.

**2** Cover; cook on Low heat setting 6 to 8 hours (or on High heat setting 3 to 4 hours).

**3** Stir zucchini and eggplant into squash mixture. If needed, increase heat setting to High; cover and cook about 30 minutes longer or until zucchini and eggplant are tender. Serve topped with basil.

**1 SERVING:** Calories 80; Total Fat 1.5g (Saturated Fat 0g; Trans Fat 0g); Cholesterol 0mg; Sodium 1020mg; Total Carbohydrate 11g (Dietary Fiber 4g); Protein 6g **EXCHANGES:** 2 Vegetable, ½ Fat **CARBOHYDRATE CHOICES:** 1

- 8 cups cubed peeled seeded butternut squash (about 3 lb)
- 1 large apple, peeled, chopped
- 1 large onion, cut into 1-inch pieces
- 1 teaspoon ground cinnamon
- ½ teaspoon ground nutmeg
- ½ teaspoon salt
- ⅛ teaspoon pepper
- 1 carton (32 oz) chicken broth (4 cups)
- ½ cup half-and-half or milk
- ½ cup real maple syrup
- ¾ cup plain yogurt or sour cream
- 2 tablespoons chopped fresh chives

# maple–butternut squash soup

**prep time:** 25 minutes **start to finish:** 7 hours 40 minutes **8 servings** (1⅓ cups each)

**1** Spray 4- to 5-quart slow cooker with cooking spray. In cooker, mix squash, apple, onion, cinnamon, nutmeg, salt and pepper. Pour broth over vegetable mixture.

**2** Cover; cook on Low heat setting 7 to 8 hours (or on High heat setting 3 hours 30 minutes to 4 hours).

**3** Pour about 3 cups of the soup mixture into blender. Cover; blend until smooth. Pour into 8-cup measuring cup or heat-proof pitcher. Blend remaining soup mixture in 2 more batches; pour into measuring cup. Pour pureed soup back into slow cooker. Stir in half-and-half and syrup.

**4** If needed, increase heat setting to High; cover and cook about 15 minutes longer or until hot. Top each serving with yogurt; sprinkle with chives.

## time-saver

Sometimes in the fall, if you're there at the right time, you can find butternut squash already peeled and cut up at your local supermarket. If you're cutting it yourself, a good swivel-headed vegetable peeler is the tool of choice to make quick work of peeling the squash.

**1 SERVING:** Calories 190; Total Fat 3g (Saturated Fat 1.5g, Trans Fat 0g); Cholesterol 5mg; Sodium 660mg; Total Carbohydrate 34g (Dietary Fiber 2g); Protein 5g **EXCHANGES:** ½ Starch, 1½ Other Carbohydrate, 1 Vegetable, ½ Fat **CARBOHYDRATE CHOICES:** 2

A hard day's got you wishing for something fast, yet warm and comforting for dinner? In about 30 minutes, you can soothe your soul with these quick and easy skillet creations.

Ginger Asian Beef, Skillet Chicken Nachos or Shrimp Alfredo Primavera are a snap to put together and are much more satisfying than a frozen meal or take-out.

s & stir-fries sizzli

**2**

# sizzling skillets & stir-fries

- 1 tablespoon canola or vegetable oil
- 2 cloves garlic, finely chopped
- 2 cups marinara sauce
- 2 cups water
- 1 package (9 oz) refrigerated fettuccine
- 1 bag (12 oz) frozen cut green beans, thawed
- 2 cups cubed cooked chicken
- ½ cup grated Parmesan cheese

# parmesan chicken

**prep time:** 20 minutes  **start to finish:** 25 minutes  **4 servings**

**1** In 12-inch skillet, heat oil over medium heat. Add garlic; cook about 30 seconds, stirring occasionally, until softened. Stir in marinara sauce and water. Cover; heat to boiling over medium heat.

**2** Add fettuccine and green beans; stir to separate fettuccine. Return to boiling. Cover; boil 3 to 5 minutes or until beans are tender.

**3** Stir in chicken. Cook 3 to 4 minutes, stirring occasionally until chicken is heated.

**4** Remove from heat. Sprinkle with cheese. Cover; let stand 2 minutes to melt cheese.

## time-saver

To quickly thaw the green beans, place in a colander or strainer. Rinse with cool water until thawed. Drain well.

**1 SERVING:** Calories 590; Total Fat 18g (Saturated Fat 4.5g; Trans Fat 0g); Cholesterol 115mg; Sodium 1090mg; Total Carbohydrate 71g (Dietary Fiber 6g); Protein 36g **EXCHANGES:** 3½ Starch, 2½ Vegetable, 3 Very Lean Meat, 2½ Fat **CARBOHYDRATE CHOICES:** 5

## Ingredients

⅓ cup Italian dressing

4 boneless skinless chicken breasts (about 1¼ lb)

¼ cup water

2 medium carrots, sliced (1 cup)

2 medium stalks celery, sliced (1 cup)

¼ cup coarsely chopped drained sun-dried tomatoes in oil

1 teaspoon dried rosemary leaves, crushed

1 can (19 oz) cannellini beans, drained, rinsed

# tuscan rosemary chicken and white beans

**prep time:** 30 minutes    **start to finish:** 30 minutes    **4 servings**

**1** In 12-inch skillet, heat dressing over medium-high heat. Add chicken; cook 2 to 3 minutes on each side or until lightly browned.

**2** Reduce heat to medium-low. Add water, carrots, celery, tomatoes and rosemary to skillet. Cover; simmer about 10 minutes or until carrots are crisp-tender and juice of chicken is clear when center of thickest part is cut (170°F).

**3** Stir in beans. Cover; cook 5 to 6 minutes or until beans are thoroughly heated.

## easy variation

Substitute 8 boneless skinless chicken thighs for the chicken breasts to make this dish even more economical.

**1 SERVING:** Calories 390; Total Fat 9g (Saturated Fat 2g; Trans Fat 0g); Cholesterol 85mg; Sodium 340mg; Total Carbohydrate 33g (Dietary Fiber 8g); Protein 42g **EXCHANGES:** 1½ Starch, ½ Other Carbohydrate, 5½ Very Lean Meat, 1 Fat **CARBOHYDRATE CHOICES:** 2

# fettuccine with chicken and vegetables

prep time: 20 minutes    start to finish: 20 minutes    **4 servings**

**1** Cook and drain fettuccine and broccoli together as directed on fettuccine package. Toss with 2 tablespoons of the dressing. Cover to keep warm.

**2** Meanwhile, in 12-inch nonstick skillet, heat 2 tablespoons of the dressing over medium-high heat. Add chicken, onion and garlic-pepper blend; cook 4 to 6 minutes, stirring occasionally, until chicken is no longer pink in center.

**3** Stir bell peppers and remaining ¼ cup dressing into chicken mixture. Cook 2 to 3 minutes, stirring occasionally, until warm. Serve chicken mixture over fettuccine and broccoli. Serve with cheese.

## quick prep

1 package (9 oz) refrigerated fettuccine

2 cups small fresh broccoli florets

½ cup Italian dressing

1 lb chicken breast strips for stir-fry

1 medium red onion, cut into thin wedges

¼ teaspoon garlic-pepper blend

½ cup sliced drained roasted red bell peppers (from 7-oz jar)

Shredded Parmesan cheese, if desired

## time-saver

Fresh fettuccine and packaged broccoli florets from the produce department can help you get this dish to the table faster.

**1 SERVING**: Calories 460; Total Fat 17g (Saturated Fat 2g; Trans Fat 0g); Cholesterol 75mg; Sodium 460mg; Total Carbohydrate 42g (Dietary Fiber 4g); Protein 34g **EXCHANGES**: 2 Starch, ½ Other Carbohydrate, 4 Very Lean Meat, 3 Fat **CARBOHYDRATE CHOICES**: 3

1 cup frozen bell pepper and onion stir-fry (from 1-lb bag)

½ cup frozen corn

½ cup chunky-style salsa

1 can (15 oz) black beans with cumin and chili spices, undrained

1 pkg (9 oz) frozen cooked southwest-seasoned chicken breast strips

2 cups water

1½ cups uncooked couscous

¼ cup chopped fresh cilantro

# southwest chicken and couscous

**prep time:** 25 minutes   **start to finish:** 25 minutes   **4 servings**

**1** Spray 12-inch nonstick skillet with cooking spray. Add stir-fry vegetables to skillet; cook 2 to 3 minutes, stirring frequently, until crisp-tender.

**2** Stir in corn, salsa, beans and frozen chicken. Heat to boiling. Reduce heat to low; cover and simmer about 5 minutes, stirring occasionally, until chicken is thoroughly heated (break up large pieces of chicken with spoon as mixture cooks).

**3** Meanwhile, heat water to boiling. Stir in couscous. Remove from heat; cover and let stand 5 minutes.

**4** Fluff couscous with fork; spoon onto serving plates. Top with chicken mixture. Sprinkle with cilantro.

## easy variation

For delicious handheld sandwiches, omit the couscous, spoon the chicken mixture onto flour tortillas and roll up.

**1 SERVING:** Calories 470; Total Fat 3.5g (Saturated Fat 1g; Trans Fat 0g); Cholesterol 30mg; Sodium 790mg; Total Carbohydrate 79g (Dietary Fiber 11g); Protein 29g **EXCHANGES:** 4 Starch, 1 Other Carbohydrate, 2½ Very Lean Meat **CARBOHYDRATE CHOICES:** 5

# dijon chicken

**prep time:** 30 minutes   **start to finish:** 30 minutes   **4 servings**

## quick prep

½ cup whipping cream

¼ cup Dijon mustard

½ teaspoon salt

1 tablespoon olive or vegetable oil

2 cans (15 oz each) whole potatoes, drained, halved lengthwise

1¼ lb boneless skinless chicken thighs, cut into bite-size pieces

2 medium red bell peppers, cut into strips (about 2 cups)

2 cups frozen baby sweet peas

**1** In small bowl, mix whipping cream, mustard and salt; set aside.

**2** In 12-inch nonstick skillet, heat oil over medium-high heat. Add potatoes and chicken; cook 5 minutes, stirring frequently.

**3** Stir in bell peppers and peas. Increase heat to high; cook about 5 minutes, stirring frequently, until chicken is no longer pink in center.

**4** Stir in mustard mixture. Cook 1 minute, stirring constantly.

## time-saver

To cut preparation time, purchase chicken breasts already cut into strips for stir-frying.

**1 SERVING:** Calories 530; Total Fat 23g (Saturated Fat 10g; Trans Fat 0.5g); Cholesterol 120mg; Sodium 1270mg; Total Carbohydrate 43g (Dietary Fiber 9g); Protein 37g **EXCHANGES:** 2 Starch, 2 Vegetable, 4 Very Lean Meat, 4 Fat **CARBOHYDRATE CHOICES:** 3

- 2 tablespoons butter or margarine
- 1 medium onion, sliced (about 1 cup)
- 1 package (8 oz) sliced fresh mushrooms (about 3 cups)
- 2 teaspoons sugar
- 1 jar (12 oz) chicken gravy
- 1 tablespoon dry sherry, if desired
- 1 deli rotisserie chicken (2 lb), cut into serving pieces, skin removed if desired
- 1 tablespoon chopped fresh parsley

# smothered chicken

**prep time:** 30 minutes   **start to finish:** 30 minutes   **4 servings**

**1** In 12-inch skillet, melt butter over medium heat. Add onion and mushrooms; cook 8 to 10 minutes, stirring occasionally, until onions are tender and beginning to brown. Stir in sugar. Cook about 3 minutes, stirring occasionally, until vegetables are very brown.

**2** Stir gravy and sherry into vegetables. Add chicken; spoon sauce over chicken. Cover; cook 5 to 10 minutes, turning chicken once, until thoroughly heated. Sprinkle with parsley.

## healthy twist

For a nutritional bonus, add sliced carrots, cut green beans or broccoli florets with the sugar; cook until crisp-tender.

**1 SERVING:** Calories 390; Total Fat 20g (Saturated Fat 7g; Trans Fat 0.5g); Cholesterol 125mg; Sodium 1150mg; Total Carbohydrate 13g (Dietary Fiber 2g); Protein 39g **EXCHANGES:** 1 Starch, 5 Lean Meat, 1 Fat **CARBOHYDRATE CHOICES:** 1

**8 oz uncooked linguine**

**1¼ lb boneless skinless chicken breasts, cut into bite-size pieces**

**½ teaspoon salt**

**¼ teaspoon pepper**

**2 tablespoons butter**

**2 medium green onions, chopped (2 tablespoons)**

**2 cloves garlic, finely chopped**

**¼ cup finely chopped drained roasted red peppers (from 7-oz jar)**

**½ lb fresh thin asparagus spears, trimmed, cut into 2-inch pieces**

**¾ cup chicken broth**

**Grated peel of 1 medium lemon (2 to 3 teaspoons)**

# quick chicken scampi

**prep time:** 25 minutes    **start to finish:** 25 minutes    **4 servings**

**1** Cook linguine as directed on package.

**2** Meanwhile, sprinkle chicken with salt and pepper. In 12-inch nonstick skillet, heat 1 tablespoon of the butter over medium-high heat until melted. Cook chicken in butter 5 to 7 minutes, stirring occasionally. Add onions, garlic, roasted peppers and asparagus; cook 2 to 3 minutes longer, stirring occasionally, until asparagus is crisp-tender and chicken is no longer pink in center. Stir in broth and remaining 1 tablespoon butter; cook until butter is melted.

**3** Drain linguine. Serve chicken mixture over linguine. Sprinkle with lemon peel.

## easy variation

If you're not in the mood for pasta, try serving the chicken mixture over your favorite variety of rice.

**1 SERVING:** Calories 500; Total Fat 12g (Saturated Fat 5g; Trans Fat 0g); Cholesterol 105mg; Sodium 800mg; Total Carbohydrate 54g (Dietary Fiber 4g); Protein 43g **EXCHANGES:** 3½ Starch, ½ Vegetable, 4½ Very Lean Meat, 1½ Fat **CARBOHYDRATE CHOICES:** 3½

# skillet chicken nachos

prep time: 20 minutes    start to finish: 20 minutes    **6 servings**

**1** In 12-inch nonstick skillet, heat oil over medium-high heat. Add chicken; cook 3 to 5 minutes, stirring occasionally, until no longer pink in center.

**2** Stir in taco seasoning mix, tomato sauce, bell pepper, beans, corn and 1 cup of the cheese. Reduce heat to medium; cook 3 to 5 minutes, stirring occasionally, until heated through and cheese is melted.

**3** Divide tortilla chips among 6 plates. Spoon chicken mixture evenly over chips. Sprinkle with remaining 1 cup cheese and cilantro.

1 tablespoon olive or vegetable oil

1¼ lb boneless skinless chicken breasts, cut into ¼-inch pieces

1 package (1 oz) taco seasoning mix

1 can (8 oz) tomato sauce

1 medium red bell pepper, chopped (1 cup)

1 can (15 oz) black beans, drained, rinsed

1 can (7 oz) whole kernel sweet corn, drained

2 cups shredded Mexican cheese blend (8 oz)

6 oz tortilla chips (about 42 chips)

¼ cup chopped fresh cilantro

## easy variation

For Skillet Beef Nachos, substitute 1 lb lean (at least 80%) ground beef for the chicken. In step 1, cook beef 5 to 7 minutes or until thoroughly cooked. Drain and proceed as directed.

**1 SERVING:** Calories 520; Total Fat 24g (Saturated Fat 9g; Trans Fat 0g); Cholesterol 95mg; Sodium 1320mg; Total Carbohydrate 38g (Dietary Fiber 5g); Protein 36g **EXCHANGES:** 2 Starch, ½ Other Carbohydrate, ½ Vegetable, 4 Very Lean Meat, 4 Fat **CARBOHYDRATE CHOICES:** 2½

- 1 cup uncooked regular long-grain white rice
- 2 cups water
- 2 tablespoons olive or vegetable oil
- 1 lb boneless skinless chicken breasts, cut into 1-inch pieces
- 1 large onion, chopped (1 cup)
- 2 medium yellow summer squash, cut in half lengthwise, then cut crosswise into ½-inch pieces (about 2 cups)
- 4 oz fresh sugar snap peas (about 1 cup)
- 2 cloves garlic, finely chopped
- ½ cup stir-fry sauce
- 1 large tomato, chopped (1 cup)

# summer chicken stir-fry

**prep time:** 30 minutes   **start to finish:** 30 minutes   **4 servings**

**1** Cook rice in water as directed on package.

**2** Meanwhile, in 12-inch nonstick skillet, heat 1 tablespoon of the oil over medium-high heat. Add chicken; cook 6 to 8 minutes, stirring occasionally, until no longer pink in center. Remove chicken from skillet; cover to keep warm.

**3** In same skillet, heat remaining 1 tablespoon oil. Cook onion, squash and peas in oil 5 minutes, stirring occasionally. Add garlic; cook 1 minute longer. Add stir-fry sauce and chicken; cook 2 to 3 minutes longer or until thoroughly heated. Remove from heat. Stir in tomato. Serve over rice.

## easy variation

This recipe can be altered to fit any family's taste buds. Just substitute 4 cups of your favorite chopped fresh vegetables for the onion, squash and sugar snap peas.

**1 SERVING:** Calories 490; Total Fat 13g (Saturated Fat 2.5g; Trans Fat 0g); Cholesterol 70mg; Sodium 1930mg; Total Carbohydrate 59g (Dietary Fiber 3g); Protein 32g **EXCHANGES:** 2½ Starch, 1 Other Carbohydrate, 1 Vegetable, 3 Lean Meat, ½ Fat **CARBOHYDRATE CHOICES:** 4

# super-quick salsa chicken

prep time: 30 minutes    start to finish: 30 minutes    **4 servings**

**1** Cook rice in water as directed on package.

**2** Meanwhile, between pieces of plastic wrap or waxed paper, place each chicken breast smooth side down; gently pound with flat side of meat mallet or rolling pin until about ¼ inch thick.

**3** In 12-inch nonstick skillet, heat 1 tablespoon of the oil over medium-high heat. Sprinkle chicken with salt and pepper. Add chicken; cook 6 to 10 minutes, turning once, until golden brown on outside and no longer pink in center. Remove chicken from skillet; cover to keep warm.

**4** In same skillet, heat remaining 1 tablespoon oil. Add zucchini; cook 3 minutes, stirring occasionally. Stir in salsa and corn. Reduce heat to medium; cook 2 minutes longer or until thoroughly heated. Serve chicken over rice; top with vegetable mixture, sour cream and cilantro.

## quick prep

- 1 cup uncooked regular long-grain white rice
- 2 cups water
- 4 boneless skinless chicken breasts (1¼ lb)
- 2 tablespoons olive or vegetable oil
- ½ teaspoon salt
- ¼ teaspoon pepper
- 1 medium zucchini, chopped (2 cups)
- 1 cup chunky-style salsa
- 1 can (11 oz) whole kernel sweet corn, drained
- ¼ cup sour cream
- 2 tablespoons chopped fresh cilantro

## time-saver

If you're short on time, skip flattening and cooking chicken breasts. Substitute 4 cups cubed cooked chicken and then add it with the salsa and corn in step 3.

**1 SERVING:** Calories 520; Total Fat 15g (Saturated Fat 4g; Trans Fat 0g); Cholesterol 95mg; Sodium 1580mg; Total Carbohydrate 58g (Dietary Fiber 2g); Protein 38g **EXCHANGES:** 2½ Starch, ½ Other Carbohydrate, 2½ Vegetable, 3½ Very Lean Meat, 2 Fat **CARBOHYDRATE CHOICES:** 4

1 tablespoon vegetable oil

1 lb boneless skinless chicken breasts, cut into ½- to ¾-inch pieces

1 clove garlic, finely chopped

1¾ cups chicken broth

1 cup uncooked orzo or rosamarina pasta (6 oz)

1 can (14.5 oz) Italian-style stewed tomatoes, undrained

1 medium zucchini, cut lengthwise in half, then cut crosswise into slices (2 cups)

2 tablespoons shredded Parmesan cheese

# chicken and orzo supper

**prep time:** 35 minutes    **start to finish:** 35 minutes    **4 servings** (1 cup each)

**1** In 12-inch nonstick skillet, heat oil over medium-high heat. Add chicken and garlic; cook 4 to 6 minutes, stirring frequently, until chicken is brown.

**2** Stir in broth and pasta. Heat to boiling. Reduce heat to medium; cover and cook 10 to 15 minutes, stirring occasionally, until pasta is tender and most of liquid is absorbed.

**3** Stir in tomatoes and zucchini. Cook uncovered 5 to 10 minutes, stirring occasionally and breaking up tomatoes with spoon, until zucchini is tender and chicken is no longer pink. Sprinkle with cheese.

## easy variation

For a change of pace and a little stronger cheese flavor, substitute shredded Asiago cheese for the Parmesan. Look for it in containers near the other cheeses.

**1 SERVING:** Calories 350; Total Fat 9g (Saturated Fat 2.5g; Trans Fat 0g); Cholesterol 70mg; Sodium 830mg; Total Carbohydrate 35g (Dietary Fiber 3g); Protein 34g **EXCHANGES:** 2 Starch, 1 Vegetable, 3½ Very Lean Meat, 1 Fat **CARBOHYDRATE CHOICES:** 2

- 1 tablespoon olive or vegetable oil
- 1 package (19.5 oz) lean Italian turkey sausages, casings removed, cut into ½-inch slices
- 1 large onion, coarsely chopped (1 cup)
- 1 cup chicken broth
- 1 cup water
- 1 cup uncooked orzo or rosamarina pasta (6 oz)
- 1 lb fresh asparagus spears, trimmed, cut into 1-inch pieces
- 2 tablespoons sliced pimientos (from 4-oz jar)

# asparagus and turkey sausage skillet

**prep time:** 15 minutes    **start to finish:** 25 minutes    **4 servings**

**1** In 12-inch nonstick skillet, heat oil over medium-high heat. Add sausage and onion; cook 2 minutes, stirring occasionally.

**2** Stir in broth and water. Heat to boiling. Stir in orzo; boil 2 minutes. Add asparagus and pimientos. Reduce heat to medium; cover and return to boiling. Cook 8 to 10 minutes or until pasta is tender.

## easy variation

Frozen asparagus is a great substitute for the fresh. One 9- or 10-ounce box (about 1½ cups) is the right amount.

**1 SERVING:** Calories 470; Total Fat 19g (Saturated Fat 4g; Trans Fat 0.5g); Cholesterol 125mg; Sodium 1140mg; Total Carbohydrate 34g (Dietary Fiber 3g); Protein 40g **EXCHANGES:** 2 Starch, 1½ Vegetable, 1½ Very Lean Meat, 2 Lean Meat, 2½ Fat **CARBOHYDRATE CHOICES:** 2

**Betty Crocker The Big Book of Slow Cooker, Casseroles & More**

1¾ cups uncooked instant brown rice

2 cups water

¼ teaspoon salt

2 teaspoons vegetable oil

1 lb turkey breast strips for stir-fry

1 medium red bell pepper, cut into thin strips

2 cups small broccoli florets

1 can (10½ oz) ready-to-serve low-sodium chicken broth soup

4 teaspoons cornstarch

4 teaspoons curry powder

½ teaspoon ground ginger

¼ teaspoon salt

# curried turkey stir-fry

**prep time:** 30 minutes    **start to finish:** 30 minutes    **4 servings** (1¼ cups each)

**1** Cook brown rice as directed on package, using water and ¼ teaspoon salt.

**2** Meanwhile, in 12-inch nonstick skillet, heat oil over medium-high heat. Add turkey; cook 5 to 8 minutes, stirring frequently, until browned. Stir in bell pepper and broccoli. Cook 2 minutes.

**3** In small bowl, mix remaining ingredients. Stir into turkey and vegetables. Heat to boiling. Reduce heat; cover and cook 2 to 3 minutes or until vegetables are crisp-tender and turkey is no longer pink in center. Serve over brown rice.

## healthy twist

Brown rice is light tan in color because it still has the bran covering. It provides more fiber than white rice, which has had the bran covering removed.

**1 SERVING:** Calories 470; Total Fat 7g (Saturated Fat 1.5g; Trans Fat 0g); Cholesterol 75mg; Sodium 530mg; Total Carbohydrate 71g (Dietary Fiber 8g); Protein 37g **EXCHANGES:** 4½ Starch, 1 Vegetable, 3 Very Lean Meat **CARBOHYDRATE CHOICES:** 4

3 cups uncooked bow-tie (farfalle) pasta (6 oz)

2 cups cubed cooked turkey breast

½ cup basil pesto

½ cup coarsely chopped roasted red bell peppers (from 7-oz jar)

¼ cup sliced ripe olives, if desired

# pesto, turkey and pasta

**prep time:** 20 minutes   **start to finish:** 20 minutes   **4 servings**

**1** In 3-quart saucepan, cook and drain pasta as directed on package.

**2** In same saucepan, mix pasta, turkey, pesto and roasted peppers. Heat over low heat, stirring constantly, until hot. Garnish with olives.

## easy variation

Rotini pasta can be substituted for the bow-tie pasta.

**1 SERVING:** Calories 670; Total Fat 22g (Saturated Fat 4.5g; Trans Fat 0g); Cholesterol 40mg; Sodium 1530mg; Total Carbohydrate 87g (Dietary Fiber 6g); Protein 30g **EXCHANGES:** 3 Starch, 1 Other Carbohydrate, 3½ Lean Meat, 2½ Fat **CARBOHYDRATE CHOICES:** 6

# beefy italian ramen skillet

**prep time:** 30 minutes    **start to finish:** 35 minutes    **4 servings**

**1** Break blocks of noodles in half (reserve one seasoning packet; discard second packet). Set aside.

**2** In 10-inch skillet, cook beef and pepperoni over medium-high heat 5 to 7 minutes, stirring occasionally, until beef is thoroughly cooked; drain.

**3** Stir in tomatoes, water and reserved seasoning packet. Heat to boiling. Stir in noodles and bell pepper. Cook 3 to 5 minutes, stirring occasionally, until noodles are tender. Remove skillet from heat.

**4** Sprinkle cheese around edge of noodle mixture. Cover; let stand about 5 minutes or until cheese is melted.

## healthy twist

Sodium is kept low in this recipe because it calls for only one of the seasoning packets.

2 packages (3 oz each) beef-flavor ramen noodle soup mix

1 lb lean (at least 80%) ground beef

24 slices pepperoni (1 to 1¼ inches in diameter)

1 can (14.5 oz) diced tomatoes with basil, garlic and oregano, undrained

1 cup water

1 small green bell pepper, cut into ½-inch pieces (½ cup)

1 cup shredded mozzarella cheese (4 oz)

**1 SERVING:** Calories 570; Total Fat 34g (Saturated Fat 14g; Trans Fat 2g); Cholesterol 120mg; Sodium 960mg; Total Carbohydrate 27g (Dietary Fiber 2g); Protein 39g **EXCHANGES:** 2 Starch, 1 Vegetable, 3½ Medium-Fat Meat, 2 Fat **CARBOHYDRATE CHOICES:** 2

- 1 tablespoon butter or margarine
- 1 medium bell pepper (any color), coarsely chopped (1 cup)
- 1½ cups sliced fresh mushrooms (about 5 oz)
- 4 boneless beef top loin steaks (New York, Kansas City or strip steaks), about ¾ inch thick (6 oz each)
- ½ teaspoon garlic salt
- ¼ teaspoon coarse ground black pepper
- ¼ cup teriyaki baste and glaze (from 12-oz bottle)
- 2 tablespoons water

# simple teriyaki steak dinner

**prep time:** 20 minutes    **start to finish:** 20 minutes    **4 servings**

**1** In 12-inch nonstick skillet, melt butter over medium-high heat. Add bell pepper; cook 2 minutes, stirring frequently. Stir in mushrooms. Cook 2 to 3 minutes, stirring frequently, until vegetables are tender. Remove vegetables from skillet; cover to keep warm.

**2** Sprinkle steaks with garlic salt and pepper. In same skillet, cook steaks over medium heat 6 to 8 minutes, turning once or twice, until desired doneness.

**3** Return vegetables to skillet. Stir teriyaki glaze and water into vegetable mixture; spoon over steaks. Cook about 1 minute, stirring vegetables occasionally, until thoroughly heated.

**1 SERVING:** Calories 370; Total Fat 23g (Saturated Fat 9g; Trans Fat 1g); Cholesterol 105mg; Sodium 1040mg; Total Carbohydrate 6g (Dietary Fiber 1g); Protein 34g **EXCHANGES:** ½ Other Carbohydrate, ½ Vegetable, 3½ Medium-Fat Meat, 1 Fat **CARBOHYDRATE CHOICES:** ½

1 lb lean (at least 80%)
  ground beef

2 cups thinly sliced celery
  (3½ medium stalks)

1 medium red bell pepper,
  coarsely chopped
  (1 cup)

1 can (8 oz) sliced water
  chestnuts, drained

1 bottle (12 oz) teriyaki
  baste and glaze

2 cups coleslaw mix
  (shredded cabbage
  and carrots)

3 cups chow mein noodles

# ground beef chow mein

**prep time:** 25 minutes    **start to finish:** 25 minutes    **6 servings** (1¼ cups each)

**1** In 12-inch nonstick skillet, cook beef over medium-high heat 5 to 7 minutes, stirring frequently, until beef is thoroughly cooked. Stir in celery and bell pepper. Cook 3 to 4 minutes, stirring frequently, until vegetables are crisp-tender; drain.

**2** Stir water chestnuts and teriyaki glaze into beef mixture. Cook about 2 minutes, stirring frequently, until hot and bubbly. Remove from heat.

**3** Stir in coleslaw mix. Serve over noodles.

## healthy twist

The fat from the ground beef is just enough to cook the vegetables evenly. To keep the fat content of the recipe lower, we drain it off after the vegetables are cooked.

**1 SERVING:** Calories 360; Total Fat 16g (Saturated Fat 4.5g; Trans Fat 0.5g); Cholesterol 45mg; Sodium 2940mg; Total Carbohydrate 34g (Dietary Fiber 4g); Protein 21g **EXCHANGES:** 1½ Starch, 2 Vegetable, 2 Medium-Fat Meat, 1½ Fat **CARBOHYDRATE CHOICES:** 2

**1 lb lean (at least 80%) ground beef**

**1 package (1 oz) taco seasoning mix**

**1½ cups water**

**1 cup chunky-style salsa**

**1 cup frozen corn**

**1½ cups uncooked instant rice**

**¾ cup shredded taco-seasoned cheese (3 oz)**

**1 cup shredded lettuce**

**1 medium tomato, chopped (¾ cup)**

**Sour cream, if desired**

# beef taco rice skillet

**prep time:** 20 minutes    **start to finish:** 30 minutes    **5 servings**

**1** In 10-inch skillet, cook beef over medium heat 8 to 10 minutes, stirring occasionally, until thoroughly cooked; drain.

**2** Stir in taco seasoning mix, water, salsa and corn. Heat to boiling. Stir in rice; boil 1 minute. Remove from heat; cover and let stand 8 minutes.

**3** Fluff rice mixture with fork; sprinkle with cheese. Cover; let stand 1 to 2 minutes or until cheese is melted. Sprinkle lettuce around edge of skillet; sprinkle tomato in circle next to lettuce. Serve with sour cream.

## easy variation

You can substitute shredded Monterey Jack or Cheddar for the taco-seasoned cheese if you have it on hand.

**1 SERVING:** Calories 420; Total Fat 16g (Saturated Fat 8g; Trans Fat 1g); Cholesterol 75mg; Sodium 1190mg; Total Carbohydrate 45g (Dietary Fiber 2g); Protein 24g **EXCHANGES:** 3 Starch, 2 Medium-Fat Meat, 1 Fat **CARBOHYDRATE CHOICES:** 3

# beef, summer squash and sweet potato curry

prep time: 40 minutes    start to finish: 40 minutes    **6 servings**

**1** Cook rice in water as directed on package.

**2** Meanwhile, in 12-inch skillet, cook beef and onion over medium-high heat 5 to 7 minutes, stirring occasionally, until beef is thoroughly cooked and onion is tender; drain.

**3** Add gingerroot, curry powder, cumin and salt to skillet; cook 1 minute, stirring occasionally. Stir in sweet potato, tomatoes and broth. Heat to boiling. Reduce heat; cover and simmer 10 minutes or until potato is almost tender.

**4** Stir in zucchini. Cover; cook 5 to 10 minutes longer or until potato and zucchini are just tender. Serve beef mixture over rice. Top each serving with about 1 tablespoon yogurt.

- 1 cup uncooked regular long-grain white rice
- 2 cups water
- 1 lb lean (at least 80%) ground beef
- 1 medium onion, chopped (½ cup)
- 1 tablespoon grated gingerroot
- 2 tablespoons curry powder
- 1 teaspoon ground cumin
- 1 teaspoon salt
- 1 large sweet potato, peeled, cut into ½-inch cubes (3 cups)
- 1 can (14.5 oz) diced tomatoes, undrained
- 1 cup reduced-sodium chicken broth
- 2 medium zucchini, cut in half lengthwise, then cut crosswise into ½-inch slices (2 cups)
- ½ cup plain yogurt

## easy variation

Fresh unpeeled gingerroot, tightly wrapped, can be frozen up to 6 months. To use, slice off a piece of frozen ginger and return the rest to the freezer. If you don't have it on hand, use ¼ teaspoon ground ginger instead and add with the other spices.

**1 SERVING**: Calories 420; Total Fat 10g (Saturated Fat 4g; Trans Fat 0.5g); Cholesterol 50mg; Sodium 1030mg; Total Carbohydrate 58g (Dietary Fiber 4g); Protein 22g **EXCHANGES**: 3½ Starch, 1 Vegetable, 1 High-Fat Meat **CARBOHYDRATE CHOICES**: 4

1 lb lean (at least 80%) ground beef

½ teaspoon salt

½ teaspoon pepper

2 tablespoons all-purpose flour

1 package (8 oz) sliced fresh mushrooms (about 3 cups)

1½ cups beef broth

⅓ cup whipping cream

4 teaspoons Dijon mustard

1 lb unpeeled Yukon Gold or red potatoes, cut into ½-inch cubes (3 medium)

2 medium carrots, thinly sliced (1 cup)

2 tablespoons chopped fresh parsley

# skillet ground beef stew

**prep time:** 20 minutes   **start to finish:** 30 minutes   **4 servings**

**1** In 12-inch nonstick skillet, cook beef over medium-high heat 5 to 7 minutes, stirring occasionally, until thoroughly cooked; drain. Stir in salt, pepper and flour. Add mushrooms; cook 3 minutes, stirring occasionally.

**2** In small bowl, mix broth, whipping cream and mustard with whisk. Add to beef mixture. Stir in potatoes and carrots.

**3** Reduce heat to medium-low; cover and cook 15 minutes or until vegetables are tender and sauce is slightly thickened. Sprinkle with parsley.

**1 SERVING:** Calories 410; Total Fat 21g (Saturated Fat 9g; Trans Fat 1g); Cholesterol 100mg; Sodium 830mg; Total Carbohydrate 30g (Dietary Fiber 4g); Protein 25g **EXCHANGES:** 2 Starch, 2½ High-Fat Meat **CARBOHYDRATE CHOICES:** 2

# ginger asian beef

prep time: 30 minutes    start to finish: 30 minutes    **5 servings**

## quick prep

1 lb lean (at least 80%) ground beef

1 box (5.6 oz) beef pasta skillet-meal mix

3⅔ cups hot water

2 tablespoons soy sauce

1 tablespoon honey

1 teaspoon ground ginger

1 bag (16 oz) frozen stir-fry vegetables

**1** In 10-inch skillet, cook beef over medium heat 8 to 10 minutes, stirring occasionally, until thoroughly cooked; drain.

**2** Stir in sauce mix and uncooked pasta (from skillet-meal mix box), water, soy sauce, honey and ginger. Heat to boiling, stirring occasionally.

**3** Stir in frozen vegetables. Reduce heat; cover and simmer 10 minutes, stirring occasionally. Uncover; cook until sauce is desired thickness.

## easy variation

Lean ground turkey is a great substitute for the ground beef in this recipe.

**1 SERVING:** Calories 310; Total Fat 11g (Saturated Fat 4g; Trans Fat 0.5g); Cholesterol 55mg; Sodium 1110mg; Total Carbohydrate 31g (Dietary Fiber 3g); Protein 21g **EXCHANGES:** 1½ Starch, 1 Vegetable, 2 Medium-Fat Meat **CARBOHYDRATE CHOICES:** 2

8 oz uncooked spaghetti

4 medium carrots, thinly
sliced (2 cups)

8 oz fresh sugar snap peas

1 can (14 oz) coconut milk
(not cream of coconut)

1 tablespoon packed
brown sugar

2 to 3 teaspoons Thai
red curry paste

1 tablespoon soy sauce

½ cup crunchy peanut
butter

2 tablespoons lime juice

1 lb lean (at least 80%)
ground beef

1 tablespoon grated
gingerroot

½ teaspoon salt

# thai peanut noodle and beef skillet

**prep time:** 30 minutes    **start to finish:** 30 minutes    **6 servings**

**1** In 5- to 6-quart Dutch oven, cook spaghetti as directed on package, adding carrots and peas during last 5 minutes of cooking time. Drain; rinse with cold water to cool. Drain again; set aside.

**2** In microwavable bowl, mix coconut milk, brown sugar, curry paste, soy sauce and peanut butter. Microwave uncovered on High 2 minutes or until hot. Add lime juice; stir with whisk until smooth. Set aside.

**3** In 12-inch nonstick skillet, cook beef over medium-high heat 5 to 7 minutes, stirring occasionally, until thoroughly cooked; drain. Stir in gingerroot and salt; cook 1 minute longer.

**4** Stir in reserved spaghetti, the vegetables and peanut sauce; toss until coated. Cook 2 to 3 minutes or until thoroughly heated.

## easy variation

Creamy peanut butter works just as well in this recipe if you prefer. Also, ¼ teaspoon ground ginger can be used instead of the fresh gingerroot.

**1 SERVING**: Calories 620; Total Fat 34g (Saturated Fat 18g; Trans Fat 0.5g); Cholesterol 45mg; Sodium 760mg; Total Carbohydrate 51g (Dietary Fiber 6g); Protein 27g **EXCHANGES**: 3 Starch, ½ Vegetable, 3 High-Fat Meat, 1½ Fat **CARBOHYDRATE CHOICES**: 3½

# deluxe pizza goulash

prep time: 35 minutes    start to finish: 40 minutes    **6 servings** (1⅓ cups each)

**1** Cook and drain macaroni as directed on package.

**2** Meanwhile, in 12-inch skillet, cook beef and onion over medium-high heat 5 to 7 minutes, stirring occasionally, until beef is thoroughly cooked; drain. Stir in macaroni, pepperoni, mushrooms and pizza sauce.

**3** Reduce heat to medium; cover and cook 8 to 10 minutes, stirring occasionally, until hot. Remove from heat. Sprinkle with cheese. Cover; let stand 2 to 3 minutes or until cheese is melted.

2 cups uncooked elbow macaroni (8 oz)

½ lb lean (at least 80%) ground beef

1 small onion, chopped (¼ cup)

1 package (3.5 oz) sliced pepperoni

1 jar (4.5 oz) sliced mushrooms, drained

2 cans (15 oz each) pizza sauce

1 cup shredded mozzarella cheese (4 oz)

## easy variation

Don't have pizza sauce on hand? Use a 26-ounce jar of tomato pasta sauce instead. You can spice up the flavor with a pinch of dried oregano.

**1 SERVING:** Calories 450; Total Fat 21g (Saturated Fat 8g; Trans Fat 0g); Cholesterol 45mg; Sodium 1160mg; Total Carbohydrate 43g (Dietary Fiber 5g); Protein 22g **EXCHANGES:** 2½ Starch, 1 Vegetable, 2 Medium-Fat Meat, 2 Fat **CARBOHYDRATE CHOICES:** 3

- **1 lb boneless beef sirloin steak, cut into 4 serving pieces**
- **¾ teaspoon seasoned salt**
- **½ teaspoon garlic-pepper blend**
- **2 tablespoons butter or margarine**
- **1½ cups frozen bell pepper and onion stir-fry (from 1-lb bag)**
- **1 bag (20 oz) refrigerated home-style potato slices**
- **1 cup shredded American-Cheddar cheese blend (4 oz)**

# cheesy steak and potato skillet

**prep time:** 30 minutes    **start to finish:** 30 minutes    **4 servings**

**1** Sprinkle beef pieces with ¼ teaspoon of the seasoned salt and ¼ teaspoon of the garlic-pepper blend. In 12-inch nonstick skillet, cook beef over medium-high heat 3 to 4 minutes, turning once or twice, until brown and desired doneness. Remove from skillet; cover to keep warm.

**2** In same skillet, melt butter over medium heat. Add stir-fry vegetables; cook 2 minutes, stirring frequently. Add potatoes; sprinkle with remaining ½ teaspoon seasoned salt and ¼ teaspoon garlic-pepper blend. Cook uncovered 8 to 10 minutes, stirring frequently, until tender.

**3** Place beef in skillet with potatoes, pushing potatoes around beef. Cook 1 to 2 minutes, turning beef once, until hot. Sprinkle with cheese. Cover; heat until cheese is melted.

## healthy twist

This easy skillet dish has everything going for it—it's high in calcium and iron and low in carbohydrates.

**1 SERVING:** Calories 470; Total Fat 19g (Saturated Fat 11g; Trans Fat 0.5g); Cholesterol 120mg; Sodium 700mg; Total Carbohydrate 33g (Dietary Fiber 2g); Protein 40g **EXCHANGES:** 2 Starch, 1 Vegetable, 4½ Lean Meat, 1 Fat **CARBOHYDRATE CHOICES:** 2

- 1 box (6 oz) herb roasted chicken-flavor long-grain and wild rice mix
- 2 cups water
- 4 cups fresh broccoli florets (about ½ lb)
- 1 tablespoon canola or vegetable oil
- ½ teaspoon salt
- ¼ teaspoon freshly ground pepper
- 4 boneless pork loin chops, ¾ inch thick (about 1⅓ lb)

# pork chops with broccoli and rice

**prep time:** 30 minutes  **start to finish:** 30 minutes  **4 servings**

**1** In 12-inch nonstick skillet, mix rice, seasoning package from rice mix and water. Heat to boiling over medium heat. Cover; cook 7 minutes. Add broccoli; cook 3 minutes longer.

**2** Spoon rice and broccoli onto 4 dinner plates. Cover to keep warm.

**3** Wipe out skillet. In same skillet, heat oil over medium-high heat. Sprinkle salt and pepper over pork; place in skillet. Cook 4 to 6 minutes or until golden brown. Turn pork; cook 4 to 5 minutes longer or until pork is no longer pink and meat thermometer inserted in center reads 160°F. Serve pork with rice and broccoli.

**1 SERVING:** Calories 400; Total Fat 22g (Saturated Fat 7g; Trans Fat 0g); Cholesterol 90mg; Sodium 560mg; Total Carbohydrate 16g (Dietary Fiber 2g); Protein 34g **EXCHANGES:** ½ Starch, ½ Fruit, 4½ Lean Meat, 1½ Fat **CARBOHYDRATE CHOICES:** 1

1 package (9 oz) refrigerated fettuccine

2 cans (15 oz each) tomato sauce with Italian herbs

1 bag (1 lb) frozen bell pepper and onion stir-fry, thawed, drained

1 ring (1 lb) fully cooked reduced-fat Polska-kielbasa sausage, cut into ½-inch pieces

Finely shredded Parmesan cheese, if desired

# sausage with fettuccine

**prep time:** 15 minutes   **start to finish:** 15 minutes   **4 servings**

**1** Cook and drain fettuccine as directed on package; keep warm.

**2** In same saucepan, stir tomato sauce, stir-fry vegetables and sausage. Heat to boiling. Serve sausage mixture over fettuccine, or toss fettuccine with sausage mixture. Serve with cheese.

## easy variation

Alfredo pasta sauce (26-oz jar) can be substituted for the tomato sauce with herbs.

**1 SERVING:** Calories 450; Total Fat 11g (Saturated Fat 2.5g; Trans Fat 0g); Cholesterol 60mg; Sodium 3010mg; Total Carbohydrate 62g (Dietary Fiber 6g); Protein 28g **EXCHANGES:** 3 Starch, 1 Other Carbohydrate, 1 Vegetable, 2½ Lean Meat **CARBOHYDRATE CHOICES:** 4

- 1 tablespoon vegetable oil
- 1 lb boneless pork loin chops, cut into thin strips
- ½ teaspoon garlic-pepper blend
- 1¾ cups chicken broth
- ½ cup sweet-and-sour sauce
- 2 tablespoons chili sauce
- 1½ cups uncooked medium egg noodles (3 oz)
- 8 oz fresh sugar snap peas (about 2 cups)
- 1 small red bell pepper, cut into thin strips
- ¼ cup cashew pieces

# sweet-and-sour noodles 'n pork

prep time: 30 minutes    start to finish: 30 minutes    **4 servings** (1 cup each)

**1** In 12-inch nonstick skillet, heat oil over medium-high heat. Add pork; sprinkle with garlic-pepper blend. Cook 3 to 5 minutes, stirring frequently, until brown.

**2** Stir in broth, sweet-and-sour sauce and chili sauce. Heat to boiling. Stir in noodles. Cover; cook over medium heat 5 minutes.

**3** Stir in peas and bell pepper. Cover; cook 5 to 8 minutes, stirring occasionally, until vegetables and noodles are tender. Sprinkle with cashews.

## easy variation

An easy substitute for the pork chops is lean pork tenderloin.

**1 SERVING:** Calories 410; Total Fat 18g (Saturated Fat 4.5g; Trans Fat 0g); Cholesterol 90mg; Sodium 700mg; Total Carbohydrate 32g (Dietary Fiber 4g); Protein 33g **EXCHANGES:** 1 Starch, 1 Other Carbohydrate, 1 Vegetable, 4 Lean Meat, 1 Fat **CARBOHYDRATE CHOICES:** 2

3 cups uncooked bow-tie (farfalle) pasta (9 oz)

2 slices bacon, cut into ½-inch pieces

1½ cups frozen sweet peas

¼ cup water

1 lb uncooked deveined peeled medium shrimp, thawed if frozen, tail shells removed

¾ cup refrigerated Alfredo sauce (from 10-oz container)

2 tablespoons chopped fresh chives

# shrimp alfredo primavera

**prep time:** 20 minutes   **start to finish:** 20 minutes   **4 servings** (1½ cups each)

**1** Cook and drain pasta as directed on package.

**2** Meanwhile, in 12-inch nonstick skillet, cook bacon over medium heat 4 to 5 minutes, stirring occasionally, until crisp. Stir in peas; cook 2 minutes, stirring occasionally.

**3** Add water. Cover; cook 3 to 5 minutes or until peas are tender and water has evaporated. Add shrimp; cook 2 to 3 minutes, stirring occasionally, until shrimp are pink.

**4** Stir in Alfredo sauce and pasta. Cook over medium-low heat, stirring occasionally, until thoroughly heated. Sprinkle with chives.

**1 SERVING:** Calories 510; Total Fat 20g (Saturated Fat 10g; Trans Fat 0.5g); Cholesterol 215mg; Sodium 720mg; Total Carbohydrate 54g (Dietary Fiber 5g); Protein 32g **EXCHANGES:** 3 Starch, 1 Vegetable, 3 Very Lean Meat, 3½ Fat **CARBOHYDRATE CHOICES:** 3

**2 tablespoons olive or vegetable oil**

**1 package (5.9 oz) chicken-and-garlic rice and vermicelli mix**

**1 cup frozen bell pepper and onion stir-fry (from 1-lb bag)**

**1¾ cups chicken broth**

**¾ cup water**

**1 dried bay leaf**

**½ lb fully cooked chorizo sausage, cut into bite-size pieces**

**½ cup frozen baby sweet peas**

**1 deli rotisserie chicken (2 lb), cut into 6 serving pieces**

**1 cup cooked deveined peeled medium shrimp, thawed if frozen, tail shells removed**

# weeknight paella

**prep time:** 30 minutes    **start to finish:** 30 minutes    **6 servings** (1½ cups each)

**1** In 12-inch skillet, heat oil over medium-high heat. Add rice mix and stir-fry vegetables; cook 2 to 3 minutes, stirring constantly, until rice mix begins to brown.

**2** Stir in broth, water, bay leaf and seasoning packet from rice mix. Heat to boiling. Reduce heat to low; cover and simmer 5 minutes.

**3** Stir in sausage and peas. Add chicken. Heat to boiling over medium-high heat. Reduce heat to low; cover and simmer 10 minutes.

**4** Stir in shrimp. Cover; cook about 5 minutes or until shrimp and chicken are thoroughly heated. Remove bay leaf before serving.

## time-saver

Chorizo is a spicy Spanish pork sausage sold fresh or fully cooked. Using the cooked variety is definitely a time-saver, but you can use fresh instead. Just be sure to cook it thoroughly before adding to the recipe.

**1 SERVING:** Calories 440; Total Fat 26g (Saturated Fat 8g; Trans Fat 0g); Cholesterol 155mg; Sodium 1330mg; Total Carbohydrate 12g (Dietary Fiber 0g); Protein 41g **EXCHANGES:** ½ Starch, 1 Vegetable, 5½ Lean Meat, 2 Fat **CARBOHYDRATE CHOICES:** 1

1 tablespoon canola
   or vegetable oil

1 large onion, coarsely
   chopped (1 cup)

4 cups water

4 cups uncooked medium
   egg noodles (8 oz)

1 package (8 oz) sliced
   fresh mushrooms
   (about 3 cups)

2 cans (5 oz each) solid
   white tuna in water,
   drained

1 jar (16 oz) Alfredo pasta
   sauce

1 cup seasoned croutons,
   coarsely crushed

# tuna-noodle skillet supper

**prep time:** 20 minutes    **start to finish:** 25 minutes    **6 servings**

**1** In 12-inch nonstick skillet, heat oil over medium-high heat. Add onion; cook 2 to 3 minutes, stirring frequently, until softened.

**2** Stir in water and noodles. Cover; heat to boiling. Boil 4 minutes.

**3** Stir in mushrooms, tuna and pasta sauce (sauce will be thin). Reduce heat to medium; simmer uncovered 4 to 6 minutes or until mushrooms are tender, sauce has slightly thickened and noodles are tender.

**4** Remove from heat; let stand 5 minutes. Just before serving, top with croutons.

## time-saver

Use frozen chopped onions to cut prep time. Look for them near the frozen breaded onion rings in the store.

**1 SERVING:** Calories 520; Total Fat 30g (Saturated Fat 16g; Trans Fat 1g); Cholesterol 120mg; Sodium 540mg; Total Carbohydrate 38g (Dietary Fiber 2g); Protein 24g **EXCHANGES:** 1½ Starch, 1 Fruit, 3 Lean Meat, 4 Fat **CARBOHYDRATE CHOICES:** 2½

**2 teaspoons canola or vegetable oil**

**1 bag (1 lb) frozen stir-fry vegetables (about 4½ cups)**

**1 tablespoon canola or vegetable oil**

**4 tilapia fillets, about ½ inch thick (about 1¼ lb)**

**4 tablespoons peanut sauce**

# thai tilapia with peanut sauce

**prep time:** 20 minutes  **start to finish:** 20 minutes  **4 servings**

**1** In 12-inch nonstick skillet, heat 2 teaspoons oil over high heat. Add frozen vegetables; cook 4 to 5 minutes, stirring frequently, until crisp-tender. Remove vegetables from skillet; cover to keep warm.

**2** Add 1 tablespoon oil to same skillet; reduce heat to medium-high. Add fish fillets; cook 3 minutes. Turn fish; spoon and spread 1 tablespoon peanut sauce over each fillet to cover. Cook about 4 minutes longer or until fish flakes easily with fork. Serve fish with vegetables.

## healthy twist

This is a great low-calorie, lower-fat main dish. Complete the meal with a chopped fresh vegetable salad and your favorite low-fat dressing—Asian flavored would taste great with the tilapia.

**1 SERVING:** Calories 260; Total Fat 11g (Saturated Fat 1.5g; Trans Fat 0g); Cholesterol 75mg; Sodium 160mg; Total Carbohydrate 9g (Dietary Fiber 3g); Protein 31g **EXCHANGES:** ½ Fruit, 4½ Very Lean Meat, 1½ Fat **CARBOHYDRATE CHOICES:** ½

# bow-ties with salmon and tarragon mustard sauce

**prep time:** 30 minutes    **start to finish:** 30 minutes    **6 servings**

- 1 package (16 oz) bow-tie (farfalle) pasta
- 1 tablespoon olive or vegetable oil
- 1 medium onion, chopped (½ cup)
- 1 tablespoon chopped fresh tarragon leaves
- 1 tablespoon chopped fresh parsley
- ¼ cup dry white wine or chicken broth
- 1 cup whipping cream or half-and-half
- 2 teaspoons stone-ground mustard
- 2 packages (3 to 4 oz each) sliced salmon (smoked or cured), cut into ½-inch-wide strips
- ½ cup freshly grated or shredded Parmesan cheese

**1** Cook and drain pasta as directed on package.

**2** Meanwhile, in 10-inch skillet, heat oil over medium heat. Add onion, tarragon and parsley; cook about 5 minutes, stirring frequently, until onion is tender. Stir in wine. Cook uncovered about 4 minutes or until wine has evaporated.

**3** Stir in whipping cream and mustard. Heat to boiling. Reduce heat; simmer uncovered 5 to 10 minutes or until sauce is slightly thickened.

**4** Add pasta, salmon and ¼ cup of the cheese; toss gently until pasta is evenly coated. Sprinkle with remaining ¼ cup cheese.

## do-ahead

You can cook the pasta up to 3 days ahead of time. Rinse with cold water, toss with a little olive oil and store in a resealable food-storage plastic bag in the refrigerator. Reheat in the microwave or plunge briefly into boiling water.

**1 SERVING:** Calories 490; Total Fat 13g (Saturated Fat 6g; Trans Fat 0g); Cholesterol 45mg; Sodium 500mg; Total Carbohydrate 69g (Dietary Fiber 4g); Protein 24g **EXCHANGES:** 4½ Starch, 1½ Very Lean Meat, 2 Fat **CARBOHYDRATE CHOICES:** 4½

When time is tight, cooks-on-the-go can depend on one-pot wonders that provide a protein, vegetable and possibly a starch in a single pan.

Fire up the stove and prepare Pizza Chicken, Santa Fe Turkey Breast or Seafood-Stuffed Pasta Shells. Serve a simple side salad and fresh bread to round out the meals.

sh meals casserole

# casseroles & other one-dish meals

1½ lb boneless skinless chicken thighs

½ teaspoon salt

¼ teaspoon pepper

1 small onion, sliced

2 medium bell peppers, cut into strips

2 cups tomato pasta sauce (from 26-oz jar)

5⅓ cups uncooked rotini pasta (16 oz)

1 cup shredded mozzarella cheese (4 oz)

# pizza chicken

**prep time:** 15 minutes   **start to finish:** 4 hours 15 minutes   **8 servings**

**1** Sprinkle chicken with salt and pepper. In 3- to 4-quart slow cooker, place chicken. Top with onion and bell peppers. Add pasta sauce.

**2** Cover; cook on Low heat setting 4 to 6 hours.

**3** About 15 minutes before serving, cook and drain pasta as directed on package. Place pasta on platter. Top with chicken and sauce. Sprinkle with cheese.

## easy variation

You could use penne pasta instead of the rotini in this easy dish that truly does taste like a pizza!

**1 SERVING:** Calories 470; Total Fat 13g (Saturated Fat 4.5g; Trans Fat 0g); Cholesterol 60mg; Sodium 800mg; Total Carbohydrate 59g (Dietary Fiber 5g); Protein 30g **EXCHANGES:** 4 Starch, 2½ Lean Meat, ½ Fat **CARBOHYDRATE CHOICES:** 4

# chicken and pinto tostadas

prep time: 20 minutes   start to finish: 8 hours 40 minutes   **8 servings**

**1** In 3- to 3½-quart slow cooker, place chicken. In small bowl, mix salsa, water and taco seasoning mix; pour over chicken.

**2** Cover; cook on Low heat setting 8 to 10 hours.

**3** Remove chicken from cooker; place on cutting board. Using 2 forks, pull into shreds. Return chicken to juices in cooker. Stir in beans. Increase heat setting to High; cover and cook 15 to 20 minutes longer or until thoroughly heated.

**4** Spoon chicken mixture over tostada shells. Top with lettuce, sour cream and guacamole.

## easy variation

If you don't have tostada shells, just break taco shells in half. Place the halves on each plate, and top with the chicken and bean mixture.

**1 SERVING:** Calories 290; Total Fat 13g (Saturated Fat 4.5g; Trans Fat 0g); Cholesterol 55mg; Sodium 570mg; Total Carbohydrate 24g (Dietary Fiber 5g); Protein 20g **EXCHANGES:** 1½ Starch, 2 Lean Meat, 1 Fat **CARBOHYDRATE CHOICES:** 1½

## chicken cacciatore

**prep time:** 15 minutes    **start to finish:** 8 hours 25 minutes    **6 servings**

2½ lb boneless skinless chicken thighs (about 12)

1 jar (4.5 oz) sliced mushrooms, drained

2 cans (6 oz each) Italian-style tomato paste

1¾ cups chicken broth (from 32-oz carton)

½ cup white wine, if desired

1½ teaspoons dried basil leaves

½ teaspoon salt

1 dried bay leaf

12 oz uncooked linguine

¼ teaspoon dried thyme leaves

1 tablespoon cornstarch

Shredded Parmesan cheese, if desired

**1** Spray 3- to 4-quart slow cooker with cooking spray. In cooker, place chicken. Add mushrooms, tomato paste, broth, wine, basil, salt and bay leaf; gently stir to mix.

**2** Cover; cook on Low heat setting 8 to 10 hours.

**3** About 15 minutes before serving, cook and drain linguine as directed on package. Remove chicken from cooker; place on serving platter. Cover to keep warm. Stir thyme into sauce in cooker. Increase heat setting to High. In small bowl, mix ¼ cup sauce from cooker and the cornstarch until smooth; stir into remaining sauce in cooker.

**4** Cover; cook on High heat setting 10 minutes longer, stirring frequently. Remove bay leaf. Serve chicken and sauce over linguine. Sprinkle with cheese.

### easy variation

One 26-ounce jar of tomato pasta sauce can be substituted for the tomato paste, chicken broth and white wine.

**1 SERVING:** Calories 620; Total Fat 17g (Saturated Fat 5g; Trans Fat 0g); Cholesterol 120mg; Sodium 1110mg; Total Carbohydrate 63g (Dietary Fiber 6g); Protein 53g **EXCHANGES:** 2 Starch, 2 Other Carbohydrate, 1 Vegetable, 6 Lean Meat **CARBOHYDRATE CHOICES:** 4

- 8 boneless skinless chicken thighs (2 lb)
- 1 bottle (13.5 oz) Thai peanut sauce
- 2 medium carrots, sliced (¾ cup)
- 4 medium green onions, sliced (½ cup)
- 1 cup uncooked converted white rice
- 2¼ cups water
- ¼ cup chopped cocktail peanuts
- 2 tablespoons chopped fresh cilantro
- ½ cup chopped red bell pepper, if desired

# thai peanut chicken

**prep time:** 10 minutes  **start to finish:** 5 hours 10 minutes  **6 servings**

**1** Spray 3- to 4-quart slow cooker with cooking spray. In cooker, place chicken. In medium bowl, mix peanut sauce, carrots and onions; pour over chicken.

**2** Cover; cook on Low heat setting 5 to 6 hours.

**3** About 20 minutes before serving, cook rice in water as directed on package; spoon onto serving platter. With slotted spoon, remove chicken from cooker; place over rice. Pour sauce from cooker over chicken. Sprinkle with peanuts, cilantro and red bell pepper.

## time-saver

Bottled sauces are great recipe time-savers. Look for the Thai peanut sauce in the Asian-foods section of the supermarket.

**1 SERVING:** Calories 490; Total Fat 21g (Saturated Fat 3g; Trans Fat 0g); Cholesterol 60mg; Sodium 1370mg; Total Carbohydrate 46g (Dietary Fiber 1g); Protein 29g **EXCHANGES:** 2 Starch, 1 Other Carbohydrate, 3 Lean Meat, 2 Fat **CARBOHYDRATE CHOICES:** 3

# cajun-seasoned chicken

**prep time:** 15 minutes   **start to finish:** 8 hours 15 minutes   **4 servings**

- 3 slices bacon, chopped
- ½ cup chopped green bell pepper
- ¼ cup chopped onion
- ¼ cup chopped celery
- 8 boneless skinless chicken thighs (about 1½ lb)
- 2 teaspoons Cajun seasoning
- 1 can (14.5 oz) diced tomatoes, undrained
- 1⅓ cups uncooked regular long-grain white rice
- 1⅓ cups water

**1** In 12-inch nonstick skillet, cook bacon over medium-high heat, stirring frequently, until crisp. Stir in bell pepper, onion and celery. Cook 2 to 3 minutes, stirring frequently, until crisp-tender. Into 3- to 4-quart slow cooker, spoon bacon and vegetables, using slotted spoon.

**2** Sprinkle chicken with 1 teaspoon of the Cajun seasoning; place in same skillet. Cook chicken over medium-high heat 4 to 5 minutes, turning once, until brown on both sides. Arrange chicken and any remaining drippings in skillet over vegetables in cooker. Pour tomatoes over chicken. Stir in remaining 1 teaspoon Cajun seasoning.

**3** Cover; cook on Low heat setting 8 to 9 hours.

**4** About 20 minutes before serving, cook rice in water as directed on package. Serve chicken and sauce over rice.

## easy variation

Spice this dish up a bit with hot pepper sauce—a staple in Louisiana. Then serve with warm sourdough bread and fresh green beans to complete the meal.

**1 SERVING:** Calories 570; Total Fat 17g (Saturated Fat 5g; Trans Fat 0g); Cholesterol 110mg; Sodium 1110mg; Total Carbohydrate 60g (Dietary Fiber 2g); Protein 44g **EXCHANGES:** 3½ Starch, 1 Vegetable, 4½ Lean Meat, ½ Fat **CARBOHYDRATE CHOICES:** 4

# chicken and vegetables with dumplings

prep time: 10 minutes    start to finish: 10 hours    **8 servings**

**quick prep**

2½ to 3 lb boneless skinless chicken thighs

1 lb small red potatoes (about 2½ inches in diameter)

¾ cup coarsely chopped onion

2 cups ready-to-eat baby-cut carrots

3 cans (14 oz each) chicken broth

2 cups original all-purpose baking mix

½ cup water

2 teaspoons parsley flakes

**1** In 6-quart slow cooker, place chicken, potatoes, onion and carrots. Add broth.

**2** Cover; cook on Low heat setting 9 to 10 hours.

**3** Increase heat setting to High. In medium bowl, stir together baking mix, water and parsley. Drop dough by rounded tablespoonfuls onto hot chicken mixture. Cover; cook on Low heat setting 45 to 50 minutes longer or until dumplings are dry in center.

## time-saver

Baby-cut carrots are always a great time-saver. Keep a bag or two on hand in the refrigerator for recipes or snacking anytime.

**1 SERVING**: Calories 420; Total Fat 16g (Saturated Fat 5g; Trans Fat 1g); Cholesterol 90mg; Sodium 970mg; Total Carbohydrate 34g (Dietary Fiber 3g); Protein 35g **EXCHANGES**: 2 Starch, 1 Vegetable, 4 Lean Meat, ½ Fat **CARBOHYDRATE CHOICES**: 2

**1¼ lb boneless skinless chicken thighs**

**1 package (1 oz) taco seasoning mix**

**1 tablespoon packed brown sugar**

**1 can (4.5 oz) chopped green chiles**

**1 cup frozen corn, thawed**

**1 can (10 oz) enchilada sauce**

**4 medium green onions, sliced (¼ cup)**

**1 package (4.6 oz) taco shells, heated if desired**

**3 cups shredded lettuce**

**1 medium tomato, chopped (¾ cup)**

# chile-chicken tacos

**prep time:** 15 minutes   **start to finish:** 6 hours 30 minutes   **12 tacos**

**1** Spray 3- to 4-quart slow cooker with cooking spray. Place chicken in cooker. Sprinkle with taco seasoning mix and brown sugar; toss to coat. Mix in green chiles, corn and ½ cup of the enchilada sauce. Refrigerate remaining enchilada sauce.

**2** Cover; cook on Low heat setting 6 to 7 hours.

**3** Remove chicken from cooker; place on cutting board. Using 2 forks, pull chicken into shreds; return chicken to cooker. Stir in green onions. Cover; cook on Low heat setting 15 minutes longer.

**4** Heat remaining enchilada sauce. Serve chicken mixture in taco shells with lettuce, tomatoes and warm enchilada sauce.

## easy variation

Mild, medium or hot enchilada sauce varies the flavor—and the heat—of these tacos.

**1 TACO:** Calories 170; Total Fat 7g (Saturated Fat 1.5g; Trans Fat 1g); Cholesterol 30mg; Sodium 310mg; Total Carbohydrate 16g (Dietary Fiber 2g); Protein 12g **EXCHANGES:** 1 Starch, 1½ Lean Meat, ½ Fat **CARBOHYDRATE CHOICES:** 1

¼ cup chopped oil-packed sun-dried tomatoes, drained

2 tablespoons herbes de Provence

2 tablespoons olive oil

2 tablespoons lemon juice

1 tablespoon finely chopped garlic

1 teaspoon salt

8 bone-in chicken thighs (about 2 lb), skin and fat removed

1½ cups sliced fresh mushrooms

1 cup uncooked regular long-grain white rice

1 medium carrot, shredded (¾ cup)

2 cups boiling water

1 tablespoon chopped fresh Italian (flat-leaf) parsley

2 teaspoons grated lemon peel

# country french chicken and rice

**prep time:** 25 minutes   **start to finish:** 3 hours 25 minutes   **8 servings**

**1** In heavy-duty 1-gallon resealable food-storage plastic bag, mix tomatoes, herbes de Provence, oil, lemon juice, garlic and ½ teaspoon of the salt. Add chicken thighs and mushrooms; seal bag. Turn to coat thighs and mushrooms in marinade. Refrigerate 2 to 24 hours.

**2** Heat oven to 375°F. Spray 13×9-inch (3-quart) glass baking dish with cooking spray. In baking dish, place rice, carrot and remaining ½ teaspoon salt; stir in boiling water. Place chicken thighs, mushrooms and marinade evenly over rice mixture.

**3** Cover with foil. Bake 50 to 60 minutes or until liquid is absorbed and juice of chicken is clear when thickest part is cut to bone (180°F). Sprinkle with parsley and lemon peel.

## easy variation

If herbes de Provence is not available, use any combination of dried basil, fennel seed, lavender, marjoram, rosemary, sage, summer savory, tarragon or thyme.

**1 SERVING:** Calories 260; Total Fat 10g (Saturated Fat 2.5g; Trans Fat 0g); Cholesterol 45mg; Sodium 360mg; Total Carbohydrate 23g (Dietary Fiber 1g); Protein 18g **EXCHANGES:** 1½ Starch, 2 Lean Meat, ½ Fat **CARBOHYDRATE CHOICES:** 1½

# chicken and barley risotto with edamame

**prep time:** 40 minutes    **start to finish:** 5 hours 10 minutes    **9 servings** (about 1 cup each)

1¼ lb boneless skinless chicken breasts, cut into ¾-inch cubes

1½ cups chopped onions (3 medium)

1¼ cups uncooked pearl barley

½ cup shredded carrot

2 medium cloves garlic, finely chopped

½ teaspoon salt

½ teaspoon dried thyme leaves

1 carton (32 oz) chicken broth (4 cups)

1 cup frozen shelled edamame (green) soybeans, thawed

½ cup shredded Parmesan cheese

**1** Spray 4- to 5-quart slow cooker with cooking spray. In cooker, mix chicken, onions, barley, carrot, garlic, salt, thyme and 3 cups of the broth.

**2** Cover; cook on Low heat setting 4 to 5 hours.

**3** In 2-cup microwavable measuring cup, microwave remaining 1 cup broth uncovered on High 2 to 3 minutes or until boiling. Stir thawed edamame and boiling broth into barley mixture in cooker. Increase heat setting to High; cover and cook 25 to 30 minutes longer or until edamame are tender. Stir in cheese.

## healthy twist

For a vegetarian version of this health-packed recipe, omit the chicken and use vegetable broth instead of the chicken broth. Complete the meal with a colorful salad using a variety of greens of different colors and textures.

**1 SERVING:** Calories 250; Total Fat 6g (Saturated Fat 2g, Trans Fat 0g); Cholesterol 45mg; Sodium 690mg; Total Carbohydrate 27g (Dietary Fiber 6g); Protein 23g   **EXCHANGES:** 1½ Starch, 1 Vegetable, 2 Lean Meat **CARBOHYDRATE CHOICES:** 2

**4 skinless bone-in chicken breasts (about 7 oz each)**

**1 can (15 to 16 oz) garbanzo beans, drained, rinsed**

**1 small onion, thinly sliced**

**1 small red bell pepper, chopped (½ cup)**

**1 cup fresh sugar snap peas**

**1 jar (9 oz) mango chutney**

**¾ cup water**

**2 tablespoons cornstarch**

**1½ teaspoons curry powder**

**¼ teaspoon salt**

**¼ teaspoon pepper**

**2 cups uncooked instant rice**

# chicken curry

**prep time:** 30 minutes    **start to finish:** 6 hours 30 minutes    **4 servings**

**1** In 3- to 4-quart slow cooker, layer chicken, beans, onion, bell pepper and sugar snap peas.

**2** In small bowl, mix remaining ingredients except rice; pour over mixture in cooker.

**3** Cover; cook on Low heat setting 6 to 7 hours.

**4** About 10 minutes before serving, cook rice as directed on package. Serve chicken mixture over rice.

### easy variation

It's easy to make this a traditional curry dish. Just sprinkle with toppers such as shredded coconut, chopped peanuts and raisins.

**1 SERVING:** Calories 640; Total Fat 8g (Saturated Fat 1.5g; Trans Fat 0g); Cholesterol 75mg; Sodium 1160mg; Total Carbohydrate 102g (Dietary Fiber 10g); Protein 41g **EXCHANGES:** 4 Starch, 2 Other Carbohydrate, 2 Vegetable, 3½ Very Lean Meat, 1 Fat **CARBOHYDRATE CHOICES:** 7

# jerk chicken casserole

**prep time:** 15 minutes    **start to finish:** 1 hour    **6 servings**

1¼ teaspoons salt

½ teaspoon pumpkin pie spice

¾ teaspoon ground allspice

¾ teaspoon dried thyme leaves

¼ teaspoon ground red pepper (cayenne)

1 tablespoon vegetable oil

6 boneless skinless chicken thighs

1 can (15 oz) black beans, drained, rinsed

1 large sweet potato (1 lb), peeled, cubed (3 cups)

¼ cup honey

¼ cup lime juice

2 teaspoons cornstarch

2 tablespoons sliced green onions (2 medium)

**1** Heat oven to 375°F. Spray 8-inch square (2-quart) glass baking dish with cooking spray. In small bowl, mix salt, pumpkin pie spice, allspice, thyme and red pepper. Rub mixture on all sides of chicken. In 12-inch nonstick skillet, heat oil over medium-high heat. Cook chicken in oil 2 to 3 minutes per side, until brown.

**2** In baking dish, layer beans and sweet potato. Top with browned chicken. In small bowl, mix honey, lime juice and cornstarch; add to skillet. Heat to boiling, stirring constantly. Pour over chicken in baking dish.

**3** Bake 35 to 45 minutes or until juice of chicken is clear when center of thickest part is cut (180°F) and sweet potatoes are fork tender. Sprinkle with green onions.

## easy variation

If a dry jerk seasoning or rub is available, use it to save a few minutes. This recipe uses a mild jerk seasoning rub; an authentic jerk rub will be spicier. You can substitute ¼ teaspoon ground cinnamon, ⅛ teaspoon ground ginger and ⅛ teaspoon ground nutmeg for the pumpkin pie spice.

**1 SERVING:** Calories 320; Total Fat 8g (Saturated Fat 2g; Trans Fat 0g); Cholesterol 45mg; Sodium 550mg; Total Carbohydrate 41g (Dietary Fiber 8g); Protein 20g **EXCHANGES:** 1½ Starch, 1 Other Carbohydrate, 2 Lean Meat, ½ Fat **CARBOHYDRATE CHOICES:** 3

- 1 container (15 oz) ricotta cheese
- 1 egg
- 1 cup grated Parmesan cheese
- 2 cups chopped cooked chicken
- 2 cans (10 oz each) green enchilada sauce
- 2 cans (4.5 oz each) chopped green chiles
- 1 package (8 or 9 oz) oven-ready lasagna noodles (12 noodles)
- 4 cups shredded mozzarella cheese (16 oz)

# green chile–chicken lasagna

**prep time:** 25 minutes   **start to finish:** 1 hour 35 minutes   **10 servings**

1 Heat oven to 350°F. In medium bowl, mix ricotta cheese, egg and ½ cup of the Parmesan cheese; set aside. In another medium bowl, mix chicken, enchilada sauce and green chiles.

2 In ungreased 13×9-inch (3-quart) glass baking dish, spread 1 cup of the chicken mixture. Top with 3 uncooked lasagna noodles; press gently into chicken mixture. Spread with ⅔ cup of the ricotta mixture. Sprinkle with 1 cup of the mozzarella cheese. Repeat layers 3 times. Sprinkle with remaining ½ cup Parmesan cheese.

3 Cover with foil. Bake 45 minutes. Uncover; bake 10 to 15 minutes longer or until lasagna is tender, cheese is bubbly and edges are lightly browned. Let stand 10 minutes before serving.

## time-saver

Prepare ahead of time! Make the lasagna the night before and refrigerate to be baked the next day. Just remember to add a few minutes to the bake time.

**1 SERVING:** Calories 420; Total Fat 20g (Saturated Fat 11g; Trans Fat 0g); Cholesterol 90mg; Sodium 880mg; Total Carbohydrate 28g (Dietary Fiber 1g); Protein 33g **EXCHANGES:** 1½ Starch, ½ Other Carbohydrate, 4 Lean Meat, 1 Fat **CARBOHYDRATE CHOICES:** 2

# country chicken and pasta bake

prep time: 10 minutes    start to finish: 40 minutes    **6 servings**

**1** Heat oven to 375°F. Cook and drain pasta as directed on package, using minimum cook time.

**2** In ungreased 2½-quart casserole, mix pasta and remaining ingredients except stuffing and butter.

**3** Cover casserole. Bake 20 minutes. Uncover and stir. In small bowl, mix stuffing and butter; sprinkle over casserole. Bake uncovered about 10 minutes longer or until hot and topping is brown.

## time-saver

There's no need to cook chicken for this recipe. You can use rotisserie chicken or frozen cooked chicken.

**quick prep**

2 cups uncooked radiatore (nuggets) pasta (6 oz)

3 cups cubed cooked chicken

2 jars (12 oz each) chicken gravy

1 bag (1 lb) frozen broccoli, carrots and cauliflower

¼ teaspoon dried thyme leaves

¼ teaspoon salt

½ cup herb-seasoned stuffing crumbs

2 tablespoons butter or margarine, melted

**1 SERVING:** Calories 410; Total Fat 16g (Saturated Fat 6g; Trans Fat 0g); Cholesterol 75mg; Sodium 1030mg; Total Carbohydrate 38g (Dietary Fiber 4g); Protein 28g **EXCHANGES:** 2 Starch, 1 Vegetable, 3 Medium-Fat Meat **CARBOHYDRATE CHOICES:** 2½

**Casseroles & Other One-Dish Meals**                    **127**

1 tablespoon olive oil

1 cup chopped red bell pepper

¼ cup sliced green onions (4 medium)

3 cups chopped cooked chicken

1 can (14 oz) artichoke hearts in water, drained, chopped

1 container (10 oz) refrigerated reduced-fat Alfredo pasta sauce

1 cup shredded Asiago cheese (4 oz)

½ cup reduced-fat mayonnaise

1½ cups Romano cheese croutons (from 5-oz bag), coarsely crushed

Additional sliced green onions, if desired

# chicken-artichoke casserole

**prep time:** 15 minutes  **start to finish:** 50 minutes  **6 servings** (1⅓ cups)

**1** Heat oven to 350°F. Spray 11×7-inch (2-quart) glass baking dish with cooking spray. In 6-inch skillet, heat oil over medium heat. Add bell pepper and green onions; cook 2 to 3 minutes, stirring occasionally, until bell pepper and onions start to soften.

**2** In large bowl, mix bell pepper mixture and all remaining ingredients except croutons. Spoon into baking dish. Top with croutons.

**3** Bake 30 to 35 minutes or until hot and bubbly. Sprinkle with additional sliced green onions.

## easy variation

If refrigerated Alfredo sauce is not available, use about 1 cup of Alfredo sauce from a jar. Use regular canned artichoke hearts for this recipe, not the marinated ones. Artichoke hearts are available in several sizes. Choose the least expensive, as they are chopped in this recipe.

**1 SERVING:** Calories 460; Total Fat 28g (Saturated Fat 11g; Trans Fat 1g); Cholesterol 105mg; Sodium 890mg; Total Carbohydrate 20g (Dietary Fiber 4g); Protein 30g **EXCHANGES:** 1 Starch, 1 Vegetable, 3½ Medium-Fat Meat, 2 Fat **CARBOHYDRATE CHOICES:** 1

- 1 tablespoon vegetable oil
- ½ cup chopped onion (1 medium)
- ½ cup chopped celery (1 medium stalk)
- 1 cup thinly sliced carrots (2 medium)
- 1 cup frozen cut green beans, thawed
- 2 cups chopped cooked chicken
- 1 can (10¾ oz) condensed cream of chicken soup
- 1 can (10½ oz) chicken gravy
- ½ teaspoon dried sage leaves
- 1 cup finely shredded sharp Cheddar cheese (4 oz)
- 1 refrigerated pie crust, softened as directed on box

# cheesy chicken pot pie

**prep time:** 20 minutes   **start to finish:** 1 hour 10 minutes   **4 servings**

**1** Heat oven to 375°F. In 10-inch skillet, heat oil over medium-high heat. Add onion and celery; cook 3 to 5 minutes, stirring occasionally, until crisp-tender. Stir in carrots, green beans, chicken, soup, gravy and sage. Cook until bubbly. Stir in ¾ cup of the cheese. Spoon into ungreased deep 2-quart casserole.

**2** Place pie crust over hot chicken mixture. Fold over edges to fit inside casserole. Cut small slits in surface of crust with paring knife to allow steam to escape.

**3** Bake 40 minutes. Sprinkle remaining ¼ cup cheese over crust; bake 5 to 6 minutes longer or until crust is deep golden brown and cheese is melted.

## time-saver

A food processor makes quick work of slicing veggies. Use the slicing blade to slice the carrots and the metal blade to chop the onion and celery.

**1 SERVING:** Calories 670; Total Fat 41g (Saturated Fat 15g; Trans Fat 0.5g); Cholesterol 105mg; Sodium 1460mg; Total Carbohydrate 44g (Dietary Fiber 3g); Protein 31g **EXCHANGES:** 1½ Starch, 1 Other Carbohydrate, 1 Vegetable, 3½ Medium-Fat Meat, 4½ Fat **CARBOHYDRATE CHOICES:** 3

# cheesy tater-topped chicken casserole

**1 bag (24 oz) frozen broccoli, carrots, cauliflower in a cheese-flavored sauce**

**2 cups diced cooked chicken**

**4 medium green onions, chopped (¼ cup)**

**4 cups frozen potato nuggets (from 32-oz bag)**

**½ cup finely shredded Cheddar cheese (2 oz)**

**prep time:** 10 minutes     **start to finish:** 1 hour 5 minutes     **6 servings** (1⅓ cups each)

**1** Heat oven to 375°F. In ungreased 11×7-inch (2-quart) glass baking dish, place broccoli, carrots, cauliflower and cheese sauce. Microwave uncovered on High 3 to 5 minutes, stirring once, until thawed. Stir well until cheese sauce is melted.

**2** Stir chicken and 3 tablespoons of the onions into vegetable-cheese mixture. Top with frozen potato nuggets.

**3** Bake 40 to 45 minutes or until bubbly around edges and potato nuggets are golden brown. Sprinkle with Cheddar cheese and remaining 1 tablespoon onion. Bake 5 to 10 minutes longer or until cheese is melted.

## easy variation

Substitute diced cooked turkey for the chicken and mozzarella cheese for the Cheddar.

**1 SERVING:** Calories 360; Total Fat 16g (Saturated Fat 8g; Trans Fat 3.5g); Cholesterol 50mg; Sodium 1040mg; Total Carbohydrate 33g (Dietary Fiber 6g); Protein 23g **EXCHANGES:** 2 Starch, 1 Vegetable, 2 Lean Meat, 1½ Fat **CARBOHYDRATE CHOICES:** 2

- 2 cups diced cooked chicken
- 3 cups shredded Colby–Monterey Jack cheese (12 oz)
- 1 can (4.5 oz) chopped green chiles, undrained
- ¾ cup sour cream
- 1 package (11.5 oz) flour tortillas for burritos (8 tortillas)
- 1 can (16 oz) refried beans
- 1 can (10 oz) enchilada sauce
- 4 medium green onions, sliced (¼ cup)
- 1 cup shredded lettuce
- 1 medium tomato, chopped (¾ cup)

# layered chile-chicken enchilada casserole

**prep time:** 25 minutes   **start to finish:** 1 hour 30 minutes   **8 servings**

1 Heat oven to 350°F. Spray 13×9-inch (3-quart) glass baking dish with cooking spray. In medium bowl, mix chicken, 1½ cups of the cheese, the green chiles and sour cream.

2 Layer 3 tortillas in baking dish, overlapping as necessary and placing slightly up sides of dish (cut third tortilla in half). Spread about half of the beans over tortillas. Top with about half of the chicken mixture and half of the enchilada sauce. Layer with 3 more tortillas and remaining beans and chicken mixture. Place remaining 2 tortillas over chicken mixture, overlapping slightly (do not place up sides of dish). Pour remaining enchilada sauce over top. Sprinkle with remaining 1½ cups cheese.

3 Cover with foil. Bake 45 to 55 minutes or until bubbly and thoroughly heated. Let stand 5 to 10 minutes before cutting. Garnish casserole or individual servings with onions, lettuce and tomato.

## time-saver

Make this casserole up to 8 hours in advance, then cover and refrigerate until it's time to bake it.

**1 SERVING:** Calories 470; Total Fat 25g (Saturated Fat 13g; Trans Fat 0.5g); Cholesterol 85mg; Sodium 1080mg; Total Carbohydrate 34g (Dietary Fiber 3g); Protein 27g **EXCHANGES:** 2½ Starch, 2½ Medium-Fat Meat, 2 Fat **CARBOHYDRATE CHOICES:** 2

# sage chicken and potatoes

**prep time:** 15 minutes   **start to finish:** 1 hour 15 minutes   **4 servings**

1 Heat oven to 400°F. Spray 13×9-inch (3-quart) glass baking dish with cooking spray. In baking dish, arrange chicken, potatoes and carrots. In small bowl, mix remaining ingredients; pour over chicken and vegetables.

2 Spray sheet of foil with cooking spray; place sprayed side down over baking dish. Bake 50 to 60 minutes or until vegetables are tender and juice of chicken is clear when center of thickest part is cut (170°F).

- 4 boneless skinless chicken breasts (about 1 lb)
- 3 medium unpeeled russet potatoes, cut into ¾-inch pieces (3 cups)
- 1½ cups ready-to-eat baby-cut carrots
- 1 jar (12 oz) chicken gravy
- 2 tablespoons Worcestershire sauce
- 1 teaspoon dried sage leaves
- ½ teaspoon garlic-pepper blend

## easy variation

You can use bone-in chicken breasts, but they will take a little longer to bake. Chicken is done when juice is clear when center of thickest part is cut to bone (165°F). Also, if the garlic-pepper blend is not available, use ¼ teaspoon each garlic powder and coarse ground black pepper instead.

**1 SERVING:** Calories 320; Total Fat 9g (Saturated Fat 2.5g; Trans Fat 0g); Cholesterol 75mg; Sodium 680mg; Total Carbohydrate 30g (Dietary Fiber 4g); Protein 31g **EXCHANGES:** 2 Starch, 3½ Very Lean Meat, 1 Fat **CARBOHYDRATE CHOICES:** 2

1 package (8 oz) seasoned yellow rice mix with saffron

1 cup frozen sweet peas

1 can (14.5 oz) diced tomatoes with green chiles, undrained

1 can (14 oz) artichoke hearts, drained, cut into quarters

1¾ cups chicken broth

1 cut-up whole chicken (3 to 3½ lb), skin removed if desired

½ teaspoon paprika

½ teaspoon garlic salt

# paella chicken and rice casserole

**prep time:** 15 minutes    **start to finish:** 1 hour 40 minutes    **6 servings**

**1** Heat oven to 375°F. Spray 13×9-inch (3-quart) glass baking dish with cooking spray. In baking dish, mix rice, peas, tomatoes, artichokes and broth. Arrange chicken on rice mixture. Sprinkle chicken with paprika and garlic salt.

**2** Cover with foil. Bake 45 minutes. Uncover; bake 30 to 40 minutes longer or until rice is tender and juice of chicken is clear when thickest piece is cut to bone (170°F for breasts; 180°F for thighs and legs).

## easy variation

Artichokes are a classic ingredient for paella, but if your family prefers, they can be omitted from the dish.

**1 SERVING**: Calories 350; Total Fat 14g (Saturated Fat 4g; Trans Fat 0g); Cholesterol 85mg; Sodium 1100mg; Total Carbohydrate 24g (Dietary Fiber 6g); Protein 33g **EXCHANGES**: 1½ Starch, 1 Vegetable, 4 Lean Meat **CARBOHYDRATE CHOICES**: 1

⅔ cup Thai peanut sauce (from 13.9-oz jar)

⅔ cup chicken broth

3 tablespoons peanut butter

1 bag (1 lb) frozen broccoli stir-fry vegetables

1 package (7.31 oz) refrigerated cooked stir-fry noodles, separated

2 packages (6 oz each) refrigerated grilled chicken breast strips

¼ cup chow mein noodles

¼ cup chopped peanuts

# spicy asian chicken and noodle casserole

**prep time:** 15 minutes   **start to finish:** 50 minutes   **4 servings** (1½ cups each)

**1** Heat oven to 350°F. Spray 2-quart casserole with cooking spray. In 3-quart saucepan, mix peanut sauce, broth, peanut butter, frozen vegetables and stir-fry noodles. Cook over medium-high heat 5 to 7 minutes, stirring frequently, until hot. Stir in chicken. Spoon into casserole.

**2** In small bowl, mix chow mein noodles and peanuts; sprinkle over chicken mixture.

**3** Bake uncovered about 30 minutes or until mixture is hot. Let stand 5 minutes before serving.

## easy variation

Look for the stir-fry noodles in the refrigerated section of the grocery store. If you can't find them, use two packages of any flavor of ramen noodles. Cook and drain the ramen noodles as directed on package, omitting the seasoning packet.

**1 SERVING:** Calories 190; Total Fat 10g (Saturated Fat 4g; Trans Fat 0.5g); Cholesterol 20mg; Sodium 90mg; Total Carbohydrate 21g (Dietary Fiber 1g); Protein 3g **EXCHANGES:** ½ Starch, 1 Other Carbohydrate, 2 Fat **CARBOHYDRATE CHOICES:** 1½

1½ lb turkey thighs (about 2 medium), skin removed

1 small butternut squash (about 2 lb), peeled, seeded and cut into 1½-inch pieces (3 cups)

1 medium onion, cut in half and sliced

1 can (16 oz) baked beans, undrained

1 can (14.5 oz) diced tomatoes with Italian seasonings, undrained

2 tablespoons chopped fresh parsley

# turkey–butternut squash ragout

**prep time:** 15 minutes    **start to finish:** 7 hours 15 minutes    **4 servings**

**1** Spray 3- to 4-quart slow cooker with cooking spray. In cooker, mix all ingredients except parsley.

**2** Cover; cook on Low heat setting 7 to 8 hours.

**3** Remove turkey from cooker; place on cutting board. Remove meat from bones; discard bones. Return turkey to cooker. Just before serving, sprinkle with parsley.

## healthy twist

Butternut squash, rich in color and great flavor, is an excellent source of vitamin A.

**1 SERVING:** Calories 380; Total Fat 6g (Saturated Fat 2g; Trans Fat 0g); Cholesterol 115mg; Sodium 730mg; Total Carbohydrate 46g (Dietary Fiber 10g); Protein 36g **EXCHANGES:** 3 Starch, 1 Vegetable, 3 Very Lean Meat **CARBOHYDRATE CHOICES:** 3

# wild rice and turkey casserole

**1** Heat oven to 350°F. In ungreased 2-quart casserole, mix all ingredients, including seasoning packet from rice mix.

**2** Cover casserole. Bake 45 to 50 minutes or until rice is tender. Uncover; bake 10 to 15 minutes longer or until liquid is absorbed. If desired, sprinkle with additional green onion.

## healthy twist

This super-easy casserole is low in fat and cholesterol. Keep with this healthy trend and serve it with whole wheat rolls and fresh green beans.

**1 SERVING:** Calories 180; Total Fat 8g (Saturated Fat 2g; Trans Fat 0g); Cholesterol 40mg; Sodium 600mg; Total Carbohydrate 13g (Dietary Fiber 0g); Protein 14g **EXCHANGES:** 1 Starch, 1½ Lean Meat, ½ Fat **CARBOHYDRATE CHOICES:** 1

**4 large bell peppers (any color)**

**½ lb lean (at least 80%) ground beef**

**½ cup chopped onion**

**1 clove garlic, finely chopped**

**1 can (15 oz) tomato sauce**

**½ teaspoon ground cumin**

**¼ teaspoon salt**

**¼ teaspoon ground cinnamon**

**⅛ teaspoon ground red pepper (cayenne)**

**⅔ cup uncooked couscous**

**½ cup water**

**Pine nuts, if desired**

**Fresh cilantro, if desired**

# couscous-stuffed peppers

**prep time:** 20 minutes    **start to finish:** 5 hours 20 minutes    **4 servings**

**1** Cut thin slice from stem end of each bell pepper to remove top of pepper. Remove seeds and membranes; rinse peppers. Set aside.

**2** In 10-inch skillet, cook beef, onion and garlic over medium heat about 5 minutes, stirring occasionally, until beef is brown; drain. Stir in tomato sauce, cumin, salt, cinnamon and red pepper. Stir in couscous. Divide mixture evenly among peppers.

**3** Add water to 5- to 6-quart slow cooker. Stand peppers upright in cooker.

**4** Cover; cook on Low heat setting 5 to 7 hours. Sprinkle with pine nuts and cilantro before serving.

**1 SERVING:** Calories 280; Total Fat 7g (Saturated Fat 2.5g; Trans Fat 0g); Cholesterol 35mg; Sodium 740mg; Total Carbohydrate 38g (Dietary Fiber 6g); Protein 16g **EXCHANGES:** 2 Starch, 1 Vegetable, 1 High-Fat Meat **CARBOHYDRATE CHOICES:** 2½

# philly cheese steak sandwiches

**prep time:** 15 minutes    **start to finish:** 6 hours 15 minutes    **6 sandwiches**

**1 boneless beef round steak, 1 inch thick (2 lb), trimmed of fat, cut into bite-size strips**

**2 medium onions, sliced**

**1 tablespoon garlic-pepper blend**

**2 tablespoons water**

**1 tablespoon beef bouillon granules**

**2 large green bell peppers, cut into bite-size strips**

**6 slices (¾ oz each) American cheese, cut in half**

**6 hoagie buns, split**

**1** In medium bowl, sprinkle beef and onions with garlic-pepper blend; stir to coat evenly. Spoon mixture into 3- to 4-quart slow cooker.

**2** In measuring cup, stir water and bouillon granules until granules are dissolved. Pour over mixture in cooker.

**3** Cover; cook on Low heat setting 6 to 8 hours.

**4** About 20 minutes before serving, stir in bell peppers. Place 2 cheese pieces on bottom of each bun. Using slotted spoon, spoon beef mixture over cheese. Cover with tops of buns. Beef mixture can be kept warm on Low heat setting up to 2 hours.

## easy variation

Not a fan of American cheese? Cheddar or mozzarella cheese can be used instead, for a slightly different but equally tasty sandwich.

**1 SANDWICH:** Calories 550; Total Fat 14g (Saturated Fat 7g; Trans Fat 1g); Cholesterol 105mg; Sodium 1360mg; Total Carbohydrate 56g (Dietary Fiber 4g); Protein 49g **EXCHANGES:** 2 Starch, 1 Other Carbohydrate, 1 Vegetable, 6 Very Lean Meat, 2 Fat **CARBOHYDRATE CHOICES:** 4

3 cups uncooked rotini pasta (9 oz)

1 lb bulk Italian pork sausage

1 medium onion, chopped (½ cup)

1 small bell pepper, chopped (½ cup)

¼ cup water

4 oz sliced Canadian bacon, cut into fourths

1 jar or can (14 or 15 oz) pizza sauce

1 jar (4.5 oz) sliced mushrooms, drained

¾ cup shredded pizza cheese blend (3 oz)

# sausage and pizza bake

**prep time:** 15 minutes    **start to finish:** 50 minutes    **6 servings**

1 Heat oven to 350°F. Spray 3-quart casserole with cooking spray. In 3-quart saucepan, cook and drain pasta as directed on package, using minimum cook time. Return pasta to saucepan.

2 Meanwhile, in 10-inch skillet, cook sausage and onion over medium heat 6 to 8 minutes, stirring occasionally, until sausage is no longer pink; drain.

3 Stir sausage mixture, bell pepper, water, bacon, pizza sauce and mushrooms into pasta. Spoon pasta mixture into casserole. Sprinkle with cheese.

4 Cover casserole. Bake 30 to 35 minutes or until hot and cheese is melted.

## easy variation

Pizza cheese is a blend of mozzarella and Cheddar cheeses. If unavailable, use equal parts of mozzarella and Cheddar.

**1 SERVING:** Calories 570; Total Fat 23g (Saturated Fat 9g; Trans Fat 0g); Cholesterol 50mg; Sodium 1420mg; Total Carbohydrate 62g (Dietary Fiber 5g); Protein 29g **EXCHANGES:** 3 Starch, 1 Other Carbohydrate, 3 Medium-Fat Meat, 1 Fat **CARBOHYDRATE CHOICES:** 4

Betty Crocker The Big Book of Slow Cooker, Casseroles & More

# potato-topped meat loaf casserole

prep time: 20 minutes    start to finish: 55 minutes    **6 servings**

**1** Heat oven to 350°F. Spray 8-inch square (2-quart) glass baking dish with cooking spray. In medium bowl, mix meat loaf ingredients. Press in bottom and up sides of baking dish to within ½ inch of top.

**2** In 2-quart saucepan, heat water, milk, butter and ¼ teaspoon salt to boiling. Remove from heat; stir in potatoes. Let stand 30 seconds. Stir in egg. Stir in broccoli and cheese. Spoon over meat.

**3** Bake 25 to 30 minutes or until meat loaf is thoroughly cooked and meat thermometer inserted in center of meat reads 160°F. Let stand 5 minutes; drain liquid along edges.

## time-saver

To save a little time, purchase refrigerated mashed potatoes for this recipe. Add the egg, broccoli and cheese as directed.

**MEAT LOAF**

1 lb extra-lean (at least 90%) ground beef

3 tablespoons unseasoned dry bread crumbs

3 tablespoons steak sauce

1 tablespoon dried minced onion

½ teaspoon salt

¼ teaspoon pepper

1 egg

**FILLING**

1¾ cups water

½ cup milk

2 tablespoons butter or margarine

¼ teaspoon salt

2 cups plain mashed potato mix (dry)

1 egg

1½ cups frozen chopped broccoli, thawed

½ cup shredded sharp Cheddar cheese (2 oz)

**1 SERVING:** Calories 330; Total Fat 15g (Saturated Fat 8g; Trans Fat 0.5g); Cholesterol 140mg; Sodium 610mg; Total Carbohydrate 26g (Dietary Fiber 2g); Protein 23g **EXCHANGES:** 1½ Starch, 2½ Medium-Fat Meat, ½ Fat **CARBOHYDRATE CHOICES:** 2

- 3 cups uncooked rigatoni pasta (9 oz)
- 1 lb bulk Italian pork sausage
- 1 can (28 oz) crushed tomatoes, undrained
- 3 cloves garlic, finely chopped
- 3 tablespoons chopped fresh or 1 tablespoon dried basil leaves
- 1 package (8 oz) sliced fresh mushrooms (3 cups)
- 1 jar (7 oz) roasted red bell peppers, drained, chopped
- 1 cup shredded Parmesan cheese (4 oz)
- 2½ cups shredded mozzarella cheese (10 oz)

# seven-layer rigatoni

**prep time:** 10 minutes   **start to finish:** 50 minutes   **8 servings**

1 Heat oven to 375°F. Spray 13×9-inch (3-quart) glass baking dish with cooking spray. Cook and drain pasta as directed on package, using minimum cook time.

2 Meanwhile, in 10-inch skillet, cook sausage over medium heat 5 to 7 minutes, stirring occasionally, until no longer pink; drain. In small bowl, mix tomatoes, garlic and basil.

3 In baking dish, layer half each of the pasta, sausage, mushrooms, bell peppers, Parmesan cheese, tomato mixture and mozzarella cheese; repeat layers.

4 Bake 35 to 40 minutes or until hot and cheese is golden brown.

## healthy twist

Slash the fat in this family-favorite casserole by using ¾ lb bulk turkey Italian sausage and reduced-fat mozzarella cheese.

**1 SERVING:** Calories 520; Total Fat 23g (Saturated Fat 11g; Trans Fat 0g); Cholesterol 50mg; Sodium 1220mg; Total Carbohydrate 46g (Dietary Fiber 3g); Protein 30g **EXCHANGES:** 2 Starch, ½ Other Carbohydrate, 1 Vegetable, 3 High-Fat Meat **CARBOHYDRATE CHOICES:** 3

# greek spanakopita pie

prep time: 35 minutes  start to finish: 1 hour 30 minutes  **6 servings**

1 lb lean (at least 80%) ground beef

1 cup chopped onion (1 large)

1 box (9 oz) frozen chopped spinach, thawed, squeezed to drain

¼ cup chopped fresh Italian (flat-leaf) parsley

½ teaspoon salt

¼ teaspoon pepper

1 can (15 oz) diced tomatoes with Italian-style herbs, undrained

12 sheets frozen phyllo (filo) pastry (14×9 inch), thawed

6 tablespoons butter or margarine, melted

¼ cup Italian-style bread crumbs

1 cup crumbled feta cheese (4 oz)

**1** Heat oven to 350°F. Spray 9-inch glass pie plate with cooking spray. In 10-inch skillet, cook beef and onion over medium-high heat 5 to 7 minutes, stirring occasionally, until beef is thoroughly cooked; drain.

**2** Stir spinach, parsley, salt, pepper and all but ½ cup of the tomatoes into beef mixture. Cook and stir until hot; set aside.

**3** Cover phyllo sheets with damp paper towel. Arrange sheets, layering 3 at a time, in an X shape and then in a plus (+) shape to create a spoke pattern on work surface, brushing each with butter and sprinkling with 1 teaspoon of the bread crumbs as it is added. Transfer all layers of phyllo to pie plate, gently easing down sides of pie plate and allowing excess phyllo to hang over edge.

**4** Place beef mixture in phyllo; top with cheese. Fold overhanging phyllo up and over filling, leaving 2- to 3-inch center of filling uncovered. Spoon remaining ½ cup tomatoes in center. Brush phyllo with remaining butter.

**5** Bake 40 to 50 minutes or until phyllo is golden brown. Let stand 5 minutes before serving.

## easy variation

For a more authentic Greek flavor, substitute ground lamb for the ground beef.

**1 SERVING:** Calories 400; Total Fat 25g (Saturated Fat 13g; Trans Fat 1.5g); Cholesterol 95mg; Sodium 810mg; Total Carbohydrate 24g (Dietary Fiber 3g); Protein 20g **EXCHANGES:** 1 Starch, 1 Vegetable, 2 Medium-Fat Meat, 3 Fat **CARBOHYDRATE CHOICES:** 1½

# taco casserole

**prep time:** 20 minutes   **start to finish:** 50 minutes   **4 servings**

**1** Heat oven to 350°F. In 10-inch skillet, cook beef over medium-high heat 5 to 7 minutes, stirring occasionally, until brown; drain. Reduce heat to medium. Stir in beans, tomato sauce, taco sauce, chili powder and garlic powder. Heat to boiling over medium heat, stirring occasionally.

**2** In ungreased 1½-quart casserole, place tortilla chips. Top with beef mixture. Sprinkle with onions, tomato and cheese.

**3** Bake uncovered 20 to 30 minutes or until hot and bubbly. Arrange additional tortilla chips around edge of casserole.

**Ingredients (sidebar):**

- 1 lb lean (at least 80%) ground beef
- 1 can (15 to 16 oz) chili beans in sauce, undrained
- 1 can (8 oz) tomato sauce
- 2 tablespoons taco sauce, picante sauce or salsa
- 2 to 4 teaspoons chili powder
- 1 teaspoon garlic powder
- 2 cups coarsely broken tortilla chips
- 8 medium green onions, sliced (½ cup)
- 1 medium tomato, chopped (¾ cup)
- 1 cup shredded Cheddar or Monterey Jack cheese (4 oz)
- Additional tortilla chips, if desired

## easy variation

Try lean ground turkey instead of the ground beef.

**1 SERVING:** Calories 660; Total Fat 33g (Saturated Fat 12g; Trans Fat 1.5g); Cholesterol 100mg; Sodium 1630mg; Total Carbohydrate 53g (Dietary Fiber 8g); Protein 36g **EXCHANGES:** 3 Starch, ½ Other Carbohydrate, 4 Lean Meat, 4 Fat **CARBOHYDRATE CHOICES:** 3½

# easy dinner lasagna

prep time: 30 minutes    start to finish: 1 hour 40 minutes    **12 servings**

quick prep

**1** Spray 13×9-inch (3-quart) glass baking dish with cooking spray. Cook and drain noodles as directed on package. Place in cold water.

**2** Meanwhile, in 12-inch skillet, cook beef and garlic over medium-high heat 5 to 7 minutes, stirring frequently, until beef is thoroughly cooked; drain. Stir in pasta sauce, red pepper and 1 teaspoon of the basil. Heat to boiling, stirring occasionally. Remove from heat.

**3** Heat oven to 350°F. In medium bowl, beat egg slightly. Stir in ricotta cheese and remaining ½ teaspoon basil until blended. Drain noodles. Spread about ½ cup sauce mixture over bottom of baking dish. Top with 3 noodles, 1½ cups of the sauce mixture, half of the ricotta mixture and ¾ cup of the mozzarella cheese. Repeat layers once. Top with remaining noodles, sauce and mozzarella cheese; sprinkle with Parmesan cheese.

**4** Spray 15-inch sheet of foil with cooking spray; place sprayed side down over baking dish. Bake 45 minutes. Uncover; bake 10 to 15 minutes longer or until bubbly. Let stand 10 minutes before serving. Garnish with fresh basil.

- 9 uncooked lasagna noodles
- 1 lb extra-lean (at least 90%) ground beef
- 2 cloves garlic, finely chopped
- 1 jar (25.5 oz) Italian herb pasta sauce
- ⅛ teaspoon ground red pepper (cayenne)
- 1½ teaspoons dried basil leaves
- 1 egg
- 1 container (15 oz) reduced-fat ricotta cheese
- 2 cups shredded reduced-fat mozzarella cheese (8 oz)
- ⅓ cup shredded Parmesan cheese (1⅓ oz)
- Fresh basil, if desired

## healthy twist

Three ingredients help reduce the fat in this lighter version of lasagna: extra-lean ground beef, light cheeses and only 1 egg instead of the 2. Basil and a touch of ground red pepper enhance the flavor.

**1 SERVING:** Calories 240; Total Fat 9g (Saturated Fat 4.5g; Trans Fat 0g); Cholesterol 60mg; Sodium 400mg; Total Carbohydrate 21g (Dietary Fiber 2g); Protein 20g **EXCHANGES:** 1 Starch, ½ Other Carbohydrate, 2½ Lean Meat **CARBOHYDRATE CHOICES:** 1½

1 package (9 oz)
    refrigerated fettuccine

1 egg

1 tablespoon butter
    or margarine, melted

1½ cups shredded Italian
    cheese blend (6 oz)

1¼ cups tomato pasta
    sauce (any variety)

1 bag (16 oz) frozen
    cooked Italian-style
    meatballs (32 meatballs),
    thawed

1 medium bell pepper,
    cut into thin strips

Chopped fresh parsley,
    if desired

# italian meatball pie

**prep time:** 20 minutes    **start to finish:** 1 hour 10 minutes    **6 servings**

**1** Heat oven to 350°F. Spray 9½-inch deep-dish glass pie plate with cooking spray. Cook and drain fettuccine as directed on package.

**2** In large bowl, beat egg and butter with fork or whisk. Stir in fettuccine and 1 cup of the cheese. Spoon mixture into pie plate. Using back of wooden spoon or rubber spatula, press evenly on bottom and up side of pie plate.

**3** In large bowl, toss pasta sauce, meatballs and bell pepper. Spoon into crust.

**4** Cover with foil. Bake 45 minutes. Uncover; sprinkle with remaining ½ cup cheese. Bake about 5 minutes longer or until cheese is melted. Sprinkle with parsley.

**1 SERVING:** Calories 480; Total Fat 20g (Saturated Fat 9g; Trans Fat 0.5g); Cholesterol 160mg; Sodium 1120mg; Total Carbohydrate 47g (Dietary Fiber 3g); Protein 28g **EXCHANGES:** 2 Starch, ½ Other Carbohydrate, ½ Low-Fat Milk, 1 Vegetable, 2 Medium-Fat Meat, 1½ Fat **CARBOHYDRATE CHOICES:** 3

# french pork and bean casserole

prep time: 25 minutes    start to finish: 6 hours 55 minutes    **5 servings** (1½ cups each)

## quick prep

2 slices bacon, chopped

1 lb boneless country-style pork ribs, cut into ¾-inch pieces

½ cup finely chopped onion

1 cup shredded carrots

1 can (14.5 oz) diced tomatoes, undrained

1 can (8 oz) tomato sauce

1 teaspoon dried thyme leaves

½ teaspoon pepper

2 cans (15 to 16 oz each) great northern beans, drained

½ lb cooked kielbasa, cut into ½-inch pieces

**1** In 10-inch skillet, cook bacon, pork pieces and onion over medium-high heat 8 to 10 minutes, stirring occasionally, until pork begins to brown.

**2** Spray 3- to 4-quart slow cooker with cooking spray. In cooker, place pork mixture. Stir in remaining ingredients except beans and kielbasa. Layer beans over top.

**3** Cover; cook on Low heat setting 6 to 7 hours.

**4** Stir in kielbasa. Increase heat setting to High; cover and cook 30 minutes longer or until thoroughly heated.

## easy variation

Kielbasa is a Polish pork sausage. Look for it near the other cooked sausages in the prepackaged meat section of the supermarket. If you like, turkey kielbasa can be used instead.

**1 SERVING:** Calories 610; Total Fat 27g (Saturated Fat 10g; Trans Fat 0g); Cholesterol 90mg; Sodium 920mg; Total Carbohydrate 49g (Dietary Fiber 12g); Protein 41g **EXCHANGES:** 2½ Starch, ½ Other Carbohydrate, 1 Vegetable, 4½ Medium-Fat Meat, ½ Fat **CARBOHYDRATE CHOICES:** 3

## Ingredients

- 1 lb boneless center-cut pork loin roast, cut into ¾-inch pieces
- 1 large onion, halved lengthwise, cut into 12 wedges
- 1 red bell pepper, cut into bite-size strips
- 2 medium carrots, sliced (1 cup)
- 3 cloves garlic, finely chopped
- 2 teaspoons finely chopped gingerroot
- ½ cup orange juice
- ½ cup orange marmalade
- 1½ teaspoons chili puree
- 2 tablespoons fresh lime juice
- 1 tablespoon cornstarch
- 1 teaspoon salt
- 4 oz fresh snow pea pods (1 cup), strings removed
- 3 cups hot cooked lo mein noodles or linguine

# thai orange pork lo mein

**prep time:** 30 minutes     **start to finish:** 6 hours 45 minutes     **5 servings**

**1** Spray 4- to 5-quart slow cooker with cooking spray. In cooker, mix pork, onion, bell pepper, carrots, garlic, gingerroot, orange juice, marmalade and chili puree.

**2** Cover; cook on Low heat setting 6 to 8 hours (or on High heat setting 3 to 4 hours).

**3** In small bowl, mix lime juice, cornstarch and salt. Stir cornstarch mixture and pea pods into pork mixture in cooker. If needed, increase heat setting to High; cover and cook about 15 minutes longer or until pea pods are crisp-tender. Serve with noodles.

## time-saver

Don't go all over the store trying to find chili puree! You'll find it near the Asian ingredients in your supermarket. It may be called "Thai Style." It is not the same as chili sauce, which is commonly used for making the sauce for shrimp cocktail.

**1 SERVING:** Calories 450; Total Fat 16g (Saturated Fat 3.5g, Trans Fat 0g); Cholesterol 60mg; Sodium 680mg; Total Carbohydrate 52g (Dietary Fiber 4g); Protein 24g **EXCHANGES:** 1½ Starch, 1½ Other Carbohydrate, 1 Vegetable, 2½ Lean Meat, 1½ Fat **CARBOHYDRATE CHOICES:** 3½

1½ lb boneless pork country-style ribs

1 cup frozen onions, celery, bell pepper and parsley seasoning blend (from 12-oz bag), thawed

1 can (29 oz) tomato puree

1 can (14.5 oz) diced tomatoes with basil, garlic and oregano, undrained

1 tablespoon Worcestershire sauce

1 teaspoon sugar

1 teaspoon fennel seed

1 package (8 oz) sliced fresh mushrooms (3 cups)

1 package (16 oz) spaghetti

1 tablespoon olive or vegetable oil

Grated Parmesan cheese, if desired

# chunky pork and mushroom spaghetti sauce

**prep time:** 15 minutes    **start to finish:** 8 hours 35 minutes    **8 servings** (1 cup each)

**1** In 3- to 4-quart slow cooker, mix all ingredients except mushrooms, spaghetti, oil and cheese.

**2** Cover; cook on Low heat setting 8 to 10 hours.

**3** Using 2 forks, break pork into bite-size pieces in cooker. Stir in mushrooms. Increase heat setting to High; cover and cook 15 to 20 minutes. Meanwhile, cook and drain spaghetti as directed on package.

**4** Stir oil into sauce. Serve over hot spaghetti; sprinkle with cheese.

## time-saver

The onion mixture shortens the prep time for this recipe, and it's great to have on hand for other recipes too. Look for it where the bags of chopped onion are in the frozen vegetable section—it should be nearby.

**1 SERVING:** Calories 480; Total Fat 13g (Saturated Fat 4g; Trans Fat 0g); Cholesterol 50mg; Sodium 890mg; Total Carbohydrate 62g (Dietary Fiber 6g); Protein 28g **EXCHANGES:** 3 Starch, 1 Other Carbohydrate, 1 Vegetable, 2½ Lean Meat, ½ Fat **CARBOHYDRATE CHOICES:** 4

4 slices bacon, chopped

½ lb bulk pork sausage

½ lb boneless pork tenderloin, cubed

⅓ cup diced onion

2 cloves garlic, finely chopped

2 cans (15 oz each) cannellini beans, drained

1 can (14.5 oz) diced tomatoes, undrained

½ cup chicken broth

¼ cup white wine or chicken broth

1 teaspoon dried sage leaves

1 teaspoon dried thyme leaves

¼ teaspoon pepper

1 dried bay leaf

# everyday cassoulet

**prep time:** 20 minutes    **start to finish:** 2 hours 20 minutes    **6 servings**

**1** Heat oven to 350°F. In 12-inch skillet, cook bacon over medium-high heat, stirring occasionally, until crisp. Remove bacon from skillet; set aside.

**2** In same skillet, cook sausage, cubed pork, onion and garlic, stirring occasionally, until pork is browned. Stir in bacon and remaining ingredients. Pour into ungreased 2½-quart casserole.

**3** Cover casserole. Bake 1 hour 45 minutes. Uncover; bake about 15 minutes longer or until pork is tender and flavors are blended. Remove bay leaf. Serve in soup bowls.

## easy variation

Great northern beans are an easy substitution for the cannellini beans if you prefer.

**1 SERVING:** Calories 330; Total Fat 9g (Saturated Fat 3g; Trans Fat 0g); Cholesterol 45mg; Sodium 820mg; Total Carbohydrate 34g (Dietary Fiber 8g); Protein 26g **EXCHANGES:** 2 Starch, 3 Lean Meat **CARBOHYDRATE CHOICES:** 2

# salmon paella bake

**prep time:** 15 minutes    **start to finish:** 1 hour    **6 servings**

- 1½ cups uncooked Arborio rice
- 1 medium onion, chopped (½ cup)
- 1 large red bell pepper, chopped (about 1¾ cups)
- 1 teaspoon grated lemon peel
- ¾ teaspoon salt
- ½ teaspoon crushed saffron threads
- 1 carton (32 oz) chicken broth (4 cups)
- ½ lb smoked turkey kielbasa sausage, cut into ¾-inch slices
- 1 salmon fillet (1½ lb), skin removed, cut into 6 pieces
- 1 tablespoon vegetable oil
- 2 tablespoons chopped fresh Italian (flat-leaf) parsley

**1** Heat oven to 350°F. Spray 13×9-inch (3-quart) glass baking dish with cooking spray. In baking dish, place rice, onion, bell pepper, lemon peel, ½ teaspoon of the salt and the saffron.

**2** Heat broth to boiling; stir into rice mixture. Arrange kielbasa slices over rice mixture. Cover with foil. Bake 20 minutes.

**3** Arrange salmon over rice mixture. Brush salmon with oil; sprinkle with remaining ¼ teaspoon salt. Bake uncovered 20 to 25 minutes longer or until fish flakes easily with fork, rice is tender and broth is absorbed. Sprinkle with parsley.

## easy variation

For a kick of spice, add a chopped jalapeño chile with the rice, and substitute chopped fresh cilantro for the parsley.

**1 SERVING:** Calories 450; Total Fat 14g (Saturated Fat 3.5g; Trans Fat 0g); Cholesterol 95mg; Sodium 1430mg; Total Carbohydrate 44g (Dietary Fiber 1g); Protein 37g **EXCHANGES:** 3 Starch, 4 Lean Meat **CARBOHYDRATE CHOICES:** 3

# seafood-stuffed pasta shells

**prep time:** 35 minutes    **start to finish:** 1 hour 5 minutes    **6 servings**

**1** Heat oven to 350°F. Spray 13×9-inch (3-quart) glass baking dish with cooking spray. Cook and drain pasta shells as directed on package.

**2** Meanwhile, in 12-inch nonstick skillet, melt butter over medium-high heat. Add onion and bell pepper; cook 2 to 3 minutes, stirring occasionally, until crisp-tender. Add asparagus. Cover; cook 3 to 5 minutes, stirring occasionally, until asparagus is crisp-tender. Remove from heat. Stir in shrimp, crabmeat, ½ cup of the Alfredo sauce and half of the basil.

**3** Spread about ¼ cup of the remaining Alfredo sauce over bottom of baking dish. Fill each pasta shell with about 2 tablespoons seafood mixture; arrange in dish. Spoon remaining Alfredo sauce over shells. Sprinkle with cheese and remaining basil.

**4** Bake uncovered 25 to 30 minutes or until bubbly.

## time-saver

Save time on the day you want to serve this dish. Make it up to 24 hours ahead of time. Fill cooked shells and arrange in dish with sauce as directed; cover and refrigerate. Bake as directed.

### Ingredients

18 uncooked jumbo pasta shells

1 tablespoon butter or margarine

1 medium onion, chopped (½ cup)

1 small bell pepper, chopped (½ cup)

8 oz fresh asparagus spears, trimmed, cut into 1-inch pieces (1½ cups)

1½ cups frozen cooked salad shrimp, thawed

2 cans (6 oz each) crabmeat, drained (1¾ cups)

1 jar (16 oz) Alfredo pasta sauce

2 tablespoons chopped fresh or ½ teaspoon dried basil leaves

¼ cup shredded Parmesan cheese (1 oz)

**1 SERVING**: Calories 630; Total Fat 30g (Saturated Fat 17g; Trans Fat 1g); Cholesterol 255mg; Sodium 880mg; Total Carbohydrate 50g (Dietary Fiber 4g); Protein 40g **EXCHANGES**: 3 Starch, ½ Vegetable, 4 Very Lean Meat, 5½ Fat **CARBOHYDRATE CHOICES**: 3

- 2 cups water
- 1 teaspoon salt
- 2 cups diced peeled potatoes (2 medium russet potatoes)
- 4 slices bacon, cut in half
- ⅓ cup all-purpose flour
- 2 bottles (8 oz each) clam juice
- ¼ cup whipping cream
- ½ teaspoon onion salt
- 1 cup frozen peas and carrots, thawed
- 1 cup frozen corn, thawed
- 1 tablespoon chopped fresh thyme leaves
- 6 oz cooked deveined peeled medium shrimp, tail shells removed (about 1 cup)
- 1 can (6 oz) crabmeat, drained, flaked (about 1 cup)
- 1 sheet frozen (thawed) puff pastry (from 17.3-oz package)

# seafood chowder pot pie

**prep time:** 30 minutes   **start to finish:** 1 hour 20 minutes   **6 servings**

**1** Heat oven to 400°F. Spray 11×7-inch (2-quart) glass baking dish with cooking spray. In 2-quart saucepan, heat water and salt to boiling over high heat. Add potatoes; heat to boiling. Reduce heat to medium; cover and simmer 5 to 7 minutes or until tender; drain.

**2** Meanwhile, in heavy 3-quart saucepan, cook bacon over medium heat, turning occasionally, until crisp. Remove bacon from saucepan; drain, crumble and set aside. Using whisk, stir flour into bacon fat in saucepan. Gradually stir in clam juice, whipping cream and onion salt. Heat, stirring constantly, until thickened and bubbly.

**3** Stir drained potatoes, bacon, peas and carrots, corn and thyme into cream mixture. Cook 3 to 4 minutes longer or until hot. Stir in shrimp and crabmeat. Spoon mixture into baking dish.

**4** On lightly floured surface, unfold pastry. Roll into 12×8-inch rectangle. With sharp knife, cut slits in pastry to allow steam to escape. Place pastry over hot seafood mixture in baking dish. Roll outer edges of pastry over edges of baking dish, pressing onto edges.

**5** Bake 30 to 40 minutes or until crust is deep golden brown. Let stand 10 minutes before serving.

**1 SERVING:** Calories 440; Total Fat 22g (Saturated Fat 8g; Trans Fat 1.5g); Cholesterol 145mg; Sodium 1090mg; Total Carbohydrate 42g (Dietary Fiber 3g); Protein 19g **EXCHANGES:** 2½ Starch, ½ Other Carbohydrate, 1½ Lean Meat, 3 Fat **CARBOHYDRATE CHOICES:** 3

2 cups uncooked fusilli pasta (6 oz)

1 jar (1 lb) Alfredo pasta sauce

⅓ cup dry white wine or chicken broth

1 teaspoon Italian seasoning

1 teaspoon grated lemon peel

2 cans (5 oz each) solid white albacore tuna in water, drained

1 box (9 oz) frozen sugar snap peas, thawed, drained

1 jar (4.5 oz) whole mushrooms, drained

½ cup unseasoned dry bread crumbs

2 tablespoons butter or margarine, melted

# contemporary tuna-noodle casserole

**prep time:** 20 minutes    **start to finish:** 50 minutes    **6 servings**

**1** Heat oven to 375°F. Spray 11×7-inch (2-quart) glass baking dish or 2-quart casserole with cooking spray. Cook and drain pasta as directed on package, using minimum cook time.

**2** In large bowl, stir together Alfredo sauce, wine, Italian seasoning, lemon peel, tuna, peas, mushrooms and pasta. Spoon into baking dish.

**3** In small bowl, stir together bread crumbs and butter; sprinkle over mixture in baking dish.

**4** Bake 25 to 30 minutes or until topping is golden brown.

## easy variation

Land lovers can substitute 2 cups cut-up cooked chicken for the tuna.

**1 SERVING:** Calories 530; Total Fat 29g (Saturated Fat 18g; Trans Fat 1g); Cholesterol 100mg; Sodium 730mg; Total Carbohydrate 41g (Dietary Fiber 3g); Protein 24g **EXCHANGES:** 2½ Starch, 2½ Lean Meat, 4 Fat **CARBOHYDRATE CHOICES:** 3

2 large onions, chopped (2 cups)

2 medium stalks celery, finely chopped (1 cup)

5 cloves garlic, finely chopped

1 can (28 oz) diced tomatoes, undrained

1 bottle (8 oz) clam juice

1 can (6 oz) tomato paste

½ cup dry white wine or water

1 tablespoon red wine vinegar

1 tablespoon olive oil

2½ teaspoons Italian seasoning

¼ teaspoon sugar

¼ teaspoon crushed red pepper flakes

1 dried bay leaf

1 lb halibut, whitefish, sea bass or other medium-firm fish fillets, cut into 1-inch pieces

¾ lb uncooked deveined peeled medium shrimp, thawed if frozen, tail shells removed

1 can (6½ oz) chopped clams with juice, undrained

1 can (6 oz) crabmeat, drained, cartilage removed and flaked

¼ cup chopped fresh parsley

# cioppino

**prep time:** 20 minutes   **start to finish:** 4 hours 5 minutes   **8 servings**

**1** In 5- to 6-quart slow cooker, mix all ingredients except fish, shrimp, clams, crabmeat and parsley.

**2** Cover; cook on High heat setting 3 to 4 hours.

**3** Stir in fish, shrimp, clams and crabmeat. Reduce heat setting to Low; cover and cook 30 to 45 minutes longer or until fish flakes easily with fork. Remove bay leaf. Stir in parsley.

## healthy twist

A variety of tasty fish make up this delicious healthful dish. Halibut is a great low-fat fish, perfect for this recipe as it tends to hold its shape.

**1 SERVING:** Calories 220; Total Fat 6g (Saturated Fat 1g; Trans Fat 0g); Cholesterol 115mg; Sodium 560mg; Total Carbohydrate 14g (Dietary Fiber 3g); Protein 26g **EXCHANGES:** ½ Other Carbohydrate, 1 Vegetable, 3 Lean Meat **CARBOHYDRATE CHOICES:** 1

1 large onion, chopped
(1 cup)

1 medium green bell
pepper, chopped
(1 cup)

2 medium stalks celery,
chopped (1 cup)

3 cloves garlic, finely
chopped

1 can (28 oz) diced
tomatoes, undrained

2 cups chopped fully
cooked smoked
sausage

1 tablespoon parsley
flakes

½ teaspoon dried thyme
leaves

½ teaspoon salt

¼ teaspoon pepper

¼ teaspoon red pepper
sauce

¾ lb uncooked deveined
peeled medium shrimp,
thawed if frozen

4 cups hot cooked rice

# jambalaya

**prep time:** 20 minutes  **start to finish:** 8 hours 20 minutes  **8 servings**

**1** Spray 3- to 6-quart slow cooker with cooking spray. In cooker, mix all ingredients except shrimp and rice.

**2** Cover; cook on Low heat setting 7 to 8 hours (or High heat setting 3 to 4 hours).

**3** Stir in shrimp. Cover; cook about 1 hour longer or until shrimp are pink. Serve jambalaya with rice.

## easy variation

If you prefer more "heat," sprinkle additional red pepper sauce on this Cajun favorite just before serving.

**1 SERVING:** Calories 280; Total Fat 10g (Saturated Fat 3g; Trans Fat 0g); Cholesterol 90mg; Sodium 630mg; Total Carbohydrate 30g (Dietary Fiber 2g); Protein 16g **EXCHANGES:** 1½ Starch, 1½ Vegetable, 1 High-Fat Meat, ½ Fat **CARBOHYDRATE CHOICES:** 2

# black bean enchiladas

prep time: 20 minutes    start to finish: 50 minutes    **10 enchiladas**

**1** Heat oven to 350°F. Spray 11×7-inch (2-quart) glass baking dish with cooking spray. In 10-inch skillet, heat oil over medium heat. Add onion and cumin; cook 4 to 5 minutes, stirring occasionally, until onion is tender. Stir in corn, salsa, beans and 1 cup of the cheese. Remove from heat.

**2** On microwavable plate, place stack of tortillas; cover with microwavable paper towel. Microwave on High 1 minute to soften. Spread ¼ cup bean mixture down center of each tortilla. Roll up tightly; place seam side down in baking dish.

**3** Spoon remaining bean mixture on top. Pour enchilada sauce over enchiladas, spreading to coat all tortillas. Sprinkle with remaining 1 cup cheese.

**4** Bake 25 to 30 minutes or until cheese is melted and sauce is bubbly around edges. Garnish with remaining ingredients.

1 tablespoon vegetable oil

½ cup chopped onion (1 medium)

1 teaspoon ground cumin

1 cup frozen corn, thawed

¾ cup medium chunky-style salsa

1 can (15 oz) black beans, drained, rinsed

2 cups shredded Monterey Jack cheese (8 oz)

10 corn tortillas (6 inch)

1 can (10 oz) enchilada sauce

Chopped avocado, ripe olives, sour cream and cilantro, if desired

## easy variation

Like variety? Why not make Hominy Enchiladas by substituting one can of hominy for the black beans? You can also vary the spice by using mild, medium or hot salsa and enchilada sauce.

**1 ENCHILADA:** Calories 240; Total Fat 10g (Saturated Fat 4.5g; Trans Fat 0g); Cholesterol 20mg; Sodium 390mg; Total Carbohydrate 27g (Dietary Fiber 6g); Protein 10g **EXCHANGES:** 1 Starch, 1 Other Carbohydrate, 1 Lean Meat, 1 Fat **CARBOHYDRATE CHOICES:** 2

- 3 medium carrots, sliced (1½ cups)
- 1 medium onion, chopped (½ cup)
- 1 cup water
- 2 teaspoons sugar
- 1 teaspoon Italian seasoning
- ½ teaspoon salt
- ¼ teaspoon pepper
- 1 can (28 oz) diced tomatoes, undrained
- 1 can (15 to 16 oz) garbanzo beans, drained, rinsed
- 1 can (6 oz) Italian-style tomato paste
- 2 cloves garlic, finely chopped
- 1½ cups frozen cut green beans, thawed
- 1 cup uncooked elbow macaroni (3½ oz)
- ½ cup shredded Parmesan cheese (2 oz)

# mediterranean minestrone casserole

**prep time:** 20 minutes **start to finish:** 6 hours 40 minutes **5 servings** (1⅓ cups each)

**1** In 3- to 4-quart slow cooker, mix all ingredients except green beans, macaroni and cheese.

**2** Cover; cook on Low heat setting 6 to 8 hours.

**3** Stir in green beans and macaroni. Increase heat setting to High. Cover; cook about 20 minutes longer or until beans and macaroni are tender. Sprinkle with cheese.

## healthy twist

Looking to get a healthy dose of vegetables? This vegetarian main dish has carrots, onions, tomatoes and green beans, in addition to fiber-rich garbanzos.

**1 SERVING:** Calories 345; Total Fat 6g (Saturated Fat 2g; Trans Fat 0g); Cholesterol 10mg; Sodium 1060mg; Total Carbohydrate 67g (Dietary Fiber 13g); Protein 19g **EXCHANGES:** 4 Starch, 1 Vegetable **CARBOHYDRATE CHOICES:** 4½

# easy cheesy manicotti

prep time: 25 minutes    start to finish: 1 hour 45 minutes    **7 servings** (2 shells each)

**quick prep**

- 1 jar (26 oz) chunky-style tomato pasta sauce
- 2 boxes (9 oz each) frozen chopped spinach, thawed, well drained
- 1 container (12 oz) small-curd cottage cheese (1½ cups)
- ⅓ cup grated Parmesan cheese
- 1 teaspoon dried oregano leaves, crumbled
- ¼ teaspoon pepper
- 1 package (8 oz) manicotti shells (14 shells)
- ¼ cup water
- 2 cups shredded mozzarella cheese (8 oz)

**1** Heat oven to 350°F. In ungreased 13×9-inch (3-quart) glass baking dish, spread about one-third of the pasta sauce.

**2** In large bowl, mix spinach, cottage cheese, Parmesan cheese, oregano and pepper. Fill uncooked manicotti shells with spinach mixture; place on sauce in baking dish.

**3** In medium bowl, mix remaining pasta sauce and water. Pour sauce mixture evenly over shells, covering completely.

**4** Cover with foil. Bake 1 hour. Sprinkle with mozzarella cheese. Cover; bake 15 to 20 minutes longer or until shells are tender.

## time-saver

Having guests for dinner? Save time on the day they're coming. Make this dish up to 24 hours ahead of time; cover and refrigerate. Then, bake as directed. Or cover tightly, label and freeze up to 1 month; bake about 2 hours.

**1 SERVING**: Calories 440; Total Fat 15g (Saturated Fat 7g; Trans Fat 0g); Cholesterol 30mg; Sodium 1000mg; Total Carbohydrate 52g (Dietary Fiber 5g); Protein 25g **EXCHANGES**: 2 Starch, 1 Other Carbohydrate, 1 Vegetable, 2½ Medium-Fat Meat **CARBOHYDRATE CHOICES**: 3½

1 box (9 oz) frozen
   chopped spinach

1 tablespoon butter
   or margarine

¼ cup chopped onion
   (1 small)

1 tablespoon all-purpose
   flour

1¼ cups half-and-half
   or milk

1 package (16 oz)
   shelf-stable gnocchi

1 cup shredded Gruyère
   cheese (4 oz)

½ cup shredded Muenster
   cheese (2 oz)

⅛ teaspoon ground
   nutmeg

1 large plum (Roma)
   tomato, thinly sliced

1 teaspoon olive oil

# cheesy gnocchi florentine

**prep time:** 20 minutes    **start to finish:** 50 minutes    **4 servings**

**1** Heat oven to 350°F. Spray 1½-quart casserole with cooking spray. Cook spinach as directed on box; drain in colander or large strainer. Press spinach to remove excess moisture. Set aside.

**2** Meanwhile, in 2-quart saucepan, melt butter. Add onion; cook 2 to 3 minutes, stirring frequently, until tender. Stir in flour. Gradually stir in half-and-half. Stir in gnocchi; heat to boiling. Remove from heat. Stir in cheeses and nutmeg.

**3** Spoon about 2 cups of the gnocchi mixture into casserole. Top with spinach, then remaining gnocchi mixture. Top with tomato slices; brush with olive oil.

**4** Bake uncovered about 30 minutes or until bubbly and browned on top and gnocchi is tender.

## easy variation

Three cups frozen gnocchi from a 16-ounce bag can be substituted for the shelf-stable gnocchi. Then make as directed. Also, Swiss cheese could be substituted for the Gruyère.

**1 SERVING:** Calories 550; Total Fat 40g (Saturated Fat 21g; Trans Fat 3g); Cholesterol 160mg; Sodium 580mg; Total Carbohydrate 19g (Dietary Fiber 2g); Protein 27g **EXCHANGES:** 1 Starch, 3½ Medium-Fat Meat, 4½ Fat **CARBOHYDRATE CHOICES:** 1

# creamy tortellini casserole

prep time: 20 minutes    start to finish: 35 minutes    **4 servings** (1½ cups each)

**1** Heat oven to 350°F. Spray 1½-quart casserole with cooking spray. In 3-quart saucepan, melt butter over medium heat. Add carrot, onion and mushrooms. Cook about 5 minutes, stirring occasionally, until mushrooms are tender.

**2** Stir in flour and salt. Gradually add milk, stirring constantly. Cook and stir until mixture is bubbly; remove from heat. Stir in cheese, peas and tortellini. Spoon into casserole. Sprinkle with crackers.

**3** Bake uncovered about 15 minutes or until edge begins to bubble.

2 tablespoons butter or margarine

1 small carrot, shredded (½ cup)

1 medium onion, chopped (½ cup)

1 package (8 oz) sliced fresh mushrooms (about 3 cups)

2 tablespoons all-purpose flour

½ teaspoon salt

2 cups milk

4 oz Gouda cheese, shredded (1 cup)

¾ cup frozen sweet peas, thawed

1 package (9 oz) refrigerated cheese-filled tortellini

½ cup finely crushed buttery crackers

## easy variation

Tortellini comes in a variety of fillings. Try spinach or red pepper filled tortellini. Or, if you want to add a little meat to the dish, choose tortellini filled with chicken or prosciutto.

**1 SERVING:** Calories 435; Total Fat 24g (Saturated Fat 13g; Trans Fat 0g); Cholesterol 110mg; Sodium 770mg; Total Carbohydrate 35g (Dietary Fiber 4g); Protein 20g **EXCHANGES:** 2 Starch, 1 Vegetable, 2 Medium-Fat Meat, 2 Fat **CARBOHYDRATE CHOICES:** 2

1 jar (26 to 28 oz) tomato pasta sauce

2 red bell peppers, chopped

1 medium onion, chopped (½ cup)

2 boxes (9 oz each) frozen chopped spinach, thawed, squeezed to drain

1 can (8 oz) tomato sauce

9 uncooked lasagna noodles

1 jar (16 oz) Alfredo pasta sauce

15 slices (1 oz each) provolone cheese

¼ cup grated Parmesan cheese

# red pepper–spinach lasagna

**prep time:** 30 minutes    **start to finish:** 5 hours 30 minutes    **8 servings**

**1** Spray 5- to 6-quart slow cooker with cooking spray. Spread ¾ cup of the tomato pasta sauce in bottom of cooker.

**2** In large bowl, mix bell peppers, onion and spinach; stir in remaining tomato pasta sauce and the tomato sauce.

**3** In cooker, layer 3 lasagna noodles, broken into pieces to fit, over sauce. Top with ⅓ of the Alfredo pasta sauce (about ½ cup), spreading to cover noodles completely. Top with 5 of the cheese slices, overlapping if necessary. Top with ⅓ of the vegetable mixture (about 2 cups), spreading evenly.

**4** Repeat layering twice. Sprinkle Parmesan cheese over top.

**5** Cover; cook on Low heat setting 5 to 6 hours. Garnish with fresh oregano or basil leaves, if desired.

## time-saver

Frozen spinach can be quickly thawed using the microwave. Place frozen blocks of spinach in a 10-inch-square microwavable dish. Place in microwave oven and cook on High 3 minutes. Break up blocks and continue cooking in microwave 3 minutes longer, just until completely thawed. Drain well, squeezing out as much liquid as possible.

**1 SERVING:** Calories 630; Total Fat 37g (Saturated Fat 21g, Trans Fat 1g); Cholesterol 95mg; Sodium 1460mg; Total Carbohydrate 48g (Dietary Fiber 5g); Protein 26g  **EXCHANGES:** 1½ Starch, 1½ Low-Fat Milk, 2 Vegetable, ½ Lean Meat, 5½ Fat  **CARBOHYDRATE CHOICES:** 3

3 medium bell peppers, cut into 1-inch pieces

3 medium zucchini or summer squash, cut in half lengthwise, then cut crosswise into ½-inch slices

1 medium onion, cut into 8 wedges, separated into pieces

1 package (8 oz) sliced fresh mushrooms

Cooking spray

½ teaspoon salt

¼ teaspoon pepper

12 uncooked lasagna noodles

1 package (5 to 6 oz) chèvre (goat) cheese

1 container (7 oz) refrigerated basil pesto

2 cups tomato pasta sauce

2 cups shredded Italian cheese blend (8 oz)

# roasted vegetable lasagna with goat cheese

**prep time:** 25 minutes    **start to finish:** 1 hour 10 minutes    **8 servings**

**1** Heat oven to 450°F. Spray 15×10×1-inch pan with cooking spray. In pan, place bell peppers, zucchini, onion and mushrooms in single layer. Spray vegetables with cooking spray; sprinkle with salt and pepper. Roast 15 to 20 minutes, turning vegetables once, until crisp-tender.

**2** Meanwhile, cook and drain noodles as directed on package, using minimum cook time. In medium bowl, crumble chèvre into pesto; stir.

**3** Spray 13×9-inch (3-quart) glass baking dish with cooking spray. In baking dish, spread ½ cup of the pasta sauce. Top with 3 noodles; spread with half of the pesto mixture and 2 cups of the vegetables. Add 3 noodles; layer with ¾ cup pasta sauce, 1 cup shredded cheese blend and 2 cups vegetables. Add 3 noodles; layer with remaining pesto mixture and vegetables. Top with remaining 3 noodles; layer with remaining ¾ cup pasta sauce and 1 cup shredded cheese.

**4** Reduce oven temperature to 375°F. Bake 20 to 30 minutes or until hot. Let stand 10 minutes before serving.

**1 SERVING:** Calories 520; Total Fat 26g (Saturated Fat 10g; Trans Fat 0g); Cholesterol 30mg; Sodium 990mg; Total Carbohydrate 47g (Dietary Fiber 5g); Protein 22g **EXCHANGES:** 1½ Starch, 1 Other Carbohydrate, 2 Vegetable, 2 High-Fat Meat, 2 Fat **CARBOHYDRATE CHOICES:** 3

3 cups uncooked rigatoni pasta (9 oz)

2 medium stalks celery, sliced (1 cup)

1 small carrot, shredded (½ cup)

1 container (8 oz) sour cream-and-chive dip

1 cup shredded Colby cheese (4 oz)

1 cup shredded Monterey Jack or brick cheese (4 oz)

¼ cup grated Parmesan cheese

¼ cup milk

1 tablespoon chopped fresh or 1 teaspoon dried basil leaves

¼ cup Italian-style bread crumbs

1 tablespoon butter or margarine, melted

# three-cheese rigatoni

**prep time:** 15 minutes    **start to finish:** 45 minutes    **6 servings**

**1** Heat oven to 375°F. Cook and drain pasta as directed on package. Return to saucepan.

**2** Stir remaining ingredients except bread crumbs and butter into pasta. Spoon into ungreased 2-quart casserole. In small bowl, mix bread crumbs and butter; sprinkle around edge of casserole.

**3** Bake uncovered 25 to 30 minutes or until hot and bubbly.

## time-saver

Prepare the casserole as directed, but do not sprinkle on bread crumbs. Cover the casserole and refrigerate up to 24 hours. To bake, top with bread crumb mixture. Bake uncovered at 375°F about 50 minutes or until hot.

**1 SERVING:** Calories 470; Total Fat 23g (Saturated Fat 14g; Trans Fat 0g); Cholesterol 60mg; Sodium 640mg; Total Carbohydrate 49g (Dietary Fiber 3g); Protein 20g **EXCHANGES:** 3 Starch, 1 Vegetable, 1 High-Fat Meat **CARBOHYDRATE CHOICES:** 3½

# savory slow-cooked grains

**prep time:** 25 minutes    **start to finish:** 6 hours 55 minutes    **6 servings**

**1** In 3- to 4-quart slow cooker, mix all ingredients except walnuts and parsley.

**2** Cover; cook on Low heat setting 6 hours 30 minutes to 7 hours 30 minutes.

**3** Stir before serving. Sprinkle with walnuts and parsley.

\*To toast walnuts, cook in skillet over medium heat 5 to 7 minutes, stirring frequently until walnuts begin to brown, then stirring constantly until light brown.

## healthy twist

This is a great starter recipe if you're new to whole grains. Using a slow cooker is a terrific way to prepare them because some grains take awhile to cook.

---

- 1 cup uncooked long-grain brown rice
- ½ cup uncooked wild rice
- ½ cup uncooked green lentils
- 3 cups coarsely chopped fresh mushrooms (8 oz)
- 2 medium carrots, coarsely chopped (1 cup)
- 12 medium green onions, chopped (¾ cup)
- 1 container (32 oz) roasted vegetable stock or chicken broth (4 cups)
- 1 cup water
- 2 tablespoons reduced-sodium soy sauce
- 2 tablespoons dry sherry, if desired
- 2 tablespoons butter or margarine, melted
- ½ teaspoon dried thyme leaves
- ½ teaspoon garlic salt
- ¼ cup chopped walnuts, toasted\*
- ⅓ cup finely chopped parsley

---

**1 SERVING:** Calories 330; Total Fat 9g (Saturated Fat 3g; Trans Fat 0g); Cholesterol 10mg; Sodium 980mg; Total Carbohydrate 51g (Dietary Fiber 9g); Protein 12g **EXCHANGES:** 2 Starch, 1 Other Carbohydrate, 1 Vegetable, ½ Very Lean Meat, 1½ Fat **CARBOHYDRATE CHOICES:** 3½

2 tablespoons extra-virgin olive oil

2 tablespoons finely chopped onion

2 cloves garlic, finely chopped

1 package (8 oz) fresh crimini mushrooms, quartered

2 teaspoons chopped fresh rosemary leaves

1 cup uncooked Arborio rice

1¾ cups chicken or vegetable broth

½ cup white wine or water

1½ cups frozen cut green beans, thawed, drained

½ cup roasted red bell peppers (from 7-oz jar), drained, cut into strips

1 cup grated Parmesan cheese

# baked vegetable risotto

**prep time:** 15 minutes   **start to finish:** 45 minutes   **4 servings**

1 Heat oven to 400°F. Spray 2½-quart casserole with cooking spray. In 12-inch nonstick skillet, heat oil over medium heat. Add onion, garlic, mushrooms and rosemary; cook 3 to 5 minutes, stirring frequently, until mushrooms begin to soften.

2 Stir in rice. Cook 2 minutes, stirring constantly. Stir in broth and wine; heat to boiling. Remove from heat; pour into casserole.

3 Cover casserole. Bake 15 minutes. Stir in green beans, roasted peppers and ½ cup of the cheese. Cover; bake 10 to 15 minutes longer or until liquid is absorbed and rice is tender. Stir in remaining ½ cup cheese.

## easy variation

If your family prefers, you could add a cup of chopped cooked ham or chicken to this meatless dish. Add it when you add the rice to the skillet.

**1 SERVING:** Calories 410; Total Fat 15g (Saturated Fat 6g; Trans Fat 0g); Cholesterol 20mg; Sodium 880mg; Total Carbohydrate 48g (Dietary Fiber 2g); Protein 18g **EXCHANGES:** 3 Starch, 1 Vegetable, 1 High-Fat Meat, 1 Fat **CARBOHYDRATE CHOICES:** 3

2 cans (13.8 oz each) refrigerated classic pizza crust

1 can (8 oz) pizza sauce (1 cup)

1 jar (4.5 oz) sliced mushrooms, drained

¼ cup sliced ripe olives

1½ cups shredded mozzarella cheese (6 oz)

2 boxes (9 oz each) frozen chopped spinach, thawed, squeezed to drain

1 teaspoon olive or vegetable oil

1 tablespoon grated Parmesan cheese

# spinach pizza pie

**prep time:** 20 minutes    **start to finish:** 1 hour    **6 servings**

**1** Heat oven to 400°F. Lightly spray 9-inch glass pie plate with cooking spray. Unroll 1 can of dough. Place in pie plate; press against bottom and side of plate to form crust.

**2** In small bowl, mix pizza sauce and mushrooms; spoon into crust. Layer with olives, ¾ cup of the mozzarella cheese, the spinach and remaining ¾ cup mozzarella cheese.

**3** Unroll second can of dough. Press dough into 9-inch round; place over filling. Pinch edges of dough together to seal; roll up edge of dough or flute to form rim. Cut several slits in dough to allow steam to escape. Brush with oil; sprinkle with Parmesan cheese.

**4** Bake 35 to 40 minutes or until deep golden brown. Cut into wedges.

**1 SERVING:** Calories 500; Total Fat 16g (Saturated Fat 5g; Trans Fat 0g); Cholesterol 15mg; Sodium 1150mg; Total Carbohydrate 72g (Dietary Fiber 6g); Protein 20g **EXCHANGES:** 4½ Starch, 1 Vegetable, ½ Medium-Fat Meat, 2 Fat **CARBOHYDRATE CHOICES:** 4½

# chipotle red beans and rice casserole

**prep time:** 15 minutes    **start to finish:** 1 hour 30 minutes    **4 servings** (1½ cups each)

**1** Heat oven to 350°F. Spray 2-quart casserole or 8-inch square (2-quart) glass baking dish with cooking spray. In baking dish, mix rice, corn, beans, tomatoes, broth and chile.

**2** Cover with foil. Bake 1 hour. Uncover; stir well. Sprinkle with chips and cheese. Bake 10 to 15 minutes longer or until bubbly and rice is tender.

- 1 cup uncooked regular long-grain white rice
- 1 cup frozen corn
- 1 can (16 oz) spicy chili beans in sauce, undrained
- 1 can (14.5 oz) diced tomatoes with green chiles, undrained
- 1 can (14 oz) vegetable broth
- 1 chipotle chile in adobo sauce (from 7-oz can), chopped
- 1 cup chili cheese–flavored corn chips
- 1 cup shredded Monterey Jack cheese (4 oz)

## easy variation

Made from ground chiles, adobo sauce is quite spicy. For a little extra zip, add 1 to 2 tablespoons of the sauce to the casserole.

**1 SERVING:** Calories 510; Total Fat 14g (Saturated Fat 6g; Trans Fat 0g); Cholesterol 25mg; Sodium 1620mg; Total Carbohydrate 82g (Dietary Fiber 8g); Protein 19g **EXCHANGES:** 5½ Starch, 2 Fat **CARBOHYDRATE CHOICES:** 5

2 cups dried lentils (1 lb), sorted, rinsed

1 large onion, chopped (1 cup)

1 can (2.25 oz) sliced ripe olives, drained

2 cans (10½ oz each) condensed chicken broth

4 cups water

1 cup chopped dry-pack sun-dried tomatoes

2 teaspoons grated lemon peel

¼ cup crumbled feta cheese (1 oz)

2 medium green onions, sliced (2 tablespoons)

4 pita (pocket) breads (6 inch), each cut into 6 wedges

# greek lentils with pita wedges

**prep time:** 25 minutes   **start to finish:** 5 hours 25 minutes   **6 servings**

**1** Spray 5- to 6-quart slow cooker with cooking spray. In cooker, mix lentils, onion, olives, broth and water. In small bowl, soak tomatoes in warm water to cover while lentil mixture cooks.

**2** Cover; cook on Low heat setting 5 to 6 hours (or on High heat setting 3 to 4 hours).

**3** During last hour of cooking, drain tomatoes; stir tomatoes and lemon peel into lentils. Top with cheese and onions. Serve with pita wedges.

**1 SERVING:** Calories 400; Total Fat 4.5g (Saturated Fat 1.5g; Trans Fat 0g); Cholesterol 5mg; Sodium 900mg; Total Carbohydrate 67g (Dietary Fiber 13g); Protein 24g **EXCHANGES:** 3½ Starch, ½ Other Carbohydrate, 1½ Vegetable, 1 Lean Meat **CARBOHYDRATE CHOICES:** 4 ½

# tropical stuffed cabbage rolls

**prep time:** 40 minutes    **start to finish:** 7 hours 40 minutes    **4 servings**

8 large cabbage leaves

1 can (14 oz) light unsweetened coconut milk

½ cup pineapple preserves

1 cup cooked orzo pasta

1 medium onion, chopped (½ cup)

⅓ cup raisins

⅓ cup cashew pieces

2 teaspoons curry powder

½ teaspoon garlic salt

1 can (15 oz) black beans, drained, rinsed

Flaked coconut, if desired

Additional cashew pieces, if desired

**1** In large bowl, cover cabbage leaves with boiling water. Cover bowl; let stand about 10 minutes or until leaves are limp. Remove leaves from water; drain.

**2** Spray 3- to 4-quart slow cooker with cooking spray. In small bowl, mix coconut milk and preserves. Spread ½ cup in bottom of cooker.

**3** In medium bowl, mix pasta, onion, raisins, ⅓ cup cashew pieces, curry powder, garlic salt and beans. Place about ⅓ cup pasta mixture at stem end of each leaf. Roll leaf around pasta mixture, tucking in sides. Place as many cabbage rolls that will comfortably fit, seam sides down, in cooker. Cover with ⅓ cup of the coconut milk mixture. Repeat with remaining cabbage rolls. Pour remaining coconut mixture over rolls.

**4** Cover; cook on Low heat setting 7 to 9 hours (or on High heat setting 3 hours 30 minutes to 4 hours 30 minutes).

**5** With spatula, carefully remove cabbage rolls, one at a time, from cooker; place on serving platter.  Sprinkle rolls with flaked coconut and additional cashew pieces.

## easy variation

Try macadamia nuts in place of the cashews for a new twist on this tropical dish.

**1 SERVING:** Calories 670; Total Fat 27g (Saturated Fat 19g, Trans Fat 0g); Cholesterol 0mg; Sodium 620mg; Total Carbohydrate 91g (Dietary Fiber 16g); Protein 16g  **EXCHANGES:** 2 Starch, 3½ Other Carbohydrate, ½ Milk, 1 Vegetable, ½ High-Fat Meat, 3½ Fat  **CARBOHYDRATE CHOICES:** 6

Rosemary Roast Chicken. Smoky Apple Butter Ribs. Caramelized Onion Pot Roast. The names of these recipes alone will make mouths water.

But just wait until the roasts are baking in the oven . . . the incredible aroma will call your family to the table and signal that dinner is not only ready but is delicious as well!

es main dish favor

**4**

# main dish favorites

3- to 3½-lb whole broiler-fryer chicken

1½ lb buttercup or acorn squash, peeled and cut into ½-inch rings or slices, then cut crosswise in half

2 medium onions, cut into 1-inch wedges (2 cups)

½ cup butter or margarine, melted

¼ cup lemon juice

2 tablespoons honey

2 teaspoons dried rosemary leaves, crumbled

1 clove garlic, finely chopped

# rosemary roast chicken

**prep time:** 20 minutes    **start to finish:** 2 hours 15 minutes    **6 servings**

**1** Heat oven to 375°F. Fold wings of chicken under back. Tie or skewer drumsticks together. Place chicken, breast side up, on rack in shallow roasting pan. Arrange squash and onions around chicken.

**2** In small bowl, mix remaining ingredients; brush on chicken and vegetables just until evenly coated. Reserve remaining butter mixture. Insert ovenproof meat thermometer in chicken so tip is in thickest part of inside thigh and does not touch bone.

**3** Roast uncovered 1 hour. Brush remaining butter mixture on chicken and vegetables. Cover loosely with foil to prevent overbrowning. Bake 45 to 55 minutes longer or until thermometer reads 165°F, legs move easily when lifted or twisted, and squash is tender.

## healthy twist

Sweet and tasty butternut squash is a great source of vitamins A and C and contains healthy fiber.

**1 SERVING:** Calories 530; Total Fat 28g (Saturated Fat 13g; Trans Fat 1g); Cholesterol 190mg; Sodium 260mg; Total Carbohydrate 19g (Dietary Fiber 3g); Protein 50g **EXCHANGES:** 1 Starch, 1 Vegetable, 6½ Lean Meat, 1½ Fat **CARBOHYDRATE CHOICES:** 1

1 whole chicken (3 to 3½ lb)

1 lemon

1 teaspoon olive oil

1 tablespoon dried herbes de Provence

¼ teaspoon pepper

8 small red potatoes (1½ lb), cut into fourths

2 medium zucchini, cut into 1½-inch pieces

1 can (14.5 oz) diced tomatoes with basil, garlic and oregano, drained

½ cup chopped pitted kalamata olives

# provençal roast chicken

**prep time:** 15 minutes    **start to finish:** 2 hours 15 minutes    **6 servings**

**1** Heat oven to 400°F. In ungreased shallow roasting pan, place chicken, breast side up.

**2** Grate peel from lemon; squeeze juice. In small bowl, mix lemon peel, lemon juice and oil. Drizzle half of lemon mixture over chicken; pat herbes de Provence and pepper on skin of chicken. Place squeezed lemon halves inside chicken cavity.

**3** In large bowl, toss potatoes, zucchini, tomatoes, olives and remaining lemon mixture. Arrange vegetables around chicken in roasting pan. Insert ovenproof meat thermometer into chicken so tip is in thickest part of inside thigh and does not touch bone.

**4** Bake 1 hour 45 minutes to 2 hours or until thermometer reads 180°F, legs move easily when lifted or twisted, and vegetables are tender.

## time-saver

To easily remove the colored outer peel of the lemon (not the white) use a grater, paring knife or vegetable peeler.

**1 SERVING:** Calories 320; Total Fat 9g (Saturated Fat 2.5g; Trans Fat 0g); Cholesterol 85mg; Sodium 290mg; Total Carbohydrate 26g (Dietary Fiber 4g); Protein 31g **EXCHANGES:** 1½ Starch, 1 Vegetable, 3 Lean Meat **CARBOHYDRATE CHOICES:** 2

1 bone-in turkey breast (4 to 5 lb), thawed if frozen

2 to 3 dark-orange sweet potatoes, peeled, cut into 1-inch pieces

1 cup frozen pearl onions (from 1-lb bag), thawed

½ cup chicken broth

¼ cup orange marmalade

2 tablespoons balsamic vinegar

½ teaspoon salt

½ teaspoon dried marjoram leaves

2 cloves garlic, finely chopped

2 tablespoons cornstarch

2 tablespoons water

# turkey breast with sweet potatoes

**prep time:** 25 minutes    **start to finish:** 7 hours 25 minutes    **8 servings**

**1** Spray 5- to 6-quart slow cooker with cooking spray. Place turkey in cooker. Arrange sweet potatoes and onions around turkey. In small bowl, mix remaining ingredients except cornstarch and water; pour over turkey and vegetables.

**2** Cover; cook on Low heat setting 7 to 8 hours.

**3** Remove turkey and vegetables from cooker; place on serving platter. Cover to keep warm. If desired, skim fat from juices in cooker. Pour juices into 4-cup microwavable measuring cup. In small bowl, mix cornstarch and water until smooth; stir into juices in cup. Microwave uncovered on High 2 to 3 minutes, stirring every minute, until mixture boils and thickens. Serve with turkey and vegetables.

## healthy twist

Sweet potatoes are good sources of vitamins A and C plus a good amount of fiber. Choose a dark-orange or red variety of sweet potatoes for this recipe.

**1 SERVING:** Calories 360; Total Fat 12g (Saturated Fat 3.5g; Trans Fat 0g); Cholesterol 115mg; Sodium 320mg; Total Carbohydrate 20g (Dietary Fiber 2g); Protein 44g **EXCHANGES:** 1 Starch, 6 Very Lean Meat, 1½ Fat **CARBOHYDRATE CHOICES:** 1

- 1 boneless turkey breast (4 to 5 lb), thawed if frozen
- 1 cup chunky-style salsa
- 2 tablespoons honey
- 1 tablespoon chopped chipotle chile in adobo sauce (from 7-oz can)
- 2 tablespoons cornstarch
- 2 tablespoons water

# santa fe turkey breast

**prep time:** 15 minutes    **start to finish:** 7 hours 15 minutes    **8 servings**

**1** Spray 5- to 6-quart slow cooker with cooking spray. Place turkey in cooker. In small bowl, mix salsa, honey and chile; pour over turkey.

**2** Cover; cook on Low heat setting 7 to 8 hours.

**3** Remove turkey from cooker; place on serving platter. Cover to keep warm. Pour juices from cooker into 4-cup microwavable measuring cup. In small bowl, mix cornstarch and cold water until smooth; stir into juices in cup. Microwave uncovered on High 3 to 5 minutes, stirring every minute, until mixture boils and thickens. Serve with turkey.

## time-saver

Chipotle chiles are dried jalapeño chiles with a wonderful sweet-and-smoky flavor. To freeze the remaining chiles from the can, spoon into tablespoonful-size mounds on waxed paper. Freeze, then store in a resealable food-storage plastic bag to have ready for recipes in the future.

**1 SERVING:** Calories 340; Total Fat 13g (Saturated Fat 3.5g; Trans Fat 0g); Cholesterol 130mg; Sodium 270mg; Total Carbohydrate 9g (Dietary Fiber 0g); Protein 47g **EXCHANGES:** ½ Starch, 6½ Very Lean Meat, 1½ Fat **CARBOHYDRATE CHOICES:** ½

1 tablespoon olive or vegetable oil

1 boneless beef chuck roast (4 lb)

1 teaspoon salt

½ teaspoon pepper

6 medium onions, sliced

1½ cups beef broth

¾ cup regular or nonalcoholic beer

2 tablespoons packed brown sugar

3 tablespoons Dijon mustard

2 tablespoons cider vinegar

# caramelized onion pot roast

**prep time:** 25 minutes    **start to finish:** 8 hours 25 minutes    **12 servings**

**1** In 10-inch skillet, heat oil over medium-high heat. Add beef; cook about 10 minutes, turning occasionally, until brown on all sides. Sprinkle with salt and pepper.

**2** Spray 4- to 5-quart slow cooker with cooking spray. Place onions in cooker. Place beef on onions. In medium bowl, mix remaining ingredients; pour over beef and onions.

**3** Cover; cook on Low heat setting 8 to 10 hours.

**4** Using slotted spoon, remove beef and onions from cooker. Cut beef into slices or break into pieces. Skim fat from beef juices in cooker, if desired. Serve beef with juices.

**1 SERVING:** Calories 330; Total Fat 19g (Saturated Fat 7g; Trans Fat 1g); Cholesterol 85mg; Sodium 500mg; Total Carbohydrate 8g (Dietary Fiber 1g); Protein 29g **EXCHANGES:** ½ Other Carbohydrate, 4 Lean Meat, 1½ Fat **CARBOHYDRATE CHOICES:** ½

- 1 large sweet onion (such as Bermuda, Maui, Spanish or Walla Walla), cut in half, then cut into thin slices
- 1 boneless beef bottom round roast (3 lb)
- 3 baking potatoes, cut into 1½- to 2-inch cubes
- 2 cloves garlic, finely chopped
- 1 can (14 oz) beef broth
- 1 package (1 oz) onion soup mix (from 2-oz box)
- ¼ cup all-purpose flour

# beef roast with onions and potatoes

**prep time:** 15 minutes    **start to finish:** 9 hours 30 minutes    **6 servings**

1 In 5- to 6-quart slow cooker, place onion. If beef roast comes in netting or is tied, do not remove. Place beef on onion. Place potatoes and garlic around beef. In small bowl, mix 1¼ cups of the broth and the dry soup mix; pour over beef. (Refrigerate remaining broth.)

2 Cover; cook on Low heat setting 9 to 10 hours.

3 Using slotted spoon, remove beef and vegetables from cooker; place on serving platter. Cover to keep warm.

4 In small bowl, mix remaining ½ cup broth and the flour until smooth. Gradually stir flour mixture into juices in cooker. Increase heat setting to High; cover and cook about 15 minutes longer, stirring occasionally, until sauce has thickened. Remove netting or strings from beef. Serve sauce over beef and vegetables.

## time-saver

Save precious time in the morning by cutting the onion and chopping the garlic the night before and refrigerating. Then complete the meal by warming frozen dinner rolls while the juices are thickening in the slow cooker, and cook frozen broccoli in the microwave. Presto—it's eating time!

**1 SERVING:** Calories 350; Total Fat 7g (Saturated Fat 2.5g; Trans Fat 0g); Cholesterol 120mg; Sodium 800mg; Total Carbohydrate 23g (Dietary Fiber 2g); Protein 49g **EXCHANGES:** 1½ Starch, 6½ Very Lean Meat, ½ Fat **CARBOHYDRATE CHOICES:** 1½

# beef roast with bacon-chili gravy

prep time: 15 minutes    start to finish: 10 hours 15 minutes    **8 servings**

**quick prep**

- 4 slices bacon, cut into ½-inch pieces
- 1 beef boneless chuck roast (3 lb)
- ½ teaspoon garlic-pepper blend
- 2 medium carrots, coarsely chopped
- 1 can (4.5 oz) chopped green chiles
- ¼ cup beef broth
- ¼ cup chili sauce
- 1 tablespoon all-purpose flour

**1** In 12-inch nonstick skillet, cook bacon over medium heat, stirring occasionally, until brown and crisp. With slotted spoon, remove bacon from skillet; drain on paper towels. Reserve bacon fat in skillet.

**2** If beef roast comes in netting or is tied, do not remove. Sprinkle beef with garlic-pepper blend. Add beef to bacon fat in skillet; cook over medium heat 5 to 6 minutes, turning occasionally, until brown on both sides.

**3** Spray 4- to 5-quart slow cooker with cooking spray. Place beef in cooker. Top with bacon and carrots. In small bowl, mix green chiles, broth, chili sauce and flour; pour over mixture in cooker.

**4** Cover; cook on Low heat setting 10 to 12 hours.

**5** Place beef on platter; remove netting or strings. Stir gravy in cooker; serve with beef.

### easy variation

Save the gravy and any leftover beef for french dip sandwiches. Layer the beef onto hoagie buns, and dip into the gravy.

**1 SERVING:** Calories 360; Total Fat 22g (Saturated Fat 8g; Trans Fat 1g); Cholesterol 110mg; Sodium 360mg; Total Carbohydrate 5g (Dietary Fiber 1g); Protein 37g **EXCHANGES:** 1 Vegetable, 5 Lean Meat, 1 Fat **CARBOHYDRATE CHOICES:** ½

- 1 boneless beef chuck roast (3 lb)
- 1 teaspoon peppered seasoned salt
- ¾ cup classic-style stir-fry sauce
- 2 tablespoons ketchup
- 2 tablespoons rice vinegar
- 2 teaspoons grated gingerroot or 1 teaspoon ground ginger
- 1 bag (1 lb) frozen bell pepper and onion stir-fry, thawed

# ginger beef roast

**prep time:** 15 minutes    **start to finish:** 8 hours 35 minutes    **8 servings**

**1** Spray 12-inch nonstick skillet with cooking spray. If beef roast comes in netting or is tied, do not remove. Sprinkle beef with peppered seasoned salt; place in skillet. Cook over medium-high heat 5 to 6 minutes, turning once, until beef is brown on both sides.

**2** Spray 5- to 6-quart slow cooker with cooking spray. Place beef in cooker (if necessary, cut beef in half to fit in cooker). In small bowl, mix stir-fry sauce, ketchup, vinegar and gingerroot; pour over beef.

**3** Cover; cook on Low heat setting 8 to 9 hours.

**4** Place beef on platter; cover to keep warm. Add stir-fry vegetables to mixture in cooker. Increase heat setting to High; cover and cook 15 to 20 minutes longer or until peppers are tender. Remove netting or strings from beef. Serve pepper mixture with beef.

## time-saver

Fresh ginger gives a distinctively different flavor than ground ginger. Remove the leathery skin quickly and easily with your vegetable peeler.

**1 SERVING:** Calories 370; Total Fat 20g (Saturated Fat 7g; Trans Fat 1g); Cholesterol 105mg; Sodium 1290mg; Total Carbohydrate 10g (Dietary Fiber 0g); Protein 37g **EXCHANGES:** ½ Starch, 1 Vegetable, 5 Lean Meat, 1 Fat **CARBOHYDRATE CHOICES:** ½

1 large onion, chopped
   (1 cup)

1 medium green bell
   pepper, chopped
   (1 cup)

1 medium stalk celery,
   thinly sliced (½ cup)

1 cup barbecue sauce

1 tablespoon packed
   brown sugar

1 teaspoon ground
   mustard

1 fresh beef brisket
   (3 lb; not corned beef)

# brisket with chunky mustard-bbq sauce

**prep time:** 10 minutes   **start to finish:** 10 hours 10 minutes   **8 servings**

**1** Spray 5- to 6-quart slow cooker with cooking spray. In cooker, mix all ingredients except beef. Add beef (if necessary, cut beef in half to fit in cooker). Spoon sauce mixture over and around beef.

**2** Cover; cook on Low heat setting 10 to 12 hours. Serve sauce with beef. Serve with cooked egg noodles and cooked broccoli, if desired.

## easy variation

Use your favorite barbecue sauce in this recipe, or experiment with a new one. Add a little more zing to the beef by sprinkling a few drops of red pepper sauce in the sauce.

**1 SERVING:** Calories 320; Total Fat 12g (Saturated Fat 4.5g; Trans Fat 0.5g); Cholesterol 95mg; Sodium 400mg; Total Carbohydrate 16g (Dietary Fiber 0g); Protein 37g **EXCHANGES:** ½ Starch, 1 Vegetable, 4½ Lean Meat **CARBOHYDRATE CHOICES:** 1

**Betty Crocker The Big Book of Slow Cooker, Casseroles & More**

3 lb beef short ribs,
  cut into rib sections

½ teaspoon seasoned salt

12 small red potatoes

1½ cups ready-to-eat
  baby-cut carrots

1 can (10¾ oz) condensed
  cream of celery soup

½ cup chili sauce

2 tablespoons
  Worcestershire sauce

½ teaspoon garlic-pepper
  blend

1½ cups frozen cut green
  beans, thawed

# easy beef short rib supper

**prep time:** 15 minutes   **start to finish:** 8 hours 40 minutes   **6 servings**

**1** Spray 12-inch skillet with cooking spray. Sprinkle ribs with seasoned salt. In skillet, cook ribs (in batches, if necessary) over medium-high heat 6 to 8 minutes, turning occasionally, until browned.

**2** Spray 5- to 6-quart slow cooker with cooking spray. With fork or tongs, remove ribs from skillet; place in cooker. Add potatoes and carrots to cooker. In small bowl, mix soup, chili sauce, Worcestershire sauce and garlic-pepper blend; pour over ribs and vegetables.

**3** Cover; cook on Low heat setting 8 to 10 hours.

**4** Skim fat from liquid in cooker, if desired. Stir in green beans. Increase heat setting to High; cover and cook 15 to 25 minutes longer or until beans are tender.

## healthy twist

Browning the ribs may add an extra step— but it's well worth it. Browning before slow cooking gives the ribs a rich, savory flavor and actually removes some of the fat.

**1 SERVING:** Calories 530; Total Fat 16g (Saturated Fat 6g; Trans Fat 0.5g); Cholesterol 70mg; Sodium 920mg; Total Carbohydrate 71g (Dietary Fiber 11g); Protein 24g **EXCHANGES:** 3 Starch, 1½ Other Carbohydrate, 1 Vegetable, 2 Lean Meat, 1½ Fat **CARBOHYDRATE CHOICES:** 5

## RIBS

1 tablespoon vegetable oil

4 lb beef short ribs, cut into rib sections

1 large sweet onion (such as Bermuda, Maui, Spanish or Walla Walla), cut in half, sliced (about 3½ cups)

## SAUCE

1 bottle (12 oz) chili sauce

¾ cup apricot preserves

2 tablespoons packed brown sugar

2 tablespoons cider vinegar

2 tablespoons Worcestershire sauce

2 teaspoons ground mustard

2 cloves garlic, finely chopped

# sweet and tangy short ribs

**prep time:** 35 minutes    **start to finish:** 9 hours 35 minutes    **6 servings**

**1** In 12-inch nonstick skillet, heat oil over medium-high heat. Add ribs (in batches, if necessary); cook 6 to 8 minutes, turning occasionally, until browned.

**2** Spray 4- to 5-quart slow cooker with cooking spray. In cooker, place onion; top with ribs, removing from skillet with fork or tongs.

**3** Cover; cook on Low heat setting 8 hours.

**4** In 2-quart saucepan, cook sauce ingredients over low heat 15 to 20 minutes, stirring frequently, until sauce has thickened.

**5** Drain excess liquid from cooker. Pour sauce over ribs. Increase heat setting to High; cover and cook about 1 hour longer or until meat begins to separate from bones.

## time-saver

Make the sauce a day ahead and store it covered in the refrigerator. Then reheat before adding it to the ribs.

**1 SERVING:** Calories 470; Total Fat 20g (Saturated Fat 7g; Trans Fat 1g); Cholesterol 90mg; Sodium 880mg; Total Carbohydrate 47g (Dietary Fiber 4g); Protein 24g **EXCHANGES:** 3 Other Carbohydrate, 3½ Medium-Fat Meat, ½ Fat **CARBOHYDRATE CHOICES:** 3

# braised short ribs with mashed potatoes

**prep time:** 10 minutes    **start to finish:** 10 hours 10 minutes    **4 servings**

**4 lb beef short ribs, cut into rib sections**

**2 dried bay leaves**

**2 teaspoons Worcestershire sauce**

**1 package (1.2 oz) brown gravy mix**

**½ cup dry red wine, if desired**

**1 can (10¾ oz) condensed golden mushroom soup**

**4 servings mashed potatoes (refrigerated, instant or frozen), heated**

**1** In 3- to 4-quart slow cooker, place ribs. Top with bay leaves. In small bowl, mix Worcestershire sauce, gravy mix (dry), wine and soup; pour over ribs.

**2** Cover; cook on Low heat setting 8 to 10 hours.

**3** Spoon excess fat from top of sauce, if desired. Remove bay leaves. Serve ribs with mashed potatoes, spooning sauce over all.

## easy variation

If short ribs are too rich for your taste, you can use a 3-pound pot roast instead. It's just as delicious as the short ribs and lower in calories.

**1 SERVING:** Calories 595; Total Fat 37g (Saturated Fat 13g; Trans Fat 3.5g); Cholesterol 105mg; Sodium 1330mg; Total Carbohydrate 29g (Dietary Fiber 2g); Protein 37g **EXCHANGES:** 2 Starch, 4 High-Fat Meat, 1 Fat **CARBOHYDRATE CHOICES:** 2

- 4 lb beef short ribs, cut into rib sections
- 2 medium onions, cut into 1-inch wedges (2 cups)
- 1 package (8 oz) fresh whole mushrooms, cut in half
- 1 jar (14 oz) tomato pasta sauce (any variety)

# italian beef short ribs

**prep time:** 10 minutes **start to finish:** 2 hours 40 minutes **6 servings**

**1** Heat oven to 350°F. Place ribs and onions in ungreased 13×9-inch (3-quart) glass baking dish. Cover and bake 1 hour. Drain and discard fat.

**2** Add mushrooms to ribs and onions in dish. Pour pasta sauce over all. Cover tightly with foil and bake about 1 hour 30 minutes longer or until ribs are tender. If desired, skim off and discard any excess fat from top.

## easy variation

Spoon the ribs and tomato-mushroom sauce over hot cooked pasta. A crisp Caesar salad complements the flavors of this short rib meal.

**1 SERVING:** Calories 340; Total Fat 20g (Saturated Fat 7g; Trans Fat 1g); Cholesterol 70mg; Sodium 380mg; Total Carbohydrate 17g (Dietary Fiber 2g); Protein 24g **EXCHANGES:** ½ Starch, 2 Vegetable, 2½ Medium-Fat Meat, 1½ Fat **CARBOHYDRATE CHOICES:** 1

# pepper steak

prep time: 15 minutes    start to finish: 7 hours 30 minutes    **6 servings**

**quick prep**

1½ lb boneless beef round steak

2 medium onions, cut into ¼-inch slices

1 clove garlic, finely chopped

½ teaspoon finely chopped gingerroot or ¼ teaspoon ground ginger

1 cup beef broth

3 tablespoons soy sauce

2 tablespoons cornstarch

¼ cup cold water

2 medium green peppers, cut into ¾-inch strips

2 medium tomatoes, cut into eighths

6 cups hot cooked rice

**1** Trim fat from beef. Cut beef into 6 serving pieces. Spray 12-inch skillet with cooking spray; heat over medium-high heat. Add beef to skillet; cook about 8 minutes, turning once, until brown.

**2** In 3- to 6-quart slow cooker, layer beef, onions, garlic and gingerroot. In small bowl, mix broth and soy sauce; pour over beef.

**3** Cover; cook on Low heat setting 7 to 9 hours.

**4** In another small bowl, mix cornstarch and water. Gradually stir cornstarch mixture into beef mixture. Stir in bell peppers. Increase heat setting to High; cover and cook 10 to 12 minutes or until slightly thickened.

**5** Stir in tomatoes. Cover; cook on High heat setting 3 minutes longer or just until tomatoes are thoroughly heated. Serve over rice.

## healthy twist

Sodium is already fairly low in this recipe, but you can trim it even more by using reduced-sodium soy sauce.

**1 SERVING:** Calories 365; Total Fat 4g (Saturated Fat 1g; Trans Fat 0g); Cholesterol 60mg; Sodium 680mg; Total Carbohydrate 56g (Dietary Fiber 3g); Protein 29g **EXCHANGES:** 3 Starch, 2 Vegetable, 2 Very Lean Meat **CARBOHYDRATE CHOICES:** 3½

- 1 boneless beef round steak (3 lb), cut into 9 serving pieces
- 1 jar (16 oz) chunky-style salsa
- 1 package (0.87 oz) brown gravy mix
- 1 bag (16 oz) frozen home-style egg noodles

# salsa swiss steak with noodles

**prep time:** 10 minutes    **start to finish:** 8 hours 10 minutes    **9 servings**

**1** In 3- to 4-quart slow cooker, place beef pieces. In small bowl, mix salsa and gravy mix; pour over beef.

**2** Cover; cook on Low heat setting 8 to 10 hours.

**3** About 15 minutes before serving, cook and drain noodles as directed on package. Serve beef and sauce over noodles.

## healthy twist

Talk about easy—only three ingredients that cook during the day, then you make the noodles, and dinner is ready. Mix it up by serving this southwestern steak dinner with long-grain brown rice instead of noodles.

**1 SERVING:** Calories 250; Total Fat 6g (Saturated Fat 2g; Trans Fat 0g); Cholesterol 95mg; Sodium 500mg; Total Carbohydrate 17g (Dietary Fiber 1g); Protein 33g **EXCHANGES:** 1 Starch, 4 Lean Meat **CARBOHYDRATE CHOICES:** 1

1½ lb extra-lean (at least 90%) ground beef

½ cup Italian-style dry bread crumbs

½ cup pepperoni-flavored pizza sauce (from 14-oz jar)

¼ teaspoon salt

¼ teaspoon pepper

2 cloves garlic, finely chopped

1 egg

¼ cup shredded Italian-style six-cheese blend or mozzarella cheese (1 oz)

Additional pizza sauce, heated, if desired

# mini italian meat loaves

**prep time:** 10 minutes    **start to finish:** 45 minutes    **6 servings** (2 loaves each)

**1** Heat oven to 350°F. In large bowl, mix all ingredients except cheese and additional pizza sauce. Press beef mixture into 12 regular-size muffin cups (cups will be very full). Place muffin pan on cookie sheet in oven to catch any spillover.

**2** Bake about 30 minutes or until meat thermometer inserted in center of loaves in middle of muffin pan reads 160°F.

**3** Sprinkle 1 teaspoon cheese over each loaf. Bake 1 to 2 minutes longer or until cheese is melted. Immediately remove from cups. Serve with pizza sauce.

## healthy twist

Extra-lean ground beef is recommended for this recipe to keep shrinkage to a minimum and limit the fat that accumulates during baking. Reduce the fat even more by using fat-free egg product and reduced-fat cheese.

**1 SERVING:** Calories 240; Total Fat 12g (Saturated Fat 4.5g; Trans Fat 0.5g); Cholesterol 110mg; Sodium 430mg; Total Carbohydrate 9g (Dietary Fiber 0g); Protein 26g **EXCHANGES:** ½ Starch, 3½ Lean Meat **CARBOHYDRATE CHOICES:** ½

1 egg, beaten

1 cup milk

1 tablespoon
Worcestershire sauce

1½ lb lean (at least 80%)
ground beef

3 slices bread, finely
chopped (1½ cups
lightly packed)

1 small onion, chopped
(¼ cup)

½ teaspoon salt

½ teaspoon ground
mustard

¼ teaspoon pepper

½ cup ketchup, chili sauce
or barbecue sauce

# meat loaf

**prep time:** 20 minutes    **start to finish:** 1 hour 40 minutes    **6 servings**

**1** Heat oven to 350°F. In large bowl, mix all ingredients except ketchup. Spread mixture in ungreased 9×5-inch loaf pan, or shape into 9×5-inch loaf in ungreased 13×9-inch pan. Spread ketchup over top.

**2** Bake uncovered 1 hour to 1 hour 15 minutes or until meat thermometer inserted in center of loaf reads at least 160°F.

**3** Drain meat loaf. Let stand 5 minutes. Remove from pan.

## easy variation

You can use either ½ cup dry bread crumbs, ½ cup crushed seasoned crackers or ¾ cup quick-cooking oats instead of the bread.

**1 SERVING:** Calories 290; Total Fat 15g (Saturated Fat 6g; Trans Fat 1g); Cholesterol 110mg; Sodium 610mg; Total Carbohydrate 15g (Dietary Fiber 0g); Protein 24g **EXCHANGES:** 1 Starch, 3 Medium-Fat Meat, ½ Fat **CARBOHYDRATE CHOICES:** 1

- 1½ teaspoons seasoned salt
- 1 teaspoon garlic-pepper blend
- 1 tablespoon vegetable oil
- 4 boneless pork loin chops, ½ inch thick (about 1 lb)
- 1 cup ready-to-eat baby-cut carrots
- 4 small red potatoes, cut in half
- 1 onion, cut into thin wedges
- 1 small yellow summer squash, thinly sliced
- 1 tablespoon olive oil
- ¼ cup chopped fresh basil

# pork chops with summer vegetable medley

**prep time:** 20 minutes     **start to finish:** 3 hours 35 minutes     **4 servings**

**1** In very small bowl, mix seasoned salt and garlic-pepper blend. Sprinkle half of seasoning mixture over pork. In 12-inch skillet, heat vegetable oil over medium-high heat. Add pork chops; cook about 4 minutes, turning once, just until browned.

**2** Spray 4- to 5-quart slow cooker with cooking spray. Place pork chops in cooker, top with carrots, potatoes and onion.

**3** Cover, cook on Low heat setting 3 to 4 hours.

**4** In medium bowl, mix squash, olive oil, basil and remaining half of seasoning mixture; place on top of vegetable mixture in cooker. Increase heat setting to High; cover and cook 10 to 15 minutes longer or until squash is crisp-tender.

## easy variation

Huge crop of zucchini from the garden this year? Substitute it for the yellow squash. Because the zucchini is cooked of only a short time, it will maintain its bright green color.

**1 SERVING:** Calories 390; Total Fat 15g (Saturated Fat 4g, Trans Fat 0g); Cholesterol 65mg; Sodium 590mg; Total Carbohydrate 37g (Dietary Fiber 5g); Protein 27g **EXCHANGES:** 2 Starch, 1½ Vegetable, 2½ Lean Meat, 1½ Fat **CARBOHYDRATE CHOICES:** 2½

1 package (6 oz) herb
stuffing mix

2 medium stalks celery,
chopped (1 cup)

1 medium tart cooking
apple, peeled, chopped

1 medium onion, chopped
(½ cup)

1 cup dried cherries

¼ cup butter or margarine,
melted

1 cup chicken broth

6 pork boneless loin
chops, about ½ inch
thick

# pork chops with apple-cherry stuffing

**prep time:** 15 minutes    **start to finish:** 6 hours 15 minutes    **6 servings**

**1** Spray 4- to 5-quart slow cooker with cooking spray. In large bowl, mix all ingredients except pork. Place half of stuffing mixture in cooker; top with pork. Spoon remaining stuffing mixture over pork.

**2** Cover; cook on Low heat setting 6 to 8 hours.

## easy variation

Dried cranberries or blueberries can be a delicious substitute for the cherries.

**1 SERVING:** Calories 365; Total Fat 17g (Saturated Fat 4g; Trans Fat 0g); Cholesterol 65mg; Sodium 500mg; Total Carbohydrate 35g (Dietary Fiber 8g); Protein 26g **EXCHANGES:** 1 Starch, 1 Fruit, 1 Vegetable, 3 Lean Meat, 1 Fat **CARBOHYDRATE CHOICES:** 2

# maple-sage pork roast

**prep time:** 30 minutes   **start to finish:** 8 hours 30 minutes   **8 servings**

**1** Spray 4- to 5-quart slow cooker with cooking spray. If pork roast comes in netting or is tied, remove netting or strings. In cooker, place pork. In small bowl, mix syrup, garlic, sage, bouillon granules and ½ cup of the water; spoon over pork. Arrange squash, carrots and onions around pork.

**2** Cover; cook on Low heat setting 8 to 9 hours.

**3** Using slotted spoon, remove pork and vegetables from cooker; cover to keep warm. If desired, skim fat from liquid in cooker. Pour liquid into 4-cup microwavable measuring cup. In small bowl, mix cornstarch and remaining ½ cup water until smooth; stir into liquid in cup. Microwave uncovered on High 2 to 3 minutes, stirring every minute, until mixture thickens. Serve with pork and vegetables.

1 boneless pork shoulder roast (2 to 3 lb)

2 tablespoons real maple syrup or maple-flavored syrup

1 clove garlic, finely chopped

2 teaspoons dried sage leaves

½ teaspoon beef bouillon granules

1 cup water

2 cups cubed (1½ inch) peeled butternut squash

2 cups ready-to-eat baby-cut carrots, cut in half lengthwise

2 small onions, cut into wedges

3 tablespoons cornstarch

## easy variation

Whole carrots, quartered lengthwise then cut crosswise into 2-inch sections, can be substituted for the baby carrots.

**1 SERVING:** Calories 280; Total Fat 14g (Saturated Fat 5g; Trans Fat 0g); Cholesterol 75mg; Sodium 110mg; Total Carbohydrate 14g (Dietary Fiber 2g); Protein 25g **EXCHANGES:** ½ Starch, ½ Other Carbohydrate, 3½ Lean Meat, ½ Fat **CARBOHYDRATE CHOICES:** 1

# honey barbecue–glazed pork roast with carrots and corn

**1 boneless pork shoulder roast (3 lb)**

**1 bag (1 lb) ready-to-eat baby-cut carrots**

**½ cup barbecue sauce**

**¼ cup honey**

**3 tablespoons balsamic vinegar**

**1 teaspoon seasoned salt**

**⅔ cup barbecue sauce**

**¼ cup all-purpose flour**

**1 cup frozen corn**

**prep time:** 15 minutes    **start to finish:** 8 hours 35 minutes    **6 servings**

**1** If pork roast comes in netting or is tied, remove netting or strings. Trim fat from pork. In 3- to 4-quart slow cooker, place pork. Arrange carrots around and on top of pork. In small bowl, mix ½ cup barbecue sauce, the honey, vinegar and seasoned salt; pour over pork and carrots.

**2** Cover; cook on Low heat setting 8 to 10 hours.

**3** Using slotted spoon, remove pork and vegetables from cooker; place on serving platter. Cover to keep warm.

**4** In small bowl, mix ⅔ cup barbecue sauce and the flour; gradually stir into juices in cooker. Increase heat setting to High; cover and cook about 15 minutes, stirring occasionally, until thickened.

**5** Stir in corn. Cover; cook on High heat setting 5 minutes longer. Serve sauce over pork and vegetables.

**1 SERVING:** Calories 630; Total Fat 27g (Saturated Fat 10g; Trans Fat 0g); Cholesterol 145mg; Sodium 830mg; Total Carbohydrate 46g (Dietary Fiber 3g); Protein 51g **EXCHANGES:** ½ Starch, 2 Other Carbohydrate, 1 Vegetable, 7 Lean Meat, 1 Fat **CARBOHYDRATE CHOICES:** 3

# harvest time pork roast

**prep time:** 15 minutes   **start to finish:** 1 hour 45 minutes   **6 servings**

**quick prep**

**1** Heat oven to 325°F. On rack in shallow roasting pan, place pork. In small bowl, mix marmalade, orange juice, fennel, thyme and sage. Brush half of marmalade mixture over pork.

**2** In large bowl, toss sweet potatoes and Brussels sprouts with oil, salt and pepper. Arrange vegetables around pork. Insert ovenproof meat thermometer so tip is in thickest part of pork.

**3** Roast uncovered 1 hour. Brush pork with remaining marmalade mixture; gently stir vegetables to coat with pan juices. Roast about 15 minutes longer or until thermometer reads 155°F and vegetables are tender. Remove from oven; cover pork with foil and let stand 10 minutes or until thermometer reads 160°F.

- 1 boneless pork loin roast (3 to 3½ lb)
- ½ cup orange marmalade
- 3 tablespoons orange juice
- 2 teaspoons fennel seed, crushed
- 1 teaspoon dried thyme leaves
- 1 teaspoon dried sage leaves, crushed
- 2 medium dark-orange sweet potatoes, peeled, cut into 1½-inch pieces
- 1 lb fresh Brussels sprouts, cut in half if large
- 2 teaspoons olive or vegetable oil
- ½ teaspoon salt
- ¼ teaspoon pepper

## time-saver

It's easy to prepare the veggies up to a day ahead of time. Then seal in resealable food-storage plastic bags and refrigerate until it's time to cook.

**1 SERVING:** Calories 530; Total Fat 20g (Saturated Fat 6g; Trans Fat 0g); Cholesterol 145mg; Sodium 310mg; Total Carbohydrate 35g (Dietary Fiber 5g); Protein 54g **EXCHANGES:** 1 Starch, 1 Other Carbohydrate, 1 Vegetable, 7 Lean Meat **CARBOHYDRATE CHOICES:** 2

1 package (1 oz) dried
  porcini mushrooms

1 boneless pork loin roast
  (3 lb)

1 tablespoon butter
  or margarine

1 medium onion, finely
  chopped (½ cup)

1 package (8 oz) fresh
  baby portabella
  mushrooms, finely
  chopped

½ cup herb-seasoned
  stuffing crumbs (do
  not use stuffing cubes)

2 tablespoons olive
  or vegetable oil

½ teaspoon salt

¼ teaspoon pepper

Fresh sage leaves,
  if desired

# wild mushroom–stuffed pork roast

**prep time:** 25 minutes   **start to finish:** 1 hour 30 minutes   **8 servings**

**1** Heat oven to 375°F. In small bowl, place dried porcini mushrooms. Cover mushrooms with hot water; let stand 10 minutes.

**2** Meanwhile, cut pork roast horizontally to ½ inch from one long side without cutting all the way through (pork will open like a book); set aside. In 10-inch skillet, melt butter over medium-high heat. Add onion; cook and stir about 1 minute or until tender.

**3** Drain porcini mushrooms well; chop. Add porcini and portabella mushrooms to onion in skillet; cook about 4 minutes, stirring occasionally, until mushrooms are tender. Stir in stuffing crumbs.

**4** Spoon mushroom mixture into opening in pork. Close pork over stuffing; secure with string. Place stuffed pork in ungreased shallow roasting pan. Brush with oil; sprinkle with salt and pepper. Insert ovenproof meat thermometer so tip is in center of thickest part of pork.

**5** Roast uncovered 45 to 55 minutes or until thermometer reads 155°F. Remove from oven; cover with foil and let stand 10 minutes or until thermometer reads 160°F. Remove strings from pork before carving. Garnish with sage.

**1 SERVING:** Calories 350; Total Fat 18g (Saturated Fat 6g; Trans Fat 0g); Cholesterol 115mg; Sodium 290mg; Total Carbohydrate 8g (Dietary Fiber 1g); Protein 40g **EXCHANGES:** 1 Vegetable, 5½ Lean Meat, ½ Fat **CARBOHYDRATE CHOICES:** ½

- 1 boneless pork shoulder (3 lb)
- 2 teaspoons Italian seasoning
- 1½ teaspoons fennel seed, crushed
- ¾ teaspoon salt
- ½ teaspoon celery seed
- 3 medium parsnips, peeled, cut into ¾-inch pieces (3 cups)
- 2 medium sweet potatoes, peeled, cut into ¾-inch pieces (3 cups)
- 12 cloves garlic, peeled, cut in half
- 1½ cups water

# porketta pot roast

**prep time:** 15 minutes    **start to finish:** 9 hours 15 minutes    **8 to 10 servings**

1 If pork comes in netting or is tied, do not remove. In small bowl, mix Italian seasoning, fennel seed, salt and celery seed. Pat seasoning mixture evenly onto pork. Heat 12-inch nonstick skillet over medium-high heat. Place pork in skillet; cook 5 to 10 minutes, turning several times, until brown.

2 In 4- to 5-quart slow cooker, place parsnips, sweet potatoes and garlic; pour water over vegetables. Place pork on vegetables.

3 Cover; cook on Low heat setting 9 to 10 hours.

4 Remove pork from cooker; place on cutting board. Remove netting or strings from pork. Cut pork across grain into slices; serve with vegetables and juices.

## healthy twist

Parsnips go unnoticed among the more colorful, popular vegetables in the produce aisle. This delicious root vegetable looks like a thick white carrot with creamy-yellow to white flesh. When cooked, it is sweeter than a carrot. Parsnips are a source of iron and vitamin C.

**1 SERVING:** Calories 350; Total Fat 20g (Saturated Fat 7g; Trans Fat 0g); Cholesterol 90mg; Sodium 290mg; Total Carbohydrate 16g (Dietary Fiber 3g); Protein 26g **EXCHANGES:** 1 Starch, 3 Medium-Fat Meat, 1 Fat **CARBOHYDRATE CHOICES:** 1

# orange pork tenderloin with butternut squash

prep time: 20 minutes    start to finish: 7 hours 20 minutes    **6 servings**

**1** Spray 3- to 4-quart slow cooker with cooking spray. Arrange squash around edge of cooker. Sprinkle with salt. Top with pork (it will overlap squash slightly). In small bowl, mix marmalade and garlic; spread evenly over pork.

**2** Cover; cook on Low heat setting 7 to 8 hours or until pork has slight blush of pink in center and thermometer inserted in center reads 160°F.

**3** Remove pork from cooker; place on cutting board. Cut pork into slices; serve with squash.

### quick prep

- 1 butternut squash (3 lb), peeled, cut into 2-inch pieces (6 cups)
- ½ teaspoon salt
- 2 pork tenderloins (¾ to 1 lb each)
- ¼ cup orange marmalade
- 2 cloves garlic, finely chopped

### healthy twist

Watching your salt intake? Omit the salt, and season with ¼ teaspoon pepper. This is a great healthy recipe for entertaining. Fan pork slices in a circular pattern on a platter, and spoon squash in the center. Drizzle remaining juices over pork, and garnish with slices of fresh orange and sprigs of parsley.

**1 SERVING:** Calories 260; Total Fat 6g (Saturated Fat 2g; Trans Fat 0g); Cholesterol 65mg; Sodium 490mg; Total Carbohydrate 20g (Dietary Fiber 3g); Protein 30g **EXCHANGES:** 1 Starch, ½ Other Carbohydrate, 4 Very Lean Meat, ½ Fat **CARBOHYDRATE CHOICES:** 1

## cajun pork tenderloin with vegetables

2 teaspoons Cajun or Creole seasoning

1 pork tenderloin (1 lb)

2 medium baking or Yukon gold potatoes, peeled

4 small zucchini (1 lb)

1½ cups frozen small whole onions

2 tablespoons butter or margarine, melted

½ teaspoon dried thyme leaves

¼ teaspoon salt

**prep time:** 15 minutes    **start to finish:** 1 hour    **4 servings**

**1** Heat oven to 425°F. Rub Cajun seasoning onto all sides of pork; place in ungreased 15×10×1-inch pan. Insert ovenproof meat thermometer horizontally into center of thickest part of pork.

**2** Cut potatoes and zucchini lengthwise in half. Arrange potatoes, zucchini and onions around pork. Drizzle butter over vegetables; sprinkle with thyme and salt.

**3** Bake uncovered about 35 minutes or until thermometer reads 150°F. Loosely cover pan with foil; let stand about 10 minutes or until pork has slight blush of pink in center and meat thermometer inserted in center reads 160°F. Cut pork into thin slices. Serve with vegetables.

**1 SERVING:** Calories 260; Total Fat 10g (Saturated Fat 5g; Trans Fat 0g); Cholesterol 85mg; Sodium 240mg; Total Carbohydrate 18g (Dietary Fiber 3g); Protein 28g **EXCHANGES:** 2 Vegetable, 3 Lean Meat **CARBOHYDRATE CHOICES:** 1½

6 tablespoons butter or margarine, melted

¼ cup packed brown sugar

1 tablespoon cider vinegar

1 teaspoon salt

½ teaspoon garlic powder

½ teaspoon pepper

2 medium red cooking apples, sliced (about 2 cups)

2 medium dark-orange sweet potatoes, peeled, thinly sliced (about 2½ cups)

1 medium onion, chopped (½ cup)

2 pork tenderloins (1 lb each)

# roast pork with apples and sweet potatoes

**prep time:** 15 minutes    **start to finish:** 1 hour 15 minutes    **6 servings**

**1** Heat oven to 425°F. In medium bowl, mix butter, brown sugar, vinegar, salt, garlic powder and pepper. Reserve 2 tablespoons of butter mixture. Add apples, sweet potatoes and onion to remaining butter mixture; toss to coat. Arrange apple mixture in ungreased roasting pan or 13×9-inch (3-quart) glass baking dish. Cover tightly with foil; bake 20 minutes.

**2** Meanwhile, brush pork with reserved butter mixture. Heat 10-inch nonstick skillet over medium-high heat. Add pork; cook about 3 minutes, turning to brown all sides evenly. Place pork on apple mixture.

**3** Bake uncovered 30 to 40 minutes or until pork has slight blush of pink in center and meat thermometer inserted in center reads 160°F.

## healthy twist

Pork tenderloin is a naturally lower-fat cut of meat. It's very lean and, when combined with other healthful ingredients like apples and sweet potatoes, helps make a great healthy meal.

**1 SERVING:** Calories 290; Total Fat 8g (Saturated Fat 3.5g; Trans Fat 0g); Cholesterol 80mg; Sodium 480mg; Total Carbohydrate 27g (Dietary Fiber 3g); Protein 27g **EXCHANGES:** 1 Starch, 1 Fruit, 4½ Lean Meat, ½ Fat **CARBOHYDRATE CHOICES:** 2

- 1½ lb sweet potatoes, peeled, cut into ½-inch slices
- 1 boneless pork shoulder roast (in netting or tied; 2½ lb)
- 2 tablespoons packed brown sugar
- ¼ teaspoon ground red pepper (cayenne)
- ¼ teaspoon salt
- ⅛ teaspoon pepper
- 1 clove garlic, finely chopped

# brown sugar–glazed pork with sweet potatoes

**prep time:** 10 minutes    **start to finish:** 8 hours 10 minutes    **6 servings**

**1** In 3- to 4-quart slow cooker, place sweet potatoes; place pork on potatoes. In small bowl, mix remaining ingredients; sprinkle over pork.

**2** Cover; cook on Low heat setting 8 to 10 hours.

**3** Remove pork from cooker; place on cutting board. Remove netting or strings from pork. Slice pork, or pull pork into serving pieces using 2 forks. Serve with sweet potatoes, spooning juices over pork.

**1 SERVING:** Calories 410; Total Fat 17g (Saturated Fat 6g; Trans Fat 0g); Cholesterol 90mg; Sodium 660mg; Total Carbohydrate 32g (Dietary Fiber 2g); Protein 32g **EXCHANGES:** 2 Starch, 4 Lean Meat **CARBOHYDRATE CHOICES:** 2

3 lb boneless pork country-style ribs

¾ teaspoon salt

½ teaspoon pepper

1 medium onion, sliced

½ cup apple butter

2 tablespoons packed brown sugar

1 tablespoon liquid smoke

2 cloves garlic, finely chopped

# smoky apple butter ribs

**prep time:** 15 minutes    **start to finish:** 8 hours 15 minutes    **4 servings**

**1** Sprinkle ribs with salt and pepper. In 3- to 4-quart slow cooker, place ribs. Cover with onion slices. In small bowl, mix remaining ingredients; pour over ribs and onion.

**2** Cover; cook on Low heat setting 8 to 10 hours.

**3** Remove ribs from cooker; place on serving platter. Cover to keep warm.

**4** Pour juices from cooker through strainer into 1-quart saucepan. Heat to boiling over medium-high heat. Reduce heat to medium; cook about 5 minutes or until sauce has slightly thickened. Serve sauce with ribs.

**1 SERVING:** Calories 750; Total Fat 39g (Saturated Fat 14g; Trans Fat 0g); Cholesterol 210mg; Sodium 570mg; Total Carbohydrate 28g (Dietary Fiber 2g); Protein 70g **EXCHANGES:** 2 Other Carbohydrate, 10 Lean Meat, 2 Fat **CARBOHYDRATE CHOICES:** 2

# barbecued baby back ribs

**prep time:** 20 minutes    **start to finish:** 7 hours 20 minutes    **8 servings**

## SAUCE

1⅓ cups ketchup

¾ cup chili sauce

⅔ cup packed brown sugar

¼ cup cider vinegar

3 tablespoons Worcestershire sauce

3 tablespoons Dijon mustard

2 tablespoons lemon juice

1 tablespoon liquid smoke

## RIBS

4 lb pork baby back ribs, cut into 3-rib sections

¾ teaspoon salt

¼ teaspoon pepper

1 In medium bowl, mix all sauce ingredients; set aside.

2 Spray 5- to 6-quart slow cooker with cooking spray. Sprinkle pork with salt and pepper. Place pork in cooker. Spoon about 1½ cups sauce evenly over sections.

3 Cover; cook on Low heat setting 6 to 7 hours (or on High heat setting 3 hours to 3 hours 30 minutes) or until almost tender.

4 Remove pork from cooker; place in shallow dish. Drain and discard liquid from cooker. Return pork to cooker; spoon remaining sauce evenly over each section. If needed, reduce heat setting to Low; cover and cook 1 hour longer.

## time-saver

Some butchers will cut the ribs into sections for you if you ask. This will save time and the mess of working with raw meat. Save even more time by starting with a bottled barbecue sauce—you need 2⅔ cups.

**1 SERVING:** Calories 580; Total Fat 27g (Saturated Fat 10g, Trans Fat 1g); Cholesterol 140mg; Sodium 1320mg; Total Carbohydrate 35g (Dietary Fiber 2g); Protein 48g  **EXCHANGES:** 2½ Other Carbohydrate, 7 Lean Meat, 1 Fat  **CARBOHYDRATE CHOICES:** 2

## BABY BACK RIBS

4½ lb pork loin back ribs

1 teaspoon salt

1 teaspoon pepper

## SPICY BARBECUE SAUCE

1 cup ketchup

½ cup water

⅓ cup packed brown sugar

¼ cup white vinegar

1 tablespoon celery seed

½ teaspoon red pepper sauce

½ teaspoon liquid smoke, if desired

# baby back ribs with spicy barbecue sauce

**prep time:** 50 minutes    **start to finish:** 2 hours 50 minutes    **24 servings**

**1** Heat oven to 325°F. Cut ribs into serving pieces; sprinkle with salt and pepper. Place ribs in ungreased 15×10×1-inch pan. Cover tightly with foil; bake about 2 hours 30 minutes or until tender.

**2** Meanwhile, in 2-quart saucepan, mix sauce ingredients. Heat to boiling over medium heat, stirring frequently. Reduce heat to low; simmer uncovered 15 minutes, stirring occasionally.

**3** Heat gas or charcoal grill for indirect cooking as directed by manufacturer.

**4** Place pork on unheated side of two-burner gas grill or over drip pan on charcoal grill. (If using one-burner gas grill, cook over low heat.) Cover grill; cook 15 to 20 minutes, brushing with sauce every 5 minutes, until pork is tender and no longer pink next to bones. Discard any remaining sauce.

## easy variation

If you prefer, you can finish the ribs in the oven instead of on the grill. After baking 2 hours 30 minutes in step 1, increase oven temperature to 450°F. Bake uncovered 15 to 20 minutes longer, brushing with sauce every 5 minutes, until pork is tender and no longer pink next to bones.

**1 SERVING:** Calories 550; Total Fat 38g (Saturated Fat 14g; Trans Fat 0g); Cholesterol 150mg; Sodium 750mg; Total Carbohydrate 17g (Dietary Fiber 0g); Protein 36g **EXCHANGES:** 1 Other Carbohydrate, 5 High-Fat Meat **CARBOHYDRATE CHOICES:** 1

Betty Crocker The Big Book of Slow Cooker, Casseroles & More

# lemon- and parmesan-crusted salmon

**prep time:** 10 minutes   **start to finish:** 35 minutes   **4 servings**

1 salmon fillet (1¼ lb)

2 tablespoons butter or margarine, melted

¼ teaspoon salt

¾ cup fresh white bread crumbs (about 1 slice bread)

¼ cup grated Parmesan cheese

2 tablespoons thinly sliced green onions (2 medium)

2 teaspoons grated lemon peel

¼ teaspoon dried thyme leaves

**1** Heat oven to 375°F. Spray shallow baking pan with cooking spray. Pat salmon dry with paper towel. Place salmon, skin side down, in pan; brush with 1 tablespoon of the butter. Sprinkle with salt.

**2** In small bowl, mix bread crumbs, cheese, onions, lemon peel and thyme. Stir in remaining 1 tablespoon butter. Press bread crumb mixture evenly on salmon.

**3** Bake uncovered 15 to 25 minutes or until salmon flakes easily with fork. Serve immediately.

## healthy twist

Serve salmon often. This delicious fish is a great source of important Omega-3 oils, essential for a healthy diet.

**1 SERVING:** Calories 290; Total Fat 16g (Saturated Fat 7g; Trans Fat 0g); Cholesterol 115mg; Sodium 420mg; Total Carbohydrate 4g (Dietary Fiber 0g); Protein 33g **EXCHANGES:** 5 Lean Meat **CARBOHYDRATE CHOICES:** 1

Okay…you've got the main course under control. But what should you serve along with it? This chapter's got you covered! For true comfort food, Wild Rice with Cranberries and Candied Sweet Potatoes are winning choices.

Take advantage of slow-cooking convenience for parties. Whether dining at home or taking an appetizer to a party, try crowd-pleasing Spinach-Artichoke Dip and Southwest Chicken Nachos.

**5**

# hearty sides

1 lb fresh asparagus spears

½ cup water

1 cup frozen corn

2 teaspoons Dijon mustard

2 teaspoons honey

¼ teaspoon lemon-pepper seasoning

# asparagus and corn with honey-mustard glaze

**prep time:** 20 minutes   **start to finish:** 20 minutes   **5 servings** (½ cup each)

**1** Snap off tough ends of asparagus and discard. Cut spears into 1-inch pieces.

**2** In 2-quart saucepan, heat water to boiling. Gently stir in asparagus and corn. Reduce heat; simmer uncovered 5 to 8 minutes or until asparagus is crisp tender. Drain.

**3** In small bowl, mix mustard, honey and lemon-pepper seasoning. Stir into hot vegetables.

## healthy twist

This fat-free recipe has a good amount of vitamin A and some vitamins B and C— all from the asparagus.

**1 SERVING:** Calories 60; Total Fat 0g (Saturated Fat 0g; Trans Fat 0g); Cholesterol 0mg; Sodium 70mg; Total Carbohydrate 12g (Dietary Fiber 2g); Protein 3g **EXCHANGES:** ½ Other Carbohydrate, 1 Vegetable **CARBOHYDRATE CHOICES:** 1

3 lb beets, peeled, cut into ½-slices (4½ cups)

1 cup apple juice

½ cup balsamic vinegar

2 cloves garlic, finely chopped

1 teaspoon salt

¼ cup chopped walnuts

1 tablespoon cornstarch

1 tablespoon cold water

¼ cup crumbled chèvre (goat) cheese with herbs (1 oz)

# balsamic-glazed beets with goat cheese

**prep time:** 20 minutes    **start to finish:** 3 hours 30 minutes    **8 servings** (½ cup each)

**1** Spray 3- to 4-quart slow cooker with cooking spray. In cooker, mix beets, apple juice, vinegar, garlic and salt.

**2** Cover; cook on High heat setting 3 to 4 hours.

**3** Meanwhile, to toast walnuts, sprinkle in ungreased heavy skillet. Cook over medium heat 5 to 7 minutes, stirring frequently until nuts begin to brown, then stirring constantly until nuts are light brown. Set aside.

**4** In small bowl, mix cornstarch and water; stir into beets. Cook uncovered on High heat setting 5 to 10 minutes longer or until sauce has thickened. Sprinkle with nuts and cheese.

**1 SERVING:** Calories 150; Total Fat 4g (Saturated Fat 1g; Trans Fat 0g); Cholesterol 0mg; Sodium 450mg; Total Carbohydrate 24g (Dietary Fiber 5g); Protein 4g **EXCHANGES:** 1 Other Carbohydrate, 2 Vegetable, 1 Fat **CARBOHYDRATE CHOICES:** 1½

1 cup water

5 cups fresh broccoli florets

1 tablespoon olive or vegetable oil

1 clove garlic, finely chopped

¼ cup chopped hazelnuts (filberts)

½ cup chopped drained roasted red bell peppers (from 7-oz jar)

¼ teaspoon salt

# broccoli with roasted red peppers and hazelnuts

**prep time:** 30 minutes    **start to finish:** 30 minutes    **8 servings** (½ cup each)

**1** In 2-quart saucepan, heat water to boiling. Add broccoli; cover and cook about 1 minute or just until crisp. Drain; immediately place broccoli in ice water.

**2** In 12-inch skillet, heat oil over medium heat. Add garlic and hazelnuts; cook 1 to 2 minutes, stirring frequently, until nuts are lightly toasted.

**3** Drain broccoli. Stir broccoli, roasted peppers and salt into nut mixture. Cook about 3 minutes, stirring occasionally, until broccoli is crisp-tender.

**1 SERVING:** Calories 70; Total Fat 4g (Saturated Fat 0g; Trans Fat 0g); Cholesterol 0mg; Sodium 90mg; Total Carbohydrate 5g (Dietary Fiber 2g); Protein 2g **EXCHANGES:** 1 Vegetable, 1 Fat **CARBOHYDRATE CHOICES:** ½

4 slices bacon, diced

¼ cup packed brown sugar

2 tablespoons all-purpose flour

¼ cup water

3 tablespoons white vinegar

¼ teaspoon salt

⅛ teaspoon pepper

1 medium head red cabbage (1½ lb), shredded

1 small onion, sliced

# sweet-sour red cabbage

**prep time:** 15 minutes **start to finish:** 6 hours 15 minutes **8 servings**

**1** In 10-inch skillet, cook bacon over medium heat about 5 minutes, stirring occasionally, or until bacon is crisp. Using slotted spoon, remove bacon from skillet; drain on paper towels. Reserve 1 tablespoon bacon drippings. Refrigerate bacon.

**2** Spray 3- to 4-quart slow cooker with cooking spray. In cooker, stir brown sugar, flour, water, vinegar, salt, pepper and reserved bacon drippings until well mixed. Stir in cabbage and onion.

**3** Cover; cook on Low heat setting 6 to 7 hours. Stir in bacon before serving.

## healthy twist

Any color of cabbage is tasty eaten raw or cooked. This cruciferous vegetable contains a good amount of vitamin A and C. For a sweeter touch to this recipe, add another tablespoon of brown sugar; for a more sour taste, add an extra tablespoon of vinegar.

**1 SERVING:** Calories 100; Total Fat 4g (Saturated Fat 1.5g; Trans Fat 0g); Cholesterol 0mg; Sodium 160mg; Total Carbohydrate 13g (Dietary Fiber 2g); Protein 3g **EXCHANGES:** ½ Other Carbohydrate, 1 Vegetable, 1 Fat **CARBOHYDRATE CHOICES:** 1

2 lb ready-to-eat baby-cut carrots

1 medium onion, cut in half, sliced

¼ teaspoon salt

⅓ cup honey

⅓ cup apricot preserves

2 tablespoons chopped fresh parsley

# apricot-glazed carrots

**prep time:** 10 minutes   **start to finish:** 9 hours 25 minutes   **10 servings** (½ cup each)

**1** In 4- to 5-quart slow cooker, place carrots and onion. Sprinkle with salt.

**2** Cover; cook on Low heat setting 9 to 10 hours.

**3** Discard liquid in cooker. In small bowl, mix honey and preserves; pour over carrots in cooker. Increase heat setting to High; cover and cook 10 to 15 minutes longer or until hot. Sprinkle with parsley before serving. Carrots will hold on Low heat setting up to 2 hours; stir occasionally.

## easy variation

Peach, plum, pineapple or another flavor of preserves will lend these carrots a subtly different yet equally delicious fruit flavor.

**1 SERVING:** Calories 110; Total Fat 0g (Saturated Fat 0g; Trans Fat 0g); Cholesterol 0mg; Sodium 95mg; Total Carbohydrate 27g (Dietary Fiber 3g); Protein 1g **EXCHANGES:** 1½ Other Carbohydrate, 1 Vegetable **CARBOHYDRATE CHOICES:** 2

6 medium carrots (¾ lb),
cut into julienne
(matchstick-cut) strips

4 medium green onions,
sliced (¼ cup)

⅓ cup honey

1 tablespoon butter

1 tablespoon lemon juice

½ teaspoon salt

# honeyed carrots

**prep time:** 25 minutes    **start to finish:** 25 minutes    **4 servings** (½ cup each)

**1** In 10-inch skillet, heat 1 inch water (salted if desired) to boiling. Add carrots; return to boiling. Reduce heat; cover and simmer about 5 minutes or until tender. Drain; remove from skillet. Set aside.

**2** In same skillet, cook remaining ingredients over low heat, stirring frequently, until bubbly. Stir in carrots. Cook uncovered 2 to 3 minutes, stirring occasionally, until carrots are glazed.

## healthy twist

Enjoy carrots often—they're a great source of vitamin A!

**1 SERVING:** Calories 160; Total Fat 3g (Saturated Fat 2g; Trans Fat 0g); Cholesterol 10mg; Sodium 380mg; Total Carbohydrate 32g (Dietary Fiber 3g); Protein 1g **EXCHANGES:** 1½ Other Carbohydrate, 1 Vegetable, ½ Fat **CARBOHYDRATE CHOICES:** 2

# dilled carrots and pea pods

**prep time:** 15 minutes    **start to finish:** 15 minutes    **4 servings**

1½ cups ready-to-eat baby-cut carrots (about 8 oz)

1½ cups fresh snow pea pods (about 5 oz), strings removed

1 tablespoon butter or margarine

2 teaspoons chopped fresh or ½ teaspoon dried dill weed

⅛ teaspoon salt

**1** In 2-quart saucepan, heat 1 inch water to boiling. Add carrots; cover and return to boiling. Reduce heat; cover and cook about 4 minutes or until carrots are crisp-tender. Do not drain water.

**2** Add pea pods to carrots in saucepan. Heat uncovered to boiling. Boil uncovered 2 to 3 minutes, stirring occasionally, until pea pods are crisp-tender. Drain vegetables; return to saucepan.

**3** Stir butter, dill weed and salt into vegetables until butter is melted.

## time-saver

Here's the easy way to remove the strings from pea pods. Simply snap off the stem end from each one, then pull the string across the pea pod.

**1 SERVING:** Calories 70; Total Fat 3g (Saturated Fat 2g; Trans Fat 0g); Cholesterol 10mg; Sodium 135mg; Total Carbohydrate 8g (Dietary Fiber 2g); Protein 1g **EXCHANGES:** 1½ Vegetable, ½ Fat **CARBOHYDRATE CHOICES:** ½

3 tablespoons olive oil

½ teaspoon salt

½ teaspoon grated orange peel

¼ teaspoon pepper

2 lb fresh cauliflower florets

1 cup shredded Asiago cheese (4 oz)

# roasted cauliflower with asiago and orange

**prep time:** 10 minutes   **start to finish:** 40 minutes   **10 servings** (½ cup each)

**1** Heat oven to 450°F. In large bowl, mix oil, salt, orange peel and pepper. Add cauliflower; toss until evenly coated. Place mixture in ungreased 15×10×1-inch pan.

**2** Roast 20 to 25 minutes. Stir; sprinkle with cheese. Bake 1 to 2 minutes longer or until cheese is melted.

## easy variation

It's easy to use shredded Parmesan instead of the shredded Asiago cheese.

**1 SERVING:** Calories 120; Total Fat 9g (Saturated Fat 3.5g; Trans Fat 0g); Cholesterol 10mg; Sodium 270mg; Total Carbohydrate 5g (Dietary Fiber 2g); Protein 4g **EXCHANGES:** 1 Vegetable, 2 Fat **CARBOHYDRATE CHOICES:** ½

4 slices bacon

4½ cups frozen corn, thawed

½ medium red bell pepper, chopped (½ cup)

½ cup milk

¼ cup butter or margarine, melted

1 teaspoon sugar

½ teaspoon salt

⅛ teaspoon pepper

1 container (8 oz) reduced-fat chive-and-onion cream cheese

# chive-and-onion creamed corn

**prep time:** 20 minutes   **start to finish:** 2 hours 30 minutes   **8 servings** (½ cup each)

**1** In 12-inch nonstick skillet, cook bacon over medium-high heat, turning occasionally, until crisp. Drain on paper towels. Crumble bacon.

**2** Spray 3- to 4-quart slow cooker with cooking spray. In cooker, mix corn, bell pepper, milk, butter, sugar, salt, pepper and half of the bacon. Refrigerate remaining bacon.

**3** Cover; cook on High heat setting 2 hours to 2 hours 30 minutes.

**4** Stir in cream cheese. Cover; cook on High heat setting 10 minutes longer. Stir well; sprinkle with remaining bacon. Corn can be kept warm on Low heat setting up to 1 hour.

**1 SERVING:** Calories 220; Total Fat 12g (Saturated Fat 7g; Trans Fat 0g); Cholesterol 35mg; Sodium 460mg; Total Carbohydrate 21g (Dietary Fiber 2g); Protein 6g **EXCHANGES:** 1½ Starch, 2 Fat **CARBOHYDRATE CHOICES:** 1½

# baked corn pudding

**prep time:** 20 minutes    **start to finish:** 1 hour 35 minutes    **12 servings**

**1** Heat oven to 350°F. Spray 13×9-inch (3-quart) glass baking dish or 3-quart casserole with cooking spray.

**2** In 4-quart Dutch oven, melt ⅓ cup butter over medium heat. Add onion; cook 3 to 4 minutes, stirring frequently, until tender. Stir in flour, salt and peppers until well blended. Stir in milk. Cook 4 to 5 minutes, stirring constantly, until thickened. Gradually stir in eggs. Stir in corn and parsley. Pour into baking dish.

**3** In small bowl, mix bread crumbs and 1 tablespoon melted butter; sprinkle over corn mixture.

**4** Bake uncovered 55 to 65 minutes or until mixture is set and knife inserted in center comes out clean. Let stand 5 to 10 minutes before serving.

## easy variation

You can spice up the flavor by stirring in a 4-ounce can of chopped green chiles and replacing the parsley with cilantro.

⅓ cup butter or margarine

1 large onion, chopped (1 cup)

½ cup all-purpose flour

2 teaspoons salt

½ teaspoon black pepper

½ teaspoon ground red pepper (cayenne)

3 cups milk

4 eggs, slightly beaten

2 bags (12 oz) frozen corn, thawed

½ cup chopped fresh parsley or 2 tablespoons dried parsley flakes

⅔ cup unseasoned dry bread crumbs

1 tablespoon butter or margarine, melted

**1 SERVING:** Calories 230; Total Fat 10g (Saturated Fat 5g; Trans Fat 0g); Cholesterol 90mg; Sodium 530mg; Total Carbohydrate 27g (Dietary Fiber 2g); Protein 8g **EXCHANGES:** 2 Starch, ½ Medium-Fat Meat, 1 Fat **CARBOHYDRATE CHOICES:** 2

8 slices uncooked bacon, cut into small pieces

1 cup chopped onion (about 1 large)

1 cup barbecue sauce

¾ cup regular or nonalcoholic dark beer

¼ cup packed brown sugar

2 cans (15 oz each) black beans, drained, rinsed

2 cans (15 oz each) pinto beans, drained

1 can (19 oz) cannellini beans, drained

# three-bean beer pot

**prep time:** 20 minutes    **start to finish:** 4 hours 20 minutes    **16 servings** (½ cup each)

**1** In 10-inch skillet, cook bacon and onion over medium heat 7 to 10 minutes, stirring occasionally, until bacon is crisp; drain.

**2** Spray 3- to 4-quart slow cooker with cooking spray. In cooker, place bacon mixture and remaining ingredients; mix well.

**3** Cover; cook on Low heat setting 4 to 6 hours.

## time-saver

For added convenience, look for bags of frozen chopped onions near the other frozen veggies.

**1 SERVING:** Calories 270; Total Fat 2.5g (Saturated Fat 0.5g; Trans Fat 0g); Cholesterol 0mg; Sodium 650mg; Total Carbohydrate 47g (Dietary Fiber 13g); Protein 14g **EXCHANGES:** 2 Starch, 1 Other Carbohydrate, 1 Lean Meat **CARBOHYDRATE CHOICES:** 3

# green beans with glazed shallots in lemon-dill butter

**prep time:** 15 minutes    **start to finish:** 15 minutes    **6 servings** (½ cup each)

1 lb fresh green beans, trimmed

2 tablespoons butter

2 shallots, finely chopped

½ teaspoon sugar

1 teaspoon lemon juice

1 tablespoon chopped fresh or 1 teaspoon dried dill weed

¼ teaspoon salt

**1** In 4-quart Dutch oven, heat 1 to 2 inches water to boiling. Add beans; boil uncovered 8 to 10 minutes or until crisp-tender. Drain; return to Dutch oven.

**2** Meanwhile, in 10-inch skillet, melt butter over medium heat. Add shallots; cook 2 to 3 minutes, stirring occasionally, until crisp-tender. Stir in sugar. Cook 2 to 3 minutes longer, stirring occasionally, until shallots are glazed and brown. Stir in lemon juice, dill weed and salt.

**3** Add shallot mixture to green beans; toss to coat.

## healthy twist

Frozen green beans are a great substitute for the fresh—and nutritional value will be the same. Frozen veggies are picked at the peak of freshness and frozen quickly so nutrients are retained.

**1 SERVING:** Calories 60; Total Fat 4g (Saturated Fat 2.5g; Trans Fat 0g); Cholesterol 10mg; Sodium 130mg; Total Carbohydrate 5g (Dietary Fiber 2g); Protein 1g **EXCHANGES:** 1 Vegetable, 1 Fat **CARBOHYDRATE CHOICES:** ½

- 2 bags (12 oz) frozen whole green beans, thawed
- 1 can (10¾ oz) condensed cream of celery or mushroom soup
- 1 teaspoon dried thyme leaves
- 1 clove garlic, finely chopped
- ¼ teaspoon salt
- ¼ teaspoon ground black pepper
- 1 package (8 oz) sliced fresh mushrooms (about 3 cups)
- ½ cup chopped red bell pepper
- ½ cup slivered almonds
- ½ cup half-and-half
- 1 tablespoon all-purpose flour
- 1½ cups seasoned croutons, slightly crushed

# company green bean casserole

**prep time:** 15 minutes     **start to finish:** 4 hours 45 minutes     **12 servings** (½ cup each)

**1** Spray 3- to 4-quart slow cooker with cooking spray. In cooker, mix beans, soup, thyme, garlic, salt and black pepper.

**2** Cover; cook on Low heat setting 4 to 5 hours.

**3** Add mushrooms, bell pepper and almonds to bean mixture in cooker. In 1-cup measuring cup, beat half-and-half and flour with fork until well blended; stir into bean mixture. Cover, cook on Low heat setting 30 minutes longer or until beans are crisp-tender. Before serving, sprinkle with croutons.

## healthy twist

Trim the fat and calories from this slow cooker–version of the well-known "Green Bean Casserole" recipe by substituting the reduced-fat version of condensed cream of celery or mushroom soup and using fat-free half-and-half.

**1 SERVING:** Calories 100; Total Fat 5g (Saturated Fat 1.5g, Trans Fat 0g); Cholesterol 0mg; Sodium 210mg; Total Carbohydrate 10g (Dietary Fiber 3g); Protein 3g **EXCHANGES:** ½ Starch, 1 Vegetable, 1 Fat **CARBOHYDRATE CHOICES:** ½

⅓ cup stir-fry sauce

2 teaspoons chili garlic paste

2 tablespoons vegetable oil

6 cups fresh green beans, trimmed

1 teaspoon sesame seed

# spicy stir-fried green beans

**prep time:** 20 minutes   **start to finish:** 20 minutes   **6 servings** (½ cup each)

**1** In medium bowl, mix stir-fry sauce and chili garlic paste; set aside.

**2** In 12-inch nonstick skillet, heat oil over medium-high heat. Add green beans; toss in hot oil and cook 5 to 7 minutes, stirring every minute, until bright green and crisp-tender (mixture may spatter during cooking). Beans will sizzle, blister and brown in spots. Remove skillet from heat.

**3** With slotted spoon, remove beans from skillet; add to sauce mixture in bowl. Toss to coat. Place in serving bowl; sprinkle with sesame seed.

## time-saver

Save clean-up time with a spatter guard screen to cover the pan during cooking. These handy covers are available at many department and specialty food stores.

**1 SERVING:** Calories 100; Total Fat 5g (Saturated Fat 1g; Trans Fat 0g); Cholesterol 0mg; Sodium 470mg; Total Carbohydrate 11g (Dietary Fiber 4g); Protein 2g **EXCHANGES:** ½ Other Carbohydrate, 1 Vegetable, 1 Fat **CARBOHYDRATE CHOICES:** 1

- 1 lb fresh spinach
- 1 jar (4.5 oz) whole mushrooms, drained
- 1 teaspoon dried minced onion
- ½ teaspoon salt
- ⅛ teaspoon pepper
- 1 small clove garlic, finely chopped
- ⅓ cup sour cream
- 1 tablespoon fat-free half-and-half or fat-free (skim) milk

# spinach gourmet

**prep time:** 25 minutes   **start to finish:** 25 minutes   **4 servings**

**1** Remove imperfect leaves and root ends from spinach. Wash spinach several times in water, lifting spinach out of water each time so sand sinks to bottom. Drain.

**2** In 3-quart saucepan, place spinach with just the water that clings to leaves. Cover; cook over medium heat about 5 minutes or until wilted. Drain; chop.

**3** In same saucepan, mix spinach, mushrooms, onion, salt, pepper and garlic. In small bowl, mix sour cream and half-and-half; pour over spinach mixture. Heat just to boiling, stirring occasionally.

## easy variation

To make this recipe in the oven, thaw and drain 1 lb frozen cut leaf spinach. (Omit steps 1 and 2.) Mix spinach, 2 tablespoons butter or margarine and the remaining ingredients in an ungreased 1-quart casserole. Cover and bake 1 hour.

**1 SERVING:** Calories 90; Total Fat 4.5g (Saturated Fat 2.5g; Trans Fat 0g); Cholesterol 10mg; Sodium 540mg; Total Carbohydrate 7g (Dietary Fiber 3g); Protein 4g **EXCHANGES:** 2 Vegetable, 1 Fat **CARBOHYDRATE CHOICES:** ½

# vegetables with lemon butter

prep time: 25 minutes    start to finish: 25 minutes    **12 servings**

**1** Cook green beans as directed on bag. Drain in large colander. Place on large serving platter; cover to keep warm.

**2** In 3-quart saucepan, heat 1 inch water (salted if desired) to boiling. Add Brussels sprouts. Cover; return to boiling. Reduce heat; cook uncovered 8 to 10 minutes or until stems are tender.

**3** Meanwhile, in 2-quart saucepan, heat 1 inch water (salted if desired) to boiling. Add carrots. Cover; return to boiling. Reduce heat; cook uncovered 6 to 8 minutes or until tender.

**4** Drain Brussels sprouts and carrots in colander. Place on same platter with green beans; cover to keep warm.

**5** In 1-quart saucepan, heat butter until melted. Stir in lemon peel and lemon juice. Pour butter mixture over vegetables.

**4 cups frozen whole green beans (from two 22-oz bags)**

**1½ lb fresh Brussels sprouts, cut in half**

**1 lb fresh carrots, cut into julienne (matchstick-cut) strips**

**⅓ cup butter or margarine**

**1 tablespoon grated lemon peel**

**1 tablespoon lemon juice**

## easy variation

If you have frozen Brussels sprouts on hand, use those in place of the fresh. Use about 2 cups or a 16-ounce bag.

**1 SERVING**: Calories 100; Total Fat 6g (Saturated Fat 3.5g; Trans Fat 0g); Cholesterol 15mg; Sodium 75mg; Total Carbohydrate 11g (Dietary Fiber 4g); Protein 2g **EXCHANGES**: ½ Starch, 1 Vegetable, 1 Fat **CARBOHYDRATE CHOICES**: 1

¼ cup butter or margarine

1 tablespoon chopped fresh or 1 teaspoon dried sage leaves

2 cloves garlic, finely chopped

½ lb fresh Brussels sprouts, cut in half (2 cups)

½ lb fresh parsnips, peeled, cut lengthwise into quarters, then cut into 2-inch pieces (2 cups)

½ small fresh butternut squash (about 1 lb), peeled, seeded and cut into 1-inch pieces (2 cups)

2 cups ready-to-eat baby-cut carrots

# roasted autumn vegetables

**prep time:** 20 minutes    **start to finish:** 1 hour 20 minutes    **6 servings** (1 cup each)

**1** Heat oven to 375°F. In 1-quart saucepan, melt butter. Stir in sage and garlic.

**2** In ungreased 13×9-inch pan, place remaining ingredients. Pour butter mixture over vegetables; stir to coat.

**3** Cover with foil. Bake 45 minutes. Uncover; bake about 15 minutes longer or until vegetables are tender.

## easy variation

You can use 2 cups 1-inch pieces of Yukon gold potatoes in place of the butternut squash. Garnish with fresh sage leaves.

**1 SERVING:** Calories 160; Total Fat 8g (Saturated Fat 5g; Trans Fat 0g); Cholesterol 20mg; Sodium 95mg; Total Carbohydrate 18g (Dietary Fiber 4g); Protein 2g **EXCHANGES:** 1 Other Carbohydrate, 1 Vegetable, 1½ Fat **CARBOHYDRATE CHOICES:** 1

# mixed vegetable bake

1 lb medium red potatoes (about 4), cut into ⅛-inch slices

1 large onion, cut in half, then cut into ¼-inch slices

2 medium carrots, peeled, cut into ¼-inch slices

¼ cup extra-virgin olive oil

2 teaspoons finely chopped garlic

1 teaspoon dried thyme leaves

1 teaspoon dried tarragon leaves

½ teaspoon salt

½ teaspoon pepper

1 medium red bell pepper, cut into ¼-inch slices

1 medium zucchini, cut into ¼-inch slices

**prep time:** 15 minutes    **start to finish:** 1 hour    **6 servings** (1 cup each)

**1** Heat oven to 400°F. Spray bottom of 13×9-inch (3-quart) glass baking dish with cooking spray.

**2** In baking dish, place potatoes, onion and carrots. Toss with half each of the oil, garlic, thyme, tarragon, salt and pepper. Bake 10 minutes.

**3** Meanwhile, in medium bowl, toss bell pepper and zucchini with remaining oil and seasonings.

**4** Stir bell pepper and zucchini into mixture in baking dish. Bake 30 to 35 minutes longer or until vegetables are tender, stirring halfway through bake time.

## easy variation

Use your imagination to substitute other veggies in this recipe. Try Yukon gold instead of the red potatoes or yellow squash instead of the zucchini. Any color of bell pepper would be great too.

**1 SERVING:** Calories 180; Total Fat 9g (Saturated Fat 1.5g; Trans Fat 0g); Cholesterol 0mg; Sodium 220mg; Total Carbohydrate 21g (Dietary Fiber 4g); Protein 2g **EXCHANGES:** 1 Starch, 1 Vegetable, 1½ Fat **CARBOHYDRATE CHOICES:** 1½

1½ cups uncooked
wild rice

1 tablespoon butter or
margarine, melted

½ teaspoon salt

¼ teaspoon pepper

4 medium green onions,
sliced (¼ cup)

2 cans (14 oz each)
vegetable broth

1 jar (4.5 oz) sliced
mushrooms, undrained

½ cup slivered almonds

⅓ cup sweetened dried
cranberries

# wild rice with cranberries

**prep time:** 15 minutes    **start to finish:** 4 hours 30 minutes    **6 servings**

**1** In 3- to 4-quart slow cooker, mix all ingredients except almonds and cranberries.

**2** Cover; cook on Low heat setting 4 to 5 hours.

**3** Meanwhile, in ungreased heavy skillet, cook almonds over medium-low heat 5 to 7 minutes, stirring frequently until browning begins, then stirring constantly until golden brown and fragrant; set aside.

**4** Stir almonds and cranberries into rice mixture. Cover; cook on Low heat setting 15 minutes longer.

## easy variation

Many supermarkets now carry a wide variety of dried fruits. Dried blueberries or cherries are delicious substitutes for the cranberries.

**1 SERVING:** Calories 280; Total Fat 7g (Saturated Fat 1.5g; Trans Fat 0g); Cholesterol 5mg; Sodium 840mg; Total Carbohydrate 45g (Dietary Fiber 5g); Protein 9g **EXCHANGES:** 2½ Starch, ½ Other Carbohydrate, ½ Vegetable, 1 Fat **CARBOHYDRATE CHOICES:** 3

1½ cups sliced fresh mushrooms (4 oz)

½ cup chopped carrot

½ cup chopped red bell pepper

½ cup uncooked brown rice

1 cup water

½ teaspoon salt

¼ teaspoon pepper

1 cup chopped fresh broccoli

# confetti brown rice

**prep time:** 10 minutes    **start to finish:** 3 hours    **6 servings**

1 Spray 3- to 4-quart slow cooker with cooking spray. In cooker, mix all ingredients except broccoli.

2 Cover; cook on High heat setting 2 hours 30 minutes to 3 hours 30 minutes.

3 Stir in broccoli. If needed, increase heat setting to High; cover and cook 15 to 20 minutes longer or until broccoli is crisp-tender.

## easy variation

If you like the earthy flavor and meaty texture of baby portabella mushrooms, they'd make a great substitution for the regular, white ones in this colorful side dish. Substitute orange or yellow bell pepper for the red bell pepper if you have one on hand.

**1 SERVING:** Calories 80; Total Fat 0.5g (Saturated Fat 0g, Trans Fat 0g); Cholesterol 0mg; Sodium 410mg; Total Carbohydrate 15g (Dietary Fiber 3g); Protein 2g **EXCHANGES:** ½ Starch, 1 Vegetable **CARBOHYDRATE CHOICES:** 1

- 1 cup uncooked bulgur or cracked wheat
- ½ cup dried lentils, sorted, rinsed
- 1 teaspoon ground cumin
- ¼ teaspoon salt
- 3 cloves garlic, finely chopped
- 1 can (15.25 oz) whole kernel corn, drained
- 2 cans (14 oz each) vegetable broth
- 2 medium tomatoes, chopped (1½ cups)
- 1 can (2¼ oz) sliced ripe olives, drained
- 1 cup crumbled feta cheese (4 oz)

# mediterranean bulgur and lentils

**prep time:** 15 minutes    **start to finish:** 3 hours 30 minutes    **8 servings**

**1** In 3- to 4-quart slow cooker, mix all ingredients except tomatoes, olives and cheese.

**2** Cover; cook on Low heat setting 3 to 4 hours.

**3** Stir in tomatoes and olives. Increase heat setting to High; cover and cook 15 minutes longer. Sprinkle each serving with cheese. Serve with toasted wedges of pita bread, if desired.

## healthy twist

If you've never tried the whole grain goodness of bulgur, this is a great recipe to start with. This nutritious food has a chewy, nutty texture that is a nice complement to the lentils.

**1 SERVING:** Calories 220; Total Fat 6g (Saturated Fat 3g; Trans Fat 0g); Cholesterol 15mg; Sodium 880mg; Total Carbohydrate 33g (Dietary Fiber 7g); Protein 10g **EXCHANGES:** 2 Starch, ½ Medium-Fat Meat, ½ Fat **CARBOHYDRATE CHOICES:** 2

1 tablespoon vegetable oil

2 cups chopped onions
    (2 large)

1½ cups uncooked quinoa,
    rinsed, well drained

½ teaspoon salt

½ teaspoon dried oregano
    leaves

3 cups chicken broth

1 can (15 oz) spicy chili
    beans, undrained

1 jar (7 oz) roasted red
    bell peppers, drained,
    chopped (¾ cup)

¼ cup chopped fresh
    cilantro

# southwestern quinoa

**prep time:** 10 minutes    **start to finish:** 2 hours 50 minutes    **8 servings** (¾ cup each)

**1** In 10-inch skillet, heat oil over medium heat. Add onion; cook about 5 minutes, stirring occasionally, until translucent.

**2** Spray 3- to 4-quart slow cooker with cooking spray. In cooker, mix onions, quinoa, salt, oregano, broth and beans.

**3** Cover, cook on Low heat setting 2 hours 30 minutes to 3 hours 30 minutes.

**4** With large fork, gently stir in peppers. Cover; cook on Low heat setting 10 minutes longer or until heated. Stir in cilantro.

## easy variation

Sun-dried tomatoes would make a nice change of pace instead of the roasted red bell peppers. Choose sun-dried tomatoes in oil and herbs for even more flavor. Drain and chop enough to get ¾ cup. Any leftover oil from the tomatoes can be the start to a tasty salad dressing. Simply follow a recipe for a vinaigrette, using the oil and herbs from the tomatoes for the oil called for in the recipe.

**1 SERVING:** Calories 220; Total Fat 5g (Saturated Fat 0.5g, Trans Fat 0g); Cholesterol 0mg; Sodium 920mg; Total Carbohydrate 35g (Dietary Fiber 5g); Protein 9g **EXCHANGES:** 1½ Starch, ½ Other Carbohydrate, 1 Vegetable, 1 Fat **CARBOHYDRATE CHOICES:** 2

6 medium unpeeled sweet potatoes (2 lb)

⅓ cup packed brown sugar

3 tablespoons butter or margarine

3 tablespoons water

½ teaspoon salt

# candied sweet potatoes

**prep time:** 20 minutes    **start to finish:** 40 minutes    **6 servings**

**1** In 2-quart saucepan, place sweet potatoes and enough water just to cover potatoes. Heat to boiling. Reduce heat; cover and simmer 20 to 25 minutes or until potatoes are tender when pierced with a fork.

**2** Drain potatoes. When cool enough to handle, peel potatoes and cut into ½-inch slices.

**3** In 10-inch skillet, heat remaining ingredients over medium heat, stirring constantly, until smooth and bubbly. Add potatoes; gently stir until glazed and hot.

## healthy twist

To make the sweet potatoes with only 2 grams of fat and 185 calories per serving, decrease the butter to 1 tablespoon and use a nonstick skillet.

**1 SERVING:** Calories 220; Total Fat 6g (Saturated Fat 3g; Trans Fat 0g); Cholesterol 15mg; Sodium 250mg; Total Carbohydrate 41g (Dietary Fiber 4g); Protein 2g **EXCHANGES:** ½ Starch, 2 Other Carbohydrate, 1 Fat **CARBOHYDRATE CHOICES:** 3

# slow cooker sweet potatoes

**prep time:** 15 minutes   **start to finish:** 6 hours 15 minutes   **10 servings**

## quick prep

6 medium dark-orange sweet potatoes (2 lb), peeled, cut into ½-inch cubes

1½ cups applesauce

½ cup packed brown sugar

3 tablespoons butter or margarine, melted

1 teaspoon ground cinnamon

½ cup chopped nuts

**1** In 2- to 3½-quart slow cooker, place sweet potatoes. In medium bowl, mix remaining ingredients except nuts; spoon over potatoes.

**2** Cover; cook on Low heat setting 6 to 8 hours.

**3** Meanwhile, in ungreased heavy skillet, cook nuts over medium-low heat 5 to 7 minutes, stirring frequently until browning begins, then stirring constantly until golden brown; set aside. Sprinkle nuts over sweet potatoes before serving.

## time-saver

If you're cooking a holiday meal, this side dish can be cooking in the slow cooker while your meat is roasting in the oven. If your home is the holiday gathering spot for family and friends, you can double or triple this recipe and cook it in a 5- to 6-quart slow cooker.

**1 SERVING:** Calories 210; Total Fat 7g (Saturated Fat 2.5g; Trans Fat 0g); Cholesterol 10mg; Sodium 55mg; Total Carbohydrate 34g (Dietary Fiber 3g); Protein 2g **EXCHANGES:** ½ Starch, 1½ Other Carbohydrate, ½ Vegetable, 1½ Fat **CARBOHYDRATE CHOICES:** 2

# chorizo, pecan and cheddar stuffing

**prep time:** 15 minutes    **start to finish:** 3 hours 15 minutes    **16 servings**

1 lb chorizo sausage, casing removed and crumbled, or bulk chorizo sausage

1 large onion, chopped (1 cup)

3 medium stalks celery, sliced (1½ cups)

1 package (16 oz) seasoned corn bread stuffing crumbs (5¾ cups)

⅓ cup butter or margarine, melted

½ teaspoon rubbed sage

¼ teaspoon pepper

2 cups chicken broth

1½ cups shredded sharp Cheddar cheese (6 oz)

1 cup pecan halves, toasted, if desired

**1** In 10-inch skillet, cook sausage, onion and celery over medium heat 8 to 10 minutes, stirring occasionally, until sausage is no longer pink; drain.

**2** In 4- to 5-quart slow cooker, place sausage mixture, stuffing, butter, sage and pepper. Pour broth over mixture; toss to combine.

**3** Cover; cook on Low heat setting 3 hours to 3 hours 30 minutes. Gently stir in cheese and pecans before serving.

## easy variation

Did you know that cooked chorizo can be substituted for the raw chorizo sausage? Decrease the cooking time in step one to 5 to 6 minutes or until onion and celery are crisp-tender.

**1 SERVING:** Calories 260; Total Fat 19g (Saturated Fat 9g; Trans Fat 0.5g); Cholesterol 35mg; Sodium 530mg; Total Carbohydrate 18g (Dietary Fiber 2g); Protein 6g **EXCHANGES:** 1 Starch, ½ Low-Fat Milk, 3 Fat **CARBOHYDRATE CHOICES:** 1

# butternut squash sauté

**prep time:** 30 minutes    **start to finish:** 30 minutes    **8 servings**

**2 slices bacon, cut into 1-inch pieces**

**1 medium onion, chopped (½ cup)**

**6 cups ½-inch pieces peeled butternut squash (2 small)**

**½ teaspoon chopped fresh or ⅛ teaspoon dried thyme leaves**

**⅛ teaspoon pepper**

**3 cups firmly packed baby spinach leaves**

**1** In 12-inch skillet, cook bacon over medium-low heat, stirring occasionally, until crisp. Stir in onion. Cook about 2 minutes, stirring occasionally, until onion is crisp-tender.

**2** Stir in squash, thyme and pepper. Cover; cook 8 to 10 minutes, stirring occasionally, until squash is tender. Stir in spinach just until wilted.

## healthy twist

That distinctive yellow-orange color of butternut squash comes from beta-carotene, a form of vitamin A. Winter squash, like butternut, is rich in vitamin A—key for healthy vision.

**1 SERVING:** Calories 60; Total Fat 1g (Saturated Fat 0g; Trans Fat 0g); Cholesterol 0mg; Sodium 60mg; Total Carbohydrate 11g (Dietary Fiber 2g); Protein 2g **EXCHANGES:** ½ Other Carbohydrate, 1 Vegetable **CARBOHYDRATE CHOICES:** 1

1 butternut squash (2½ lb)

¼ cup butter or margarine

2 large cloves garlic, finely chopped

¼ cup unseasoned crispy bread crumbs

⅓ cup grated Parmesan cheese

¼ teaspoon salt

⅛ teaspoon pepper

¼ cup chopped fresh parsley

# parmesan–butternut squash gratin

**prep time:** 25 minutes   **start to finish:** 1 hour 15 minutes   **6 servings** (½ cup each)

**1** Heat oven to 375°F. Spray 13×9-inch (3-quart) glass baking dish with cooking spray. Peel, halve lengthwise and seed squash; cut into ½-inch-thick slices. Arrange with slices overlapping slightly in bottom of baking dish.

**2** In 2-quart saucepan, melt butter over medium heat. Reduce heat to low. Add garlic; cook 2 to 3 minutes, stirring frequently, until garlic is soft and butter is infused with garlic flavor. Do not let butter brown.

**3** In small bowl, mix bread crumbs, cheese and 1 tablespoon of the butter-garlic mixture.

**4** Brush squash slices with remaining butter-garlic mixture. Sprinkle with salt, pepper and bread crumb mixture.

**5** Bake 30 to 40 minutes or until squash is tender when pierced with fork. Increase oven temperature to 425°F. Bake 5 to 10 minutes longer or until lightly browned. Before serving, sprinkle parsley over top.

## time-saver

Save time by making this side dish ahead. Prepare the recipe through step 4. Cover and refrigerate for up to 24 hours.

**1 SERVING**: Calories 180; Total Fat 10g (Saturated Fat 6g; Trans Fat 0g); Cholesterol 25mg; Sodium 270mg; Total Carbohydrate 18g (Dietary Fiber 2g); Protein 4g **EXCHANGES**: 1 Starch, 2 Fat **CARBOHYDRATE CHOICES**: 1

1 small buttercup or acorn squash (2 to 2½ lb)

¼ cup water

3 tablespoons packed brown sugar

2 tablespoons butter or margarine, melted

1 teaspoon grated orange peel

3 tablespoons fresh orange juice

¼ teaspoon salt

1 chipotle chile in adobo sauce (from 7-oz can), finely chopped

# spicy chipotle-orange squash

**prep time:** 15 minutes  **start to finish:** 3 hours 15 minutes  **4 servings**

**1** Cut squash in half crosswise; remove seeds and membranes. Pour water into 5- to 6-quart slow cooker. Place squash halves, cut sides up, in cooker. (If necessary, cut off pointed tip so squash stands upright.)

**2** In small bowl, mix remaining ingredients; pour into squash halves.

**3** Cover; cook on High heat setting 3 to 4 hours. Cut squash in half to serve.

## healthy twist

Skip the butter in this recipe if you're watching your fat intake. It does help to round out the flavors in the sauce, but if you're looking for ways to cut fat from your diet, this would be an easy one.

**1 SERVING:** Calories 190; Total Fat 7g (Saturated Fat 4g, Trans Fat 0g); Cholesterol 15mg; Sodium 230mg; Total Carbohydrate 29g (Dietary Fiber 6g); Protein 2g  **EXCHANGES:** ½ Starch, 1 Other Carbohydrate, 1 Vegetable, 1½ Fat  **CARBOHYDRATE CHOICES:** 2

**2 lb small red potatoes**

**2 cups ready-to-eat baby-cut carrots, cut in half lengthwise**

**1 large sweet onion (such as Bermuda, Maui, Spanish or Walla Walla), cut in half, thinly sliced**

**2 teaspoons salt**

**1 lb fresh asparagus spears, cut into 2-inch pieces**

**¼ cup olive or vegetable oil**

**6 tablespoons chopped fresh dill weed**

**1 to 2 teaspoons grated lemon peel**

**2 tablespoons Dijon mustard**

# new potatoes and spring vegetables

**prep time:** 20 minutes    **start to finish:** 5 hours 40 minutes    **18 servings** (½ cup each)

**1** Cut large potatoes in half as needed to make similar-size pieces. In 5- to 6-quart slow cooker, place carrots. Top with onion and potatoes; sprinkle with 1 teaspoon of the salt.

**2** Cover; cook on Low heat setting 5 to 6 hours.

**3** Add asparagus to cooker. Increase heat setting to High; cover and cook 15 to 20 minutes longer or until asparagus is crisp-tender.

**4** In small bowl, mix oil, dill weed, lemon peel, mustard and remaining 1 teaspoon salt. Pour over vegetables in cooker; stir to coat. Vegetables will hold on Low heat setting up to 2 hours; stir occasionally.

**1 SERVING**: Calories 80; Total Fat 3.5g (Saturated Fat 0g; Trans Fat 0g); Cholesterol 0mg; Sodium 310mg; Total Carbohydrate 12g (Dietary Fiber 2g); Protein 2g **EXCHANGES**: ½ Starch, 1 Vegetable, ½ Fat **CARBOHYDRATE CHOICES**: 1

**Betty Crocker The Big Book of Slow Cooker, Casseroles & More**

3 cups boiling water

1½ cups milk

½ cup butter or margarine, cut into pieces

½ cup sour cream

1 package (8 oz) cream cheese, cut into cubes

1 teaspoon garlic salt

¼ teaspoon pepper

4 cups plain mashed potato mix (dry)

Gravy or chopped fresh parsley, if desired

# ultimate slow cooker potatoes

**prep time:** 15 minutes    **start to finish:** 1 hour 45 minutes    **12 servings** (⅔ cup each)

**1** Spray 3- to 4-quart slow cooker with cooking spray. In cooker, mix water, milk, butter, sour cream and cream cheese with whisk until blended. Add garlic salt, pepper and mashed potatoes (dry); mix just until blended.

**2** Cover; cook on Low heat setting 1 hour 30 minutes, stirring once after 1 hour.

**3** Before serving, stir potatoes. Serve immediately, or hold in slow cooker on Low heat setting up to 3 hours, stirring every 30 minutes. If potatoes become too thick, stir in additional milk, a couple tablespoons at a time. Serve with gravy or sprinkle with chopped parsley.

## time-saver

This is truly the ultimate party recipe. It does not require last-minute preparation and this leaves you free to tend to the rest of the meal and be with your guests.

**1 SERVING:** Calories 250; Total Fat 17g (Saturated Fat 11g; Trans Fat 0.5g); Cholesterol 50mg; Sodium 230mg; Total Carbohydrate 20g (Dietary Fiber 1g); Protein 5g **EXCHANGES:** 1½ Starch, 3 Fat **CARBOHYDRATE CHOICES:** 1

**3 lb small red potatoes**

**⅓ cup water**

**1 cup sour cream–and-chive potato topper (from 12-oz container)**

**2 tablespoons ranch dressing and seasoning mix (from 1-oz package)**

**⅓ cup half-and-half**

# country ranch smashed potatoes

**prep time:** 15 minutes    **start to finish:** 5 hours 15 minutes    **12 servings** (½ cup each)

**1** Cut potatoes into halves or quarters as needed to make similar-size pieces. In 5- to 6-quart slow cooker, place potatoes. Add water; mix well to coat all pieces.

**2** Cover; cook on Low heat setting 5 to 6 hours.

**3** Gently mash potatoes with fork or potato masher. Stir in potato topper and dry dressing mix. Stir in half-and-half until potatoes are soft consistency. Potatoes can be kept warm on Low heat setting up to 1 hour; stir occasionally.

## easy variation

For delicious cheesy smashed potatoes, fold in 1 cup shredded Cheddar cheese after stirring in the half-and-half.

**1 SERVING:** Calories 140; Total Fat 4g (Saturated Fat 2.5g; Trans Fat 0g); Cholesterol 5mg; Sodium 280mg; Total Carbohydrate 23g (Dietary Fiber 2g); Protein 3g **EXCHANGES:** 1 Starch, ½ Other Carbohydrate, ½ Fat **CARBOHYDRATE CHOICES:** 1½

# twice-baked potatoes

**prep time:** 15 minutes **start to finish:** 1 hour 50 minutes **8 servings**

**1** Heat oven to 375°F. Gently scrub potatoes, but do not peel. Pierce potatoes several times with fork to allow steam to escape while potatoes bake.

**2** Bake 1 hour to 1 hour 15 minutes or until potatoes are tender when pierced in center with fork.

**3** When potatoes are cool enough to handle, cut each in half lengthwise. Scoop out inside into medium bowl, leaving a thin shell. With potato masher or electric mixer on low speed, mash potatoes until no lumps remain. Add milk in small amounts, beating after each addition with potato masher or electric mixer on low speed (amount of milk needed to make potatoes smooth and fluffy depends on kind of potatoes used).

**4** Add butter, salt and pepper; beat vigorously until potatoes are light and fluffy. Stir in cheese and chives. Fill potato shells with mashed potato mixture. Place on ungreased cookie sheet.

**5** Increase oven temperature to 400°F. Bake about 20 minutes or until hot.

## time-saver

Filled potato shells can be stored in the refrigerator or freezer (wrapped up tightly) before being baked the second time. Bake refrigerated potatoes 30 minutes, frozen potatoes about 40 minutes.

**1 SERVING:** Calories 200; Total Fat 11g (Saturated Fat 7g; Trans Fat 0g); Cholesterol 30mg; Sodium 210mg; Total Carbohydrate 20g (Dietary Fiber 2g); Protein 6g **EXCHANGES:** 1 Starch, ½ High-Fat Meat, 1½ Fat **CARBOHYDRATE CHOICES:** 1

4 large unpeeled Idaho or russet baking potatoes (8 to 10 oz each)

¼ to ½ cup milk

¼ cup butter or margarine, softened

¼ teaspoon salt

Dash pepper

1 cup shredded Cheddar cheese (4 oz)

1 tablespoon chopped fresh chives

6 medium baking potatoes

1½ cups ricotta cheese

1 cup grated Parmesan cheese

¼ cup chopped fresh parsley

¼ teaspoon pepper

1 egg, beaten

Additional chopped fresh parsley, if desired

# ricotta-stuffed potatoes

**prep time:** 25 minutes   **start to finish:** 1 hour 45 minutes   **6 servings**

1 Heat oven to 375°F. Bake potatoes about 1 hour or until tender.

2 Cut each potato in half crosswise; scoop out inside into large bowl, leaving a thin shell. Mash potatoes until no lumps remain. Stir in cheeses, ¼ cup parsley, the pepper and egg until well blended.

3 Increase oven temperature to 400°F. Cut thin slice from bottom of each potato half if needed to stand upright. Place shells on ungreased 15×10×1-inch pan with sides; fill shells with potato mixture.

4 Bake about 20 minutes or until hot. Garnish with additional parsley.

**1 SERVING:** Calories 340; Total Fat 11g (Saturated Fat 6g; Trans Fat 0g); Cholesterol 70mg; Sodium 360mg; Total Carbohydrate 41g (Dietary Fiber 4g); Protein 19g **EXCHANGES:** 2 Starch, ½ Other Carbohydrate, 2 Medium-Fat Meat **CARBOHYDRATE CHOICES:** 3

# appetizing add-ons for easy entertaining

Hot appetizers are a wonderful way to welcome guests into your home. But instead of hassling with items in the oven, put your slow cooker to work.

## cranberry barbecue meatballs

prep time: 30 minutes    start to finish: 2 hours 50 minutes    **24 servings**

**MEATBALLS**

1 lb lean (at least 80%) ground beef

½ lb ground pork

1 medium onion, finely chopped (½ cup)

¼ cup unseasoned dry bread crumbs

½ teaspoon ground mustard

½ teaspoon seasoned salt

⅛ teaspoon pepper

1 egg

**SAUCE**

1 cup barbecue sauce

½ cup cranberry-orange sauce (from 9.2-oz jar)

½ teaspoon ground mustard

½ teaspoon ground ginger

½ teaspoon salt

2 tablespoons chopped fresh parsley

1 Heat oven to 375°F. Spray 15×10×1-inch pan with cooking spray. In large bowl, mix all meatball ingredients. Shape into 1-inch meatballs. Place in pan. Bake 15 to 20 minutes or until thoroughly cooked and no longer pink in center.

2 In 2- to 2½-quart slow cooker, mix all sauce ingredients except parsley until well blended. Add meatballs.

3 Cover; cook on Low heat setting 2 to 3 hours.

4 Stir in parsley. Serve meatballs with cocktail forks or toothpicks. Meatballs will hold on Low heat setting up to 2 hours; stir occasionally.

**1 SERVING:** Calories 90; Total Fat 4g (Saturated Fat 1.5g; Trans Fat 0g); Cholesterol 25mg; Sodium 210mg; Total Carbohydrate 8g (Dietary Fiber 0g); Protein 6g **EXCHANGES:** ½ Starch, ½ Medium-Fat Meat, ½ Fat **CARBOHYDRATE CHOICES:** ½

# southwest chicken nachos

**prep time:** 15 minutes   **start to finish:** 3 hours 45 minutes   **21 servings**

1 package (16 oz) mild Mexican prepared cheese product with jalapeño peppers, cut into cubes

¾ cup chunky-style salsa

1 can (15 oz) black beans, drained, rinsed

1 package (9 oz) frozen cooked southwest-seasoned chicken breast strips, thawed, cubed

1 container (8 oz) southwest ranch sour cream dip

1 medium green bell pepper, chopped (1 cup)

1 medium red bell pepper, chopped (1 cup)

12 oz large tortilla chips

1 In 3- to 4-quart slow cooker, place cheese, salsa, beans and chicken.

2 Cover; cook on Low heat setting 3 to 4 hours, stirring once halfway through cooking.

3 Stir in sour cream dip and bell peppers. Increase heat setting to High; cover and cook about 30 minutes longer or until mixture is hot. Serve over tortilla chips. Topping will hold on Low heat setting up to 2 hours; stir occasionally.

**1 SERVING:** Calories 230; Total Fat 12g (Saturated Fat 5g; Trans Fat 0g); Cholesterol 30mg; Sodium 600mg; Total Carbohydrate 20g (Dietary Fiber 2g); Protein 11g **EXCHANGES:** 1 Starch, 1 Vegetable, 1 Medium-Fat Meat **CARBOHYDRATE CHOICES:** 1

# spinach-artichoke dip

**prep time:** 10 minutes   **start to finish:** 1 hour 10 minutes   **24 servings**

1 cup mayonnaise or salad dressing

1 cup freshly grated Parmesan cheese

1 can (14 oz) artichoke hearts, drained, coarsely chopped

1 box (9 oz) frozen chopped spinach, thawed, squeezed to drain

½ cup chopped red bell pepper

¼ cup shredded Monterey Jack or mozzarella cheese (1 oz)

Toasted baguette slices, assorted crackers or pita chips, if desired

1 Spray 1- to 2½-quart slow cooker with cooking spray. In medium bowl, mix mayonnaise and Parmesan cheese. Stir in artichoke hearts, spinach and bell pepper. Spoon into cooker. Sprinkle with Monterey Jack cheese.

2 Cover; cook on Low heat setting 1 hour to 1 hour 15 minutes. Serve warm with baguette slices. Dip will hold on Low heat setting up to 3 hours; stir occasionally.

**1 SERVING:** Calories 100; Total Fat 9g (Saturated Fat 2g; Trans Fat 0g); Cholesterol 10mg; Sodium 190mg; Total Carbohydrate 3g (Dietary Fiber 1g); Protein 3g **EXCHANGES:** 1 Vegetable, 2 Fat **CARBOHYDRATE CHOICES:** 0

You and your family work hard throughout the week. Reward them (and yourself!) with their just desserts by making one of this chapter's special confections.

Bittersweet Chocolate Cheesecake with White Truffle Sauce will appeal to chocolate fans, while fruity options like Country Apple Streusel Cake, Fresh Berry Crisp and Dulce de Leche–Banana Pie will satisfy any sweet tooth.

zzling desserts dazzling desserts dazzling desserts dazzling desserts dazzling desserts dazzling desserts

**6**

# dazzling
# desserts

**6 cups cubed French bread**

**1 package (6 oz) white chocolate baking bar, coarsely chopped**

**1 cup fat-free egg product**

**¾ cup warm water**

**1 teaspoon vanilla**

**1 can (14 oz) sweetened condensed milk (not evaporated)**

**1 cup fresh raspberries**

# white chocolate bread pudding

**prep time:** 15 minutes   **start to finish:** 3 hours 40 minutes   **8 servings**

**1** Spray 3- to 4-quart slow cooker with cooking spray. Place bread cubes in cooker. Sprinkle with chopped baking bar.

**2** In small bowl, mix remaining ingredients; pour over bread cubes and baking bar.

**3** Cover; cook on Low heat setting 3 hours 30 minutes to 4 hours or until toothpick inserted in center comes out clean. Top servings with fresh raspberries. Serve warm.

## easy variation

Here's a quick new idea. One cup of white vanilla chips can be used instead of the white chocolate baking bar.

**1 SERVING:** Calories 370; Total Fat 12g (Saturated Fat 7g; Trans Fat 0g); Cholesterol 20mg; Sodium 290mg; Total Carbohydrate 53g (Dietary Fiber 0g); Protein 11g **EXCHANGES:** 1½ Starch, 2 Other Carbohydrate, 1 High-Fat Meat, ½ Fat **CARBOHYDRATE CHOICES:** 3½

## BREAD PUDDING

6 cups cubed (1 inch) day-old French bread

1 cup fresh raspberries

2 tablespoons miniature semisweet chocolate chips

2 cups fat-free (skim) milk

½ cup fat-free egg product

¼ cup packed brown sugar

1 teaspoon vanilla

## SAUCE

½ cup granulated sugar

2 tablespoons cornstarch

¾ cup water

1 bag (12 oz) frozen unsweetened raspberries, thawed, undrained

# raspberry bread pudding

**prep time:** 25 minutes   **start to finish:** 1 hour   **8 servings** (½ cup pudding)

**1** Heat oven to 350°F. Spray bottom and sides of 8-inch square (2-quart) glass baking dish with cooking spray. In large bowl, place bread, 1 cup raspberries and chocolate chips.

**2** In medium bowl, mix milk, egg product, brown sugar and vanilla with whisk or fork until blended. Pour egg mixture over bread mixture; stir gently until bread is coated. Spread evenly in baking dish.

**3** Bake 40 to 50 minutes or until golden brown and set.

**4** Meanwhile, in 2-quart saucepan, mix granulated sugar and cornstarch. Stir in water and 1 bag thawed raspberries. Heat to boiling over medium heat, stirring constantly and pressing raspberries to release juice. Boil about 1 minute or until thick. Place small strainer over small bowl. Pour mixture through strainer to remove seeds; discard seeds. Serve sauce with warm bread pudding.

## easy variation

Instead of making the sauce from scratch, use raspberry pancake syrup.

**1 SERVING:** Calories 230; Total Fat 2g (Saturated Fat 1g; Trans Fat 0g); Cholesterol 0mg; Sodium 210mg; Total Carbohydrate 46g (Dietary Fiber 5g); Protein 7g **EXCHANGES:** 1½ Starch, 1½ Other Carbohydrate, ½ Fat **CARBOHYDRATE CHOICES:** 3

## CRUST

1¾ cups graham cracker crumbs

6 tablespoons butter or margarine, melted

## FILLING

3 packages (8 oz each) cream cheese, softened

¼ cup sugar

3 eggs

¾ cup cream of coconut

¼ cup light rum

2 teaspoons grated orange peel

1 can (8 oz) crushed pineapple in juice, drained, ½ cup juice reserved

## GLAZE

Reserved ½ cup pineapple juice

2 teaspoons cornstarch

¼ cup sugar

## GARNISH

1 can (8 oz) crushed pineapple in juice, drained

1 jar (24 oz) refrigerated sliced mango, drained, chopped

# piña colada cheesecake

**prep time:** 30 minutes    **start to finish:** 9 hours 5 minutes    **16 servings**

1 Heat oven to 325°F. Wrap outside bottom and side of 10-inch springform pan with foil to prevent leaking. Spray inside bottom and side of pan with cooking spray. In small bowl, mix crust ingredients. Press crust mixture in bottom of pan. Bake 8 to 10 minutes or until set.

2 Meanwhile, in large bowl, beat cream cheese and ¼ cup sugar with electric mixer on medium speed until light and fluffy. Beat in eggs, one at a time, just until blended. On low speed, beat in remaining filling ingredients except pineapple. Gently fold in pineapple. Pour over crust.

3 Bake 1 hour 10 minutes to 1 hour 15 minutes or until edge of cheesecake is set at least 2 inches from edge of pan but center of cheesecake still jiggles slightly when moved.

4 Run small metal spatula around edge of pan to loosen cheesecake. Turn oven off; open oven door at least 4 inches. Let cheesecake remain in oven 30 minutes. Cool in pan on cooling rack 30 minutes. Refrigerate at least 6 hours or overnight before serving.

5 In 1-quart saucepan, mix reserved ½ cup pineapple juice plus enough water to equal ⅔ cup, the cornstarch and sugar. Heat to boiling over medium heat, stirring constantly. Boil 1 minute, stirring constantly, until slightly thickened. Cool 20 minutes at room temperature.

6 In large bowl, toss glaze with pineapple and mango. Spoon onto top of cheesecake.

**1 SERVING:** Calories 360; Total Fat 25g (Saturated Fat 16g; Trans Fat 0.5g); Cholesterol 100mg; Sodium 230mg; Total Carbohydrate 27g (Dietary Fiber 1g); Protein 6g **EXCHANGES:** ½ Fruit, 1½ Other Carbohydrate, 1 High-Fat Meat, 3½ Fat **CARBOHYDRATE CHOICES:** 2

## CAKE MIXTURE

1¼ cups all-purpose flour

¾ cup sugar

¼ cup unsweetened
baking cocoa

1½ teaspoons baking
powder

½ teaspoon salt

½ cup milk

2 tablespoons butter
or margarine, melted

1 teaspoon almond
extract

1 bag (12 oz) frozen dark
sweet cherries, thawed,
coarsely chopped and
drained

## PUDDING MIXTURE

1 cup sugar

¼ cup unsweetened
baking cocoa

Dash salt

1⅓ cups boiling water

## TOPPING

¼ cup chocolate chips

¼ cup slivered almonds

# hot fudge–cherry pudding cake

**prep time:** 15 minutes    **start to finish:** 1 hour 40 minutes    **6 servings**

**1** Spray 3- to 4-quart slow cooker with cooking spray. In medium bowl, mix flour, ¾ cup sugar, ¼ cup cocoa, the baking powder and ½ teaspoon salt. Stir in milk, butter and almond extract until well blended. Stir in cherries. Spread batter evenly in cooker.

**2** In small bowl, mix all pudding mixture ingredients except water. Sprinkle evenly over batter in cooker. Carefully pour water over sugar mixture to moisten all of sugar mixture.

**3** Cover; cook on High heat setting 1 hour to 1 hour 30 minutes or until top springs back when touched lightly (center will still be soft).

**4** Turn off cooker; let cake stand uncovered 20 minutes to cool slightly. Sprinkle with chips and almonds; cover and let stand 5 minutes longer to soften chips.

**1 SERVING:** Calories 520; Total Fat 10g (Saturated Fat 4.5g; Trans Fat 0g); Cholesterol 10mg; Sodium 380mg; Total Carbohydrate 102g (Dietary Fiber 5g); Protein 6g **EXCHANGES:** 1½ Starch, ½ Fruit, 5 Other Carbohydrate, 2 Fat **CARBOHYDRATE CHOICES:** 7

# bittersweet chocolate cheesecake with white truffle sauce

**prep time:** 30 minutes    **start to finish:** 5 hours 15 minutes    **12 servings**

## CHEESECAKE

2 packages (8 oz each) cream cheese, softened

1 teaspoon vanilla

⅔ cup sugar

1 tablespoon all-purpose flour

3 eggs

8 oz bittersweet baking chocolate, melted, cooled

Fresh raspberries or strawberries, if desired

## SAUCE

1 package (6 oz) white chocolate baking bars, chopped

2 tablespoons butter or margarine

½ cup whipping cream

**1** Heat oven to 275°F. Lightly spray bottom and side of 9-inch springform pan with cooking spray. In medium bowl, beat cream cheese and vanilla with electric mixer on medium speed until smooth. Gradually add sugar, beating until fluffy. Beat in flour. Beat in eggs, one at a time. Beat in chocolate. Pour into pan.

**2** Bake about 1 hour 15 minutes or until center is set. (Do not insert knife because hole could cause cheesecake to crack.) Cool at room temperature 15 minutes.

**3** Run knife around side of pan to loosen cheesecake. Cover; refrigerate about 3 hours or until chilled.

**4** Meanwhile, in 2-quart saucepan, melt white chocolate and butter over low heat, stirring constantly (mixture will be thick and grainy). Remove from heat. Stir in whipping cream until smooth. Cover; refrigerate about 2 hours or until chilled.

**5** Run knife around side of pan to loosen cheesecake; remove side of pan. Let cheesecake stand at room temperature 15 minutes before cutting. Drizzle sauce over cheesecake. Top with berries. Store in refrigerator.

**1 SERVING:** Calories 430; Total Fat 30g (Saturated Fat 18g; Trans Fat 0.5g); Cholesterol 115mg; Sodium 160mg; Total Carbohydrate 33g (Dietary Fiber 1g); Protein 6g **EXCHANGES:** 2 Other Carbohydrate, 1 High-Fat Meat, 4½ Fat **CARBOHYDRATE CHOICES:** 2

# country apple streusel cake

prep time: 35 minutes   start to finish: 1 hour 35 minutes   **15 servings**

## STREUSEL TOPPING

¾ cup whole wheat flour

½ cup packed brown sugar

½ teaspoon ground cinnamon

½ cup cold butter or margarine

## CAKE

1½ cups whole wheat flour

1½ cups all-purpose flour

1½ cups granulated sugar

3 teaspoons baking powder

1 teaspoon salt

1¼ cups milk

¾ cup butter or margarine, softened

1½ teaspoons vanilla

3 eggs

4 cups very thinly sliced peeled apples

1 Heat oven to 350°F. Spray 13×9-inch pan with cooking spray. In small bowl, mix streusel topping ingredients with pastry blender or fork until crumbly; set aside.

2 In large bowl, beat all cake ingredients except apples with electric mixer on medium speed 3 minutes, scraping bowl frequently. Spread batter in pan. Arrange apple slices evenly over batter. Sprinkle evenly with topping.

3 Bake 55 to 60 minutes or until toothpick inserted in center comes out clean. Serve warm with ice cream or whipped cream, if desired.

## healthy twist

Even though this is a cake and a decadent dessert, it's a choice that is full of good wholesome ingredients like whole wheat flour and apples.

**1 SERVING:** Calories 400; Total Fat 17g (Saturated Fat 10g; Trans Fat 0.5g); Cholesterol 85mg; Sodium 390mg; Total Carbohydrate 55g (Dietary Fiber 3g); Protein 6g **EXCHANGES:** 2 Starch, 1½ Other Carbohydrate, 3 Fat **CARBOHYDRATE CHOICES:** 3½

3 cups all-purpose flour

2 teaspoons ground
ginger

1 teaspoon baking powder

¼ teaspoon salt

2½ cups sugar

1¼ cups butter, softened
(do not use margarine)

1 tablespoon grated
gingerroot

1 teaspoon vanilla

5 eggs

¾ cup milk

½ cup finely chopped
crystallized ginger

3 cups fresh fruit,
if desired

# triple-ginger pound cake

**prep time:** 20 minutes   **start to finish:** 3 hours 30 minutes   **24 servings**

**1** Heat oven to 350°F. Spray 12-cup fluted tube cake pan or 10-inch angel food cake pan with baking spray with flour. In medium bowl, mix flour, ground ginger, baking powder and salt; set aside.

**2** In large bowl, beat sugar, butter, gingerroot, vanilla and eggs with electric mixer on low speed 30 seconds, scraping bowl constantly. Beat on high speed 5 minutes, scraping bowl occasionally. On low speed, beat in flour mixture alternately with milk. Fold in crystallized ginger until evenly mixed. Spread in pan.

**3** Bake 50 to 60 minutes or until toothpick inserted in center comes out clean. Cool 10 minutes. Remove cake from pan to cooling rack. Cool completely, about 2 hours.

## easy variation

Serve with sliced strawberries and whipped cream.

**1 SERVING:** Calories 250; Total Fat 11g (Saturated Fat 7g; Trans Fat 0g); Cholesterol 70mg; Sodium 130mg; Total Carbohydrate 35g (Dietary Fiber 0g); Protein 3g **EXCHANGES:** 1 Starch, 1½ Other Carbohydrate, 2 Fat **CARBOHYDRATE CHOICES:** 2

**CRUST**

1 cup all-purpose flour

½ teaspoon salt

⅓ cup plus 1 tablespoon
  shortening

2 to 3 tablespoons
  cold water

**FILLING**

1 can (13.4 oz) dulce de
  leche (caramelized
  sweetened condensed
  milk)

3 ripe medium bananas

1 cup whipping cream

¼ cup powdered sugar

½ cup semisweet
  chocolate chips

1 teaspoon vegetable oil

# dulce de leche–
# banana pie

**prep time:** 20 minutes    **start to finish:** 1 hour 5 minutes    **8 servings**

**1** Heat oven to 450°F. In medium bowl, mix flour and salt. Using pastry blender, cut in shortening until particles are size of small peas. Sprinkle with water, 1 tablespoon at a time, tossing with fork until all flour is moistened.

**2** On lightly floured surface, shape dough into a ball. Flatten ball to ½-inch thickness. With floured rolling pin, roll dough into 11-inch round. Fold dough in half; place in 9-inch glass pie plate. Gently press into plate.

**3** Fold edge of dough under; flute edge. Prick dough generously with fork. Bake 9 to 12 minutes or until light golden brown. Cool completely.

**4** Spoon dulce de leche into crust; gently spread to edge. Thinly slice bananas; arrange over dulce de leche.

**5** In medium bowl, beat whipping cream and powdered sugar with electric mixer. Spread over bananas.

**6** In small resealable freezer plastic bag, place chocolate chips and oil; seal bag. Microwave on High 30 seconds; knead bag to mix melted chips and unmelted chips. Microwave 15 to 30 seconds longer or until all chips are melted and smooth. Snip off tiny corner of bag. Pipe melted chocolate mixture over whipped cream. Store pie in refrigerator.

**1 SERVING:** Calories 500; Total Fat 26g (Saturated Fat 12g; Trans Fat 2g); Cholesterol 35mg; Sodium 210mg; Total Carbohydrate 60g (Dietary Fiber 2g); Protein 7g **EXCHANGES:** 1 Starch, 3 Other Carbohydrate, ½ High-Fat Meat, 4 Fat **CARBOHYDRATE CHOICES:** 4

# toffee apple turnover pie

**prep time:** 40 minutes  **start to finish:** 1 hour 50 minutes  **4 servings**

**PASTRY**

1 cup all-purpose flour

¼ teaspoon salt

⅓ cup plus 1 tablespoon shortening

2 to 3 tablespoons cold water

**FILLING**

1½ cups sliced peeled apples (2 small)

1 tablespoon all-purpose flour

½ cup toffee bits (from 10-oz bag)

1 egg, beaten

1 tablespoon coarse white sparkling sugar

**1** Heat oven to 375°F. Line cookie sheet with sides or 15×10×1-inch pan with cooking parchment paper or foil. In medium bowl, mix 1 cup flour and the salt. Using pastry blender (or pulling 2 tables knives through ingredients in opposite directions), cut in shortening until particles are size of small peas. Sprinkle with cold water, 1 tablespoon at a time, tossing with fork until all flour is moistened and pastry almost leaves side of bowl (if necessary, 1 to 2 teaspoons more water can be added).

**2** Gather pastry into a ball. On lightly floured surface, shape pastry into flattened round. Using rolling pin, roll into 12-inch round, about ⅛ inch thick. Place on cookie sheet.

**3** In medium bowl, toss apples and 1 tablespoon flour. Mound apple mixture on half of pastry to within ¾ inch of edge. Sprinkle with toffee bits. Fold pastry in half over apple mixture. Fold ½ inch of sealed edge of pastry over; firmly press tines of fork around edge to seal. Brush top of turnover with egg. Cut 3 slits, 1 inch long, in top to allow steam to escape. Sprinkle top with sugar.

**4** Bake 30 to 40 minutes or until golden brown. Immediately remove from cookie sheet to serving plate. Cool 30 minutes before cutting.

**1 SERVING:** Calories 500; Total Fat 31g (Saturated Fat 11g; Trans Fat 3.5g); Cholesterol 75mg; Sodium 280mg; Total Carbohydrate 50g (Dietary Fiber 2g); Protein 5g **EXCHANGES:** 1 Starch, 2½ Other Carbohydrate, 6 Fat **CARBOHYDRATE CHOICES:** 3

**6 yellow- or red-skinned pears, cored from bottom leaving stems attached**

**1 cup caramel ice cream topping**

**⅓ cup real maple syrup**

**Grated lemon peel**

# caramel-maple pears

**prep time:** 15 minutes    **start to finish:** 2 hours 45 minutes    **6 servings**

**1** Spray 5- to 6-quart slow cooker with cooking spray. Place pears upright in cooker. (If all pears do not fit in bottom of cooker, place remaining pears suspended between 2 others in cooker.)

**2** In small bowl, mix ice cream topping and syrup; pour over pears.

**3** Cover; cook on High heat setting 2 hours 30 minutes to 3 hours 30 minutes.

**4** Remove pears from cooker; place upright on serving plate or in individual dessert dishes. Spoon about ¼ cup topping mixture over each pear; sprinkle with lemon peel.

## easy variation

This elegant dessert is stunning all by itself, or you can add an additional layer of flavor by stirring in ½ cup raisins or orange-flavored dried cranberries with the ice cream topping. Drizzle a little cream over the sauce that falls onto the plate, if you like.

**1 SERVING:** Calories 310; Total Fat 0g (Saturated Fat 0g, Trans Fat 0g); Cholesterol 0mg; Sodium 190mg; Total Carbohydrate 76g (Dietary Fiber 6g); Protein 1g   **EXCHANGES:** 1 Starch, ½ Fruit, 3½ Other Carbohydrate   **CARBOHYDRATE CHOICES:** 5

1 can (21 oz) apple pie
    filling

2 cups all-purpose flour

1¼ cups packed brown
    sugar

1 cup canned pumpkin
    (not pumpkin pie mix)

¾ cup fat-free egg product

⅓ cup vegetable oil

2 teaspoons baking
    powder

1 teaspoon ground
    cinnamon

½ teaspoon ground
    nutmeg

¼ teaspoon baking soda

Ice cream, if desired

# pumpkin-apple dessert

**prep time:** 15 minutes    **start to finish:** 1 hour 45 minutes    **12 servings**

**1** Spray 3½- to 6-quart slow cooker with cooking spray. Spoon pie filling into cooker; spread evenly.

**2** In large bowl, beat remaining ingredients except ice cream on low speed 1 minute, scraping bowl constantly. Beat on medium speed 2 minutes, scraping bowl occasionally. Pour batter over pie filling.

**3** Cover; cook on High heat setting 1 hour 30 minutes to 2 hours or until toothpick inserted in center comes out clean. Serve with ice cream.

**1 SERVING:** Calories 300; Total Fat 6g (Saturated Fat 1g; Trans Fat 0g); Cholesterol 0mg; Sodium 140mg; Total Carbohydrate 55g (Dietary Fiber 2g); Protein 4g **EXCHANGES:** 1½ Starch, 2 Other Carbohydrate, 1 Fat **CARBOHYDRATE CHOICES:** 3½

# caramel-apple crisp

**prep time:** 20 minutes    **start to finish:** 1 hour 10 minutes    **6 servings**

½ cup caramel topping

½ teaspoon ground cinnamon

6 large baking apples, peeled, cut into ½-inch slices (about 6 cups)

⅔ cup all-purpose flour

½ cup packed brown sugar

½ cup cold butter or margarine, cut into small pieces

⅔ cup quick-cooking oats

**1** Heat oven to 375°F. In large bowl, stir together caramel topping and cinnamon until blended. Add apples; toss until evenly coated. Spread in ungreased 8-inch square (2-quart) glass baking dish.

**2** In same bowl, mix ⅔ cup flour and the brown sugar. Using pastry blender (or pulling 2 table knives through mixture in opposite directions), cut in butter until mixture looks like coarse crumbs. Stir in oats. Crumble mixture over apples in baking dish.

**3** Bake 45 to 50 minutes or until apples are tender and topping is golden brown. If desired, serve with whipped cream and additional caramel topping.

## time-saver

Save time by coring all of the apples first. Then use a very sharp knife to cut the apples into slices of the same thickness so they'll cook evenly. To test for doneness, simply poke the tip of a sharp knife into an apple, and you'll be able to feel if it's tender.

**1 SERVING:** Calories 430; Total Fat 16g (Saturated Fat 10g; Trans Fat 0.5g); Cholesterol 40mg; Sodium 210mg; Total Carbohydrate 67g (Dietary Fiber 3g); Protein 3g **EXCHANGES:** 1 Starch, ½ Fruit, 3 Other Carbohydrate, 3 Fat **CARBOHYDRATE CHOICES:** 4½

3 cups fresh strawberries, sliced

3 tablespoons cornstarch

2 tablespoons granulated sugar

1 pint (2 cups) fresh blueberries

1 pint (2 cups) fresh raspberries

⅔ cup packed brown sugar

½ cup whole wheat flour

½ cup old-fashioned or quick-cooking oats

½ teaspoon ground cinnamon

¼ teaspoon salt

⅓ cup butter or margarine, softened

# fresh berry crisp

**prep time:** 10 minutes    **start to finish:** 40 minutes    **6 servings**

**1** Heat oven to 350°F. In 2-quart saucepan, mash 2 cups of the strawberries. Stir in cornstarch and granulated sugar. Cook over medium heat, stirring constantly, until mixture boils. Boil and stir 1 minute.

**2** Carefully stir in blueberries, raspberries and remaining strawberries. Pour berry mixture into ungreased 8-inch square (2-quart) glass baking dish or 9-inch pie plate.

**3** In small bowl, mix remaining ingredients with pastry blender or fork until crumbly; sprinkle over berry mixture.

**4** Bake about 30 minutes or until topping is golden brown. Serve warm with ice cream, if desired.

**1 SERVING:** Calories 370; Total Fat 12g (Saturated Fat 7g; Trans Fat 0g); Cholesterol 25mg; Sodium 180mg; Total Carbohydrate 62g (Dietary Fiber 7g); Protein 3g **EXCHANGES:** 1 Starch, 1 Fruit, 2 Other Carbohydrate, 2½ Fat **CARBOHYDRATE CHOICES:** 4

# metric conversion guide

## volume

| U.S. UNITS | CANADIAN METRIC | AUSTRALIAN METRIC |
| --- | --- | --- |
| ¼ teaspoon | 1 mL | 1 ml |
| ½ teaspoon | 2 mL | 2 ml |
| 1 teaspoon | 5 mL | 5 ml |
| 1 tablespoon | 15 mL | 20 ml |
| ¼ cup | 50 mL | 60 ml |
| ⅓ cup | 75 mL | 80 ml |
| ½ cup | 125 mL | 125 ml |
| ⅔ cup | 150 mL | 170 ml |
| ¾ cup | 175 mL | 190 ml |
| 1 cup | 250 mL | 250 ml |
| 1 quart | 1 liter | 1 liter |
| 1½ quarts | 1.5 liters | 1.5 liters |
| 2 quarts | 2 liters | 2 liters |
| 2½ quarts | 2.5 liters | 2.5 liters |
| 3 quarts | 3 liters | 3 liters |
| 4 quarts | 4 liters | 4 liters |

## weight

| U.S. UNITS | CANADIAN METRIC | AUSTRALIAN METRIC |
| --- | --- | --- |
| 1 ounce | 30 grams | 30 grams |
| 2 ounces | 55 grams | 60 grams |
| 3 ounces | 85 grams | 90 grams |
| 4 ounces (¼ pound) | 115 grams | 125 grams |
| 8 ounces (½ pound) | 225 grams | 225 grams |
| 16 ounces (1 pound) | 455 grams | 500 grams |
| 1 pound | 455 grams | 0.5 kilogram |

## measurements

| INCHES | CENTIMETERS |
| --- | --- |
| 1 | 2.5 |
| 2 | 5.0 |
| 3 | 7.5 |
| 4 | 10.0 |
| 5 | 12.5 |
| 6 | 15.0 |
| 7 | 17.5 |
| 8 | 20.5 |
| 9 | 23.0 |
| 10 | 25.5 |
| 11 | 28.0 |
| 12 | 30.5 |
| 13 | 33.0 |

## temperatures

| FAHRENHEIT | CELSIUS |
| --- | --- |
| 32° | 0° |
| 212° | 100° |
| 250° | 120° |
| 275° | 140° |
| 300° | 150° |
| 325° | 160° |
| 350° | 180° |
| 375° | 190° |
| 400° | 200° |
| 425° | 220° |
| 450° | 230° |
| 475° | 240° |
| 500° | 260° |

note: The recipes in this cookbook have not been developed or tested using metric measures. When converting recipes to metric, some variations in quality may be noted.

# index

Page numbers in *italics*
indicate illustrations

BETTY Crocker.com

# P

Paella
  Chicken and Rice, Casserole, 136, *137*
  Salmon Paella Bake, 162
  Weeknight, 100, *101*
Parmesan
  –Butternut Squash Gratin, 286, *287*
  Chicken, 60, *61*
  -and Lemon-Crusted Salmon, 242, *243*
Pasta. *See also* Fettuccine; Lasagna; Noodle(s)
  Asparagus and Turkey Sausage Skillet, 74, *75*
  Bow-Ties with Salmon and Tarragon Mustard Sauce, 106, *107*
  and Chicken Bake, Country, 127
  Chicken Cacciatore, 112, *113*
  Chicken Scampi, Quick, 68
  Cincinnati Chili, 30
  Ginger Asian Beef, 87
  Manicotti, Easy Cheesy, 173
  Orzo and Chicken Supper, 72, *73*
  Pesto and Turkey, 78
  Pizza Chicken, 110
  Pizza Goulash, Deluxe, 89
  Rigatoni, Seven-Layer, 148, *149*
  Rigatoni, Three-Cheese, 180
  Sausage and Pizza Bake, 146
  Shells, Seafood-Stuffed, 163
  Shrimp Alfredo Primavera, 98, *99*
  Spaghetti Sauce, Chunky Pork and Mushroom, 158, *159*
  Tortellini Casserole, Creamy, 175
Pea and Ham Soup, Golden, 45
Peanut
  Chicken, Thai, 114, *115*
  Noodle and Beef Skillet, Thai, 88
  Sauce, Tilapia with, Thai, 104, *105*
Pea Pods and Carrots, Dilled, 257
Pears, Caramel-Maple, 320, *321*

Pepper(s). *See also* Chile(s); Chipotle
  Couscous-Stuffed, 142, *143*
  Ratatouille Soup, Summer Vegetable, 54, *55*
  Red Pepper-Spinach Lasagna, 176, *177*
  Roasted Red, Broccoli with Hazelnuts and, 250, *251*
  Steak, 213
Philly Cheese Steak Sandwiches, 144, *145*
Pie(s)
  Apple Turnover, Toffee, 318, *319*
  Chicken Pot Pie, Cheesy, 130, *131*
  Dulce de Leche–Banana, 316, *317*
  Meatball, Italian, 154
  Pizza, Spinach, 184
  Seafood Chowder Pot Pie, 164, *165*
  Spanakopita, Greek, 150, *151*
Piña Colada Cheesecake, 306, *307*
Pinto and Chicken Tostadas, 111
Pizza
  Chicken, 110
  Goulash, Deluxe, 89
  Pie, Spinach, 184
  and Sausage Bake, 146
Pork. *See also* Sausage
  Baby Back Ribs, Barbecued, 238, *239*
  Baby Back Ribs with Spicy Barbecue Sauce, 240, *241*
  Bacon-Chili Gravy, Beef Roast with, 203
  and Bean Casserole, French, 155
  Brown Sugar-Glazed, with Sweet Potatoes, 234, *235*
  Cassoulet, Everyday, 160, *161*
  Chili, Chipotle, 44
  Chops with Apple-Cherry Stuffing, 222
  Chops with Broccoli and Rice, 92, *93*
  Chops with Summer Vegetable Medley, 220, *221*

  Ham and Pea Soup, Golden, 45
  Ham and Wild Rice Soup, 46, *47*
  Lo Mein, Thai Orange, 156, *157*
  Meatballs, Cranberry Barbecue, *298*, 298
  and Mushroom Spaghetti Sauce, Chunky, 158, *159*
  'n Noodles, Sweet-and-Sour, 96, *97*
  Pot Roast, Porketta, 228
  Ribs, Smoky Apple Butter, 236, *237*
  Roast, with Apples and Sweet Potatoes, 232, *233*
  Roast, Harvest Time, 225
  Roast, Honey Barbecue-Glazed, with Carrots and Corn, 224
  Roast, Maple-Sage, 223
  Roast, Wild Mushroom-Stuffed, 226, *227*
  Tenderloin, Cajun, with Vegetables, 230, *231*
  Tenderloin, Orange, with Butternut Squash, 229
Porketta Pot Roast, 228
Potato(es)
  Beef Roast with Onions and, 202
  and Chicken, Sage, 135
  Mashed, Braised Short Ribs with, 211
  Meat Loaf Casserole, -Topped, 147
  New, and Spring Vegetables, 290, *291*
  Ricotta-Stuffed, 296, *297*
  Smashed, Country Ranch, 294
  Soup, Cheesy, 50, *51*
  and Steak Skillet, Cheesy, 90, *91*
  Tater-Topped Chicken Casserole, Cheesy, 132, *133*
  Twice-Baked, 295
  Ultimate Slow Cooker, 292, *293*
Pot Pie, Chicken, Cheesy, 130, *131*
Pot Pie, Seafood Chowder, 164, *165*
Pot Roast, Caramelized Onion, 200, *201*

*BettyCrocker*.com

## Recipe Testing and Calculating Nutrition Information

**Recipe Testing:**

- Large eggs and 2% milk were used unless otherwise indicated.
- Fat-free, low-fat, low-sodium or lite products were not used unless indicated.
- No nonstick cookware and bakeware were used unless otherwise indicated. No dark-colored, black or insulated bakeware was used.
- When a pan is specified, a metal pan was used; a baking dish or pie plate means ovenproof glass was used.
- An electric hand mixer was used for mixing only when mixer speeds are specified.

**Calculating Nutrition:**

- The first ingredient was used wherever a choice is given, such as ⅓ cup sour cream or plain yogurt.
- The first amount was used wherever a range is given, such as 3- to 3½-pound whole chicken.
- The first serving number was used wherever a range is given, such as 4 to 6 servings.
- "If desired" ingredients were not included.
- Only the amount of a marinade or frying oil that is absorbed was included.

# Complete your cookbook library with these *Betty Crocker* titles

Betty Crocker 300 Calorie Cookbook

Betty Crocker Baking for Today

Betty Crocker Basics

Betty Crocker's Best Bread Machine Cookbook

Betty Crocker's Best Chicken Cookbook

Betty Crocker's Best Christmas Cookbook

Betty Crocker's Best of Baking

Betty Crocker's Best of Healthy and Hearty Cooking

Betty Crocker's Best-Loved Recipes

Betty Crocker's Bisquick® Cookbook

Betty Crocker Bisquick® II Cookbook

Betty Crocker Bisquick® Impossibly Easy Pies

Betty Crocker Celebrate!

Betty Crocker's Complete Thanksgiving Cookbook

Betty Crocker's Cook Book for Boys and Girls

Betty Crocker's Cook It Quick

Betty Crocker Cookbook, 10th Edition— The BIG RED Cookbook®

Betty Crocker Cookbook, Bridal Edition

Betty Crocker's Cookie Book

Betty Crocker's Cooking Basics

Betty Crocker's Cooking for Two

Betty Crocker's Cooky Book, Facsimile Edition

Betty Crocker Country Cooking

Betty Crocker Decorating Cakes and Cupcakes

Betty Crocker's Diabetes Cookbook

Betty Crocker Dinner Made Easy with Rotisserie Chicken

Betty Crocker Easy Everyday Vegetarian

Betty Crocker Easy Family Dinners

Betty Crocker's Easy Slow Cooker Dinners

Betty Crocker's Eat and Lose Weight

Betty Crocker's Entertaining Basics

Betty Crocker's Flavors of Home

Betty Crocker 4-Ingredient Dinners

Betty Crocker Grilling Made Easy

Betty Crocker Healthy Heart Cookbook

Betty Crocker's Healthy New Choices

Betty Crocker's Indian Home Cooking

Betty Crocker's Italian Cooking

Betty Crocker's Kids Cook!

Betty Crocker's Kitchen Library

Betty Crocker's Living with Cancer Cookbook

Betty Crocker Low-Carb Lifestyle Cookbook

Betty Crocker's Low-Fat, Low-Cholesterol Cooking Today

Betty Crocker Money Saving Meals

Betty Crocker More Slow Cooker Recipes

Betty Crocker's New Cake Decorating

Betty Crocker's New Chinese Cookbook

Betty Crocker One-Dish Meals

Betty Crocker's A Passion for Pasta

Betty Crocker's Picture Cook Book, Facsimile Edition

Betty Crocker's Quick & Easy Cookbook

Betty Crocker's Slow Cooker Cookbook

Betty Crocker's Ultimate Cake Mix Cookbook

Betty Crocker's Vegetarian Cooking

Betty Crocker Why It Works

JAMESTOWN  PUBLISHERS

# ENGLISH, YES!

## INTRODUCTORY

# Learning English Through Literature

JAMESTOWN PUBLISHERS

*a division of* NTC/CONTEMPORARY PUBLISHING GROUP
Lincolnwood, Illinois USA

"Hello, Goodbye" by John Lennon/Paul McCartney,
© 1967, Paul McCartney,
Renewed 1995 Sony/ATV Songs LLC.
Administered by EMI Blackwood Music Inc. (BMI)


Original cover and interior design: Michael Kelly
Cover illustration: Westlight / © Jim Zuckerman


ISBN: 0-89061-915-8


Published by Jamestown Publishers,
a division of NTC/Contemporary Publishing Group, Inc.,
4255 West Touhy Avenue,
Lincolnwood (Chicago), Illinois 60712-1975 U.S.A.
© 1998 NTC/Contemporary Publishing Group, Inc.
Manufactured in the United States of America.

00 01 02 03 04 VH 12 11 10 9 8 7 6 5

# CONTENTS

JAMESTOWN PUBLISHERS

# ENGLISH, YES!

## INTRODUCTORY

## Learning English Through Literature

# HELLO, GOOD-BYE

How do you say *hello* to a family member?
How do you say hello to a friend?
How do you say hello to a stranger?

# Good-bye to the Old, Hello to the New

Last month I was in my native country. I said **good-bye** to
my grandparents, my cousins, and my friends. I was **sad.**
I was a little **worried** too. What about the future?

Now I live in a **different** country. I live in the United States.
5   I am in a different school. My sister is in a different
school too. We have **new** teachers and new friends. New
experiences are good!

I am **happy** here, but a new life isn't easy. Sometimes I
remember my grandparents in my country. Sometimes
10   I remember my **old** friends. Sometimes I am **lonely.**
Then I look at their pictures and I feel better. **Part of my
heart** is with them. And part of their heart is with me.

# Hello, Good-bye

by John Lennon and Paul McCartney

You say **yes,** I say **no.**
You say **stop,** I say **go,** go, go.
**Oh no!**
You say good-bye and I say hello.
5    Hello, hello,
I don't know why you say good-bye.
I say hello.
Hello, hello,
I don't know why you say good-bye.
10    I say hello.

I say **high,** you say **low.**
You say why, and I say I don't know.
Oh no!
You say good-bye and I say hello.
15    Hello, hello,
I don't know why you say good-bye.
I say hello.
Hello, hello,
I don't know why you say good-bye.
20    I say hello.

Put an *x* in the box next to the correct answer.

*Reading Comprehension*

**1.** Last month the boy in the story was in
  ❏ a. the United States.
  ❏ b. his native country.

**2.** Now the boy is in
  ❏ a. the United States.
  ❏ b. his native country.

**3.** The boy said good-bye to his
  ❏ a. sister.
  ❏ b. grandparents.

**4.** In his new country, the boy is
  ❏ a. sad and worried.
  ❏ b. happy but sometimes lonely.

**5.** In the song, the singer says *no.* Then the singer's friend says
  ❏ a. yes.
  ❏ b. no.

**6.** The singer and her friend think the same way.
  ❏ a. Right.
  ❏ b. Wrong.

*Vocabulary*

**7.** *Good-bye* and *hello* have
  ❏ a. the same meaning.
  ❏ b. different meanings.

**8.** When you are *worried,* you are
  ❏ a. not happy. You are thinking about your problems.
  ❏ b. tired. You are ready to go to bed.

*Idioms*

**9.** In the story, the boy says part of his heart is with his old friends. The idiom *part of my heart* means
  ❏ a. part of my body.
  ❏ b. part of my feelings and thoughts.

**10.** In the song, *Oh no* means
  ❏ a. there is a problem.
  ❏ b. there is not a problem.

How many questions did you answer correctly? Circle your score. Then fill in your score on the Score Chart on page 152.

| Number Correct | 1 | 2 | 3 | 4 | 5 | 6 | 7 | 8 | 9 | 10 |
|---|---|---|---|---|---|---|---|---|---|---|
| **Score** | 10 | 20 | 30 | 40 | 50 | 60 | 70 | 80 | 90 | 100 |

# EXERCISES TO HELP YOU

*Exercise A*

**Building sentences.** Make sentences by adding the correct letter. One is done for you.

1. Last month I ____*c*____

2. I said good-bye _____

3. Sometimes I

   remember _____

4. Then I look _____

**a.** to my grandparents, my cousins, and my old friends.
**b.** my old friends.
**c.** was in my native country.
**d.** at their pictures.

Now write the sentences in the blanks below. Begin each sentence with a capital letter. End it with a period. One is done for you.

1. *Last month I was in my native country.*

2. _____

3. _____

4. _____

Do numbers 5–8 the same way. These sentences are about the song.

5. You say stop, and _____

6. You say good-bye _____

7. You say why _____

8. I don't know _____

**a.** why you say good-bye.
**b.** I say go, go, go.
**c.** and I say hello.
**d.** and I say I don't know.

5. _____

6. _____

7. _____

8. _____

*Exercise B*

**Understanding the story.** Answer each question. Complete the sentence. Look back at the story. One is done for you.

1. Where was the boy last month?

   *Last month he was in his native country* .

2. Who did the boy say good-bye to?

   *He said good-bye* .

3. The boy said good-bye. How did he feel?

   *He was* .

4. Where is the boy now?

   *He is* .

5. Is the boy in the same school or in a different school?

   *He is* .

6. How does the boy feel here in his new country?

   *He is* .

7. Who does the boy remember?

   *He remembers* .

8. What does the boy look at?

   *He looks at* .

*Exercise C*

**Using the verb *be* correctly.** Study this chart.

| The Verb *Be:* Simple Present | |
|---|---|
| **Singular** | **Plural** |
| I am | We are |
| You are | You are |
| He is | They are |
| She is | |
| It is | |

Fill in each blank. Use the present tense of the verb *be*. One is done for you.

1. The boy said good-bye.

   Now he _____*is*_____ in a new country.

2. The boy said good-bye to his grandparents.

   They _____ in the boy's native country.

3. The boy said, "I _____ happy in my new country."

4. The boy's sister is in the United States too.

   But she _____ in a different school.

5. The boy said, "We _____ in new schools."

6. The boy has new friends.

   They _____ in the United States.

7. The boy is happy in the United States.

   But sometimes he _____ lonely.

8. The boy remembers his old friends.

   They _____ a part of his heart.

## Exercise D

**Understanding vocabulary.** *Opposites* are words with different meanings. For example, *happy* and *sad* are opposites. Complete the crossword puzzle.

Look at each clue. Find the opposite in the box. Write the opposite in the puzzle. One is done for you: 1 Across is *yes*. The opposite of *yes* is *no*.

| happy hello high new no old part sad same stop yes |
| --- |

**Across** ➡

1. yes
2. different
3. good-bye
4. all
5. sad
8. happy

**Down** ⬇

1. old
2. go
3. low
6. no
7. new

## Exercise E

**Using vocabulary.** Complete each sentence. Use a word from the box in Exercise D. Use each word once.

1. You said yes, and I said yes. We said the _____ thing.

2. I said yes, and you said _____. We said different things.

3. I am happy when I say hello. But sometimes I am _____ when I say good-bye.

4. I have many _____ friends in my native country, but I have many new friends here.

**Understanding vocabulary.** Some words in the story tell about the boy's feelings. Fill in the chart. Use the feeling words in the box.

| happy | sad | worried | lonely |
|-------|-----|---------|--------|

| **"Good Feelings"** | **"Bad Feelings"** |
|---------------------|--------------------|
|                     |                    |

*Exercise G*

**Putting words in the correct order.** Make sentences by putting the words in the correct order. Write each sentence in the blank. The sentences are about the story. One is done for you.

1. friends / good-bye / I / my / to / said

   *I said good-bye to my friends*                    .

2. United States / I / in / the / live

   _____.

3. am / I / in / different / a / school

   _____.

4. new / friends / We / have

   _____.

5. remember / I / old / friends / my

   _____.

6. pictures / look / I / their / at

   _____.

**Speaking up.** Look at the conversation. Practice with two other students.

> Hello, Miss Martinez. How are you?

> Hi, Timmy. I'm fine. How are you?

# SHARING WITH OTHERS

*Activity A*

**Choral reading.** Work in two groups. Read the song on page 3.

Group 1 reads the first three lines.
Group 2 reads the next three lines.
Group 1 reads the next three lines.
Everybody reads the last line together.

*Activity B*

**Sharing ideas.** It's fun to share ideas with others. Discuss these questions with your partner or with the group. Write your answer to one of the questions.

How do you feel when you say hello to someone new?
How do you feel when you say good-bye to your family or friends?

_____

_____

_____

_____

_____

# ROOTS

What are *roots?*
How do roots help plants grow?

Like a plant, each person has roots.
What are your roots?
How are your roots part of you?

# Not Just Blue

**"What is wrong?"** Chi-Yin's mother asked. She **loved** her son very much. She saw that he was not happy.

"Nothing," Chi-Yin said. He picked up his **glass** and drank. The glass was **blue.** When he looked through it, everything

5   was blue.

"Something is wrong. You are sad," said his mother.

"Mother, what does **weird** mean?"

"I know this word in English," said his mother. "It means 'strange' or 'different.'" She smiled just a little.

10   "Some kids at school say that I am weird. They say I am not American," said Chi-Yin.

Chi-Yin's mother **twisted** the kitchen **towel** in her hands. "They are **right** and they are wrong. You were not born here. You are Chinese. But you are not weird." Chi-Yin

15   looked at his mother. He sighed.

"You are a very **special** boy. Your country has a great history. Be **proud** of your roots."

"Mother, I don't want to be different." Chi-Yin picked up his glass and looked through it. Everything was blue again.

20 "The world is interesting because people are different. Remember that, my son." Chi-Yin's mother took the glass from the **table.** "Be proud of who you are and where you come from. Because you are different, you are special."

Chi-Yin sat at the table in **silence.** He thought about his
25 mother's words. "I will remember, Mother. I'll **try hard to** remember."

Chi-Yin smiled. "It was like colors," he thought. "A **rainbow** of different colors was more **beautiful** than a rainbow of just blue."

# YOU CAN ANSWER THESE QUESTIONS

Put an *x* in the box next to the correct answer.

*Reading Comprehension*

1. The two people in the story are
   - ❑ a. a mother and a son.
   - ❑ b. a father and a daughter.

2. At the beginning of the story, Chi-Yin was
   - ❑ a. happy.
   - ❑ b. sad.

3. Children at school told Chi-Yin that he was
   - ❑ a. weird.
   - ❑ b. special.

4. Chi-Yin was born in
   - ❑ a. the United States.
   - ❑ b. China.

5. Chi-Yin's mother said that it was good to be
   - ❑ a. different.
   - ❑ b. sad.

6. The story teaches you that it is good when
   - ❑ a. everyone is alike.
   - ❑ b. people are different.

*Vocabulary*

7. The mother told the boy that he was special. *Special* means
   - ❑ a. not like everyone else.
   - ❑ b. like everyone else.

8. When you are *proud* of your roots, you are
   - ❑ a. pleased with where you come from.
   - ❑ b. worried about where you come from.

*Idioms*

9. *What is wrong?* means
   - ❑ a. What is the problem?
   - ❑ b. What is the right answer?

10. The boy said he would try hard to remember his roots. The expression *try hard to* means
   - ❑ a. do your best.
   - ❑ b. forget to do something.

How many questions did you answer correctly? Circle your score. Then fill in your score on the Score Chart on page 152.

| Number Correct | 1 | 2 | 3 | 4 | 5 | 6 | 7 | 8 | 9 | 10 |
|---|---|---|---|---|---|---|---|---|---|---|
| Score | 10 | 20 | 30 | 40 | 50 | 60 | 70 | 80 | 90 | 100 |

# EXERCISES TO HELP YOU

*Exercise A*

**Building sentences.** Make sentences by adding the correct letter.

1. The mother _____

2. She saw that her _____

3. She asked _____

4. The children said that _____

a. Chi-Yin was weird.
b. what was wrong.
c. loved her son.
d. son was sad.

Now write the sentences on the lines below. Begin each sentence with a capital letter. End it with a period.

1. _____

2. _____

3. _____

4. _____

Now do numbers 5–8 the same way.

5. Chi-Yin was _____

6. His country _____

7. Chi-Yin did not want _____

8. Because Chi-Yin is different, _____

a. has a great history.
b. he is special.
c. born in China.
d. to be different.

5. _____

6. _____

7. _____

8. _____

*Exercise B*

**Understanding the story.** Answer each question. Complete the sentence. Look back at the story.

1. What is the boy's name?

   *His name* _____.

2. Who was the boy with?

   *The boy was with* _____.

3. How did the boy feel at first?

   *He felt* _____.

4. What did the children call Chi-Yin?

   *They called* _____.

5. Where was Chi-Yin born?

   *He* _____.

6. What did the mother tell her son to be proud of?

   *The mother told her son to be* _____.

7. Why is the boy special?

   *The boy is special* _____.

8. Why is a rainbow beautiful?

   *A rainbow is beautiful because it has* _____.

*Exercise C*

**Using pronouns correctly.** Study this chart.

| Subject Pronouns | |
|---|---|
| **Singular** | **Plural** |
| I | we |
| you | you |
| he | they |
| she | |
| it | |

Fill in the blank. Use the correct subject pronoun. One is done for you.

1. The mother asked, "What is wrong?"

   _____*She*_____ saw that her son was not happy.

2. The son said nothing was wrong.

   _____ didn't want to talk about the problem.

3. The mother and boy talked together.

   _____ talked about the problem.

4. The kids at school said things to the boy.

   _____ said that he was weird.

5. The mother said to her son, "_____ are special."

6. The mother said, "You and I come from a great country.

   _____ are Chinese."

7. The boy said, "_____ don't want to be different."

8. The boy thought about what his mother said.

   _____ smiled.

*Exercise D*

**Using past tense verbs correctly.** Study this chart.

| Past Tense |
| --- |
| talk + ed   = talked |
| sigh + ed   = sighed |
| smile + ed = smiled |

Fill in the blank with the past tense. Use the verb in parentheses ( ).

**1.** The mother _____ what was wrong. (ask)

**2.** The mother _____ her son very much. (love)

**3.** The boy _____ through the glass. (look)

**4.** The boy _____ to his mother's words. (listen)

**5.** The boy _____ at the end of the story. (smile)

*Exercise E*

**Understanding irregular past tense verbs.** The past tense of some verbs does not end in *-ed.* These are irregular verbs.

| Verb | Past Tense |
| --- | --- |
| take | took |

Look at the story. Find the past tense of each verb. Complete the verb.

|  |  | **Past Tense** |
| --- | --- | --- |
| **1.** | see | _ _ w |
| **2.** | drink | _ _ a _ _ |
| **3.** | say | _ a _ _ |
| **4.** | sit | _ _ _ |
| **5.** | think | t _ _ _ g _ _ |

## Exercise F

**Using past tense verbs correctly.** Complete the sentences. Use the past tense of the verbs in Exercise E. Use each verb once.

1. Yesterday the boy _____ milk.

2. He _____ at the table.

3. He _____ about the kids at school.

4. He _____ that the world was blue through the glass.

5. He _____, "I'll try to remember my roots."

## Exercise G

**Understanding vocabulary.** Read the words in the box. Write the words in the correct place in the chart. Some are done for you.

| beautiful | blue | glass | happy | sad | table | towel |
|-----------|------|-------|-------|-----|-------|-------|

| Things | Words that Describe People or Things |
|--------|--------------------------------------|
| glass | beautiful |
| | |
| | |
| | |

## Exercise H

**Using vocabulary.** Correct the sentences about the story. Use the words in the chart in Exercise G.

1. The glass was ~~sad~~ *blue*.
2. The boy was happy.
3. A rainbow of many colors is weird.
4. The boy sat at the towel.
5. The boy picked up the table.
6. The mother twisted the glass.

*Exercise I*

**Speaking up.** Look at the conversation and then practice with a partner.

## SHARING WITH OTHERS

*Activity A*

**Acting out the story.** Work with a partner. Act out the conversation between Chi-Yin and his mother.
1. Read the words in the quotation marks; for example: "What is wrong?"
2. Perform the actions.
3. Share your acting with the group.

*Activity B*

**Sharing ideas.** It's fun to share ideas with others. Discuss these questions with your partner or with the group. Write your answer to one of the questions.

What country do you come from?
What do you know about the history of your country?

Is it easy or hard to move to a new country?
Is it easy or hard to make friends with people from the new country?

_____

_____

_____

# LIONS' TALES

*Fables* are very old stories.
People began to tell them many years ago.
Fables are usually about animals.

These stories teach us lessons about life.

What are some of the animals in fables?
Do you know any fables?

# The Lion and the Rabbit

## Fable 1

One day a **hungry** lion saw a rabbit. The rabbit was asleep. The lion wanted to eat the rabbit.

"This rabbit isn't very **big,**" said the lion to himself. "And I am very hungry." Then the lion saw something move
5   among the trees in the **forest.** It was a deer. "Yes!" thought the lion. "A deer is bigger than a rabbit. I will eat the deer."

The deer saw the lion. The deer began to run through the forest. It crashed through the trees and bushes and made a lot of **noise.** The noise woke up the rabbit. It ran away.

10   The lion ran after the deer. He tried to **catch** the deer, but the deer was very **fast.** It **escaped.**

"Now I am really hungry," thought the lion. "I will go back and eat that rabbit." When the lion **returned,** the rabbit was gone. "Now I have no food at all," **roared** the very
15   unhappy and very hungry lion.

Moral: Be happy with the things you have and don't be **greedy** for more.

# The Mouse and the Lion

## Fable 2

1  One day a mouse woke up a sleeping lion. The **angry** lion decided to eat the mouse.

"Please don't eat me," said the mouse. "You are the king of the jungle. Have mercy on me!"

5  "It's true," said the lion. "A good king **shows mercy.** You can go. I won't eat you."

"Thank you, king. I promise I will help you when you are **in trouble,**" said the happy mouse. The lion laughed.

A few days later hunters captured the lion. They tied him
10  to a tree with a strong, thick rope. The mouse heard the roar of the lion. He came to the tree. "Oh, king," said the mouse. "I am here to help you."

Lion said, "How can a **little** mouse help a **mighty** lion?"

"You'll see," said the mouse. He chewed the rope with his
15  teeth. Soon the rope broke, and the lion was **free.**

The mouse said, "Even a little mouse can **keep a promise** and **repay a favor.**"

Moral: Be nice to everyone. You may need help one day.

# YOU CAN ANSWER THESE QUESTIONS

Put an *x* in the box next to the correct answer.

## Reading Comprehension

**1.** In Fable 1, the lion first wanted to eat a
- ❑ a. deer.
- ❑ b. rabbit.

**2.** The lion decided to eat the deer because
- ❑ a. the deer was bigger.
- ❑ b. a rabbit can run faster than a deer.

**3.** In the end, the lion ate
- ❑ a. the rabbit.
- ❑ b. nothing.

**4.** In Fable 2, the lion was angry because the mouse
- ❑ a. woke him up.
- ❑ b. talked too much.

**5.** The mouse asked the lion
- ❑ a. to free him.
- ❑ b. not to eat him.

**6.** The mouse helped the lion. The mouse
- ❑ a. freed the lion from ropes.
- ❑ b. gave the lion food.

## Vocabulary

**7.** Fable 1 teaches us not to be greedy. The word *greedy* means
- ❑ a. very hungry.
- ❑ b. always wanting more.

**8.** The lion tried to catch the deer, but the deer escaped. The word *escape* means
- ❑ a. get free.
- ❑ b. run fast.

## Idioms

**9.** When you *keep a promise,* you
- ❑ a. forget to do something.
- ❑ b. do what you said.

**10.** When you *repay a favor,* you
- ❑ a. help someone who helped you.
- ❑ b. give someone money.

How many questions did you answer correctly? Circle your score. Then fill in your score on the Score Chart on page 152.

| Number Correct | 1 | 2 | 3 | 4 | 5 | 6 | 7 | 8 | 9 | 10 |
|---|---|---|---|---|---|---|---|---|---|---|
| **Score** | 10 | 20 | 30 | 40 | 50 | 60 | 70 | 80 | 90 | 100 |

*Exercise A*

**Building sentences.** Make sentences by adding the correct letter.

1. The lion wanted to _____    **a.** but the deer escaped.
                                   **b.** eat a rabbit.
2. A deer is bigger _____       **c.** the rabbit was gone.
                                   **d.** than a rabbit.
3. The lion tried to catch

   a deer, _____

4. When the lion returned, _____

Now write the sentences on the lines below. Begin each sentence with a capital letter. End it with a period.

1. _____

2. _____

3. _____

4. _____

Now do numbers 5–8 the same way. The sentences are about Fable 2.

5. The angry lion               **a.** lion to have mercy.
                                **b.** help the lion.
   decided _____             **c.** and the lion was free.
                                **d.** to eat the mouse.
6. The mouse asked the _____

7. The mouse promised to _____

8. The mouse chewed the rope, _____

5. _____

6. _____

7. _____

8. _____

**Understanding the story.** Answer each question. Write a complete sentence. Look back at the stories.

*Fable 1*

1. How did the lion feel at the start of the story?

   _He was very_ _____.

2. What animal did the lion see first?

   _He saw_ _____.

3. What animal ran fast and escaped?

   _____ _ran fast and_ _____.

4. How did the lion feel at the end of the story?

   _He was very_ _____ _and very_ _____.

*Fable 2*

5. Who woke the sleeping lion?

   _____.

6. Who captured the lion?

   _____.

7. What did the mouse hear?

   _He heard_ _____.

8. How did the mouse help the lion?

   _____.

*Exercise C*
**Using future tense verbs correctly.** Study this chart.

| Future Tense |
| --- |
| *will* + verb |
| will + go = will go |
| I will go. <br> It will run. <br> We will read. |

Fill in each blank in the story. Use the future tense of the verb in parentheses ( ). The first one is done for you.

The lion thought, "I am hungry. I ___*will eat*___ (eat) the
                                          1
rabbit." The lion saw a deer. "The deer is bigger than a rabbit.

So I _____ (catch) the deer." But the deer escaped. The
         2
lion was now very hungry. He thought, "I _____ (go)
                                             3
back, and I _____ (eat) the rabbit." When the lion
              4
returned, the rabbit was gone. The lion was unhappy. "Now I

_____ (have) no food at all," the lion thought.
     5

*Exercise D*
**Adding an adjective.** Adjectives are words that tell about people or animals. The words in the box are adjectives.

| angry | fast | greedy | hungry | little | mighty |
| --- | --- | --- | --- | --- | --- |

Complete each sentence. Use the correct word from the box.

*Fable 1*

1. The lion chased the deer because he was _____.

2. The deer was very _____, and it escaped.

3. Because the lion was _____, he had no food to eat.

*Fable 2*

4. The lion was _____ when the mouse woke him up.

5. The _____ lion was king of the jungle.

6. The lion was big, and the mouse was _____.

*Exercise E*

**Putting words in the correct order.** Make sentences by putting the words in the correct order. Write each sentence in the blank. The sentences are about Fable 2.

1. lion / captured / the / Hunters

   _____.

2. roared / anger / lion / The / with

   _____.

3. rope / mouse / chewed / The / his / teeth / the / with

   _____.

4. lion / free / was / The

   _____.

5. to / Be / nice / everyone

   _____.

*Exercise F*

**Adding vocabulary.** On the left are six words from Fable 1. Complete each sentence by adding the correct word.

catch     1. The lion saw the deer in the _____.

      He saw it move among the trees.

escaped     2. The lion ran after the deer. He tried

      to _____ it.

forest     3. The deer ran fast. It _____.

noise     4. The _____ woke up the rabbit.

      It went away.

returned     5. When the lion _____, the rabbit

      was gone.

roared     6. The lion _____ because it was very

      unhappy and very hungry.

*Exercise G*

**Understanding idioms.** Make idioms. Find the words that go together. Write the correct letter in the blank. The idioms are all in Fable 2. One is done for you.

1. keep _____d_____      **a.** the favor

2. in _____      **b.** trouble

3. show _____      **c.** mercy

4. repay _____      **d.** a promise

*Exercise H*

**Using idioms.** Complete the sentences. Use the idioms from Exercise G. Use each phrase once.

1. The lion decided not to eat the mouse. He decided to

   _____ to the mouse.

2. The mouse promised to help the lion. He promised

   to _____.

3. Hunters captured the lion. The lion was tied to a tree. The

   lion was _____.

4. The mouse helped the lion. The mouse was able

   to _____. He did what he said.

*Exercise I*

**Speaking up.** Look at the conversation. Practice it with a partner.

*Activity A*

**Pantomiming a fable.** Work in groups. Act out one of the fables.
1.  Choose which fable to act out.
2.  Make a mask for each character in the story: Draw a face on paper. Tape the face to a stick.
    > Story 1 characters: Lion, rabbit, deer
    > Story 2 characters: Lion, mouse, two hunters
3.  One person reads the fable. The others use the masks to show the action.
4.  Take turns reading the fable.

*Activity B*

**Reading fables.** Work in small groups. Find a fable. Aesop's fables are good to use.
1.  Read the fable together.
2.  Talk about what happens in the fable. Talk about what the fable teaches about life.
3.  Retell the fable to the class.
Be sure to tell these things:
> Tell about the characters. These are the animals or people in the story.
> Tell what happens at the beginning.
> Tell the important things that happen in the story.
> Tell what happens at the end.
> Tell what the fable teaches.

*Activity C*

**Sharing ideas.** It's fun to share ideas with others. Discuss these questions with your partner or with the group. Write your answer to one of the questions.

Which of the two fables do you like better? Why?

What did the lion do wrong in the first fable?
What did the lion learn in the second fable?
How are the two lions like people?

Do you know any fables with animals? Tell one of them.
What does the fable teach?

_____

_____

# THE GREEN-EYED MONSTER

In English-speaking cultures, green can mean envy or *jealousy*, red can mean anger or danger, and yellow can mean fear or cowardice.

Do these colors mean the same thing in your culture? What do these colors mean to you?

# The Green-Eyed Monster

John Lake left the house at seven o'clock. He waved good-bye to his **wife,** Lisa.

"Good-bye, darling," said Lisa. "Have a **safe** trip."

"Don't worry. I'll be back tomorrow night," said John.

5    John got into his **car** and **drove** away.

Lisa looked down at her hands. The sun made her wedding ring shine. Lisa sighed. She was not happy.

"John loves someone else," said Lisa. "I want to see the woman he loves." Lisa decided to **follow** John in her car.

10    John stopped his car a block from the house. He wasn't on a **business trip.** He was worried about Lisa. "Lisa loves someone else," he thought. "Will Lisa leave the house? Will she go and see someone else?" he wondered. Soon John saw Lisa drive by in her car. He followed her.

15　John saw Lisa **pass** him. "She is driving very fast," he thought. "I will hurry through the **alley** and **catch up with** her car."

Lisa couldn't see John's car. She decided to turn around and go through the alley. She **pressed** down on the
20　**accelerator** with her foot.

Suddenly, John and Lisa saw each other. They were both driving very fast. They couldn't stop. Their cars **crashed** into each other. Everything **went black.**

In the **hospital,** two tired doctors talked. "It is very
25　sad," said one doctor. "My **patient died.** His name was John. Before he died, he said, 'Please tell my wife that I love her.'"

"That is strange," said the other doctor. "My patient whispered, 'Tell my **husband** that I love him.' Then she died."

30　"Well, the night is over for us."

"Yes," said the younger doctor. "I'm going home to my wife. Nights like this give me the **blues,** and she can always cheer me up."

# You Can Answer These Questions

Put an *x* in the box next to the correct answer.

*Reading Comprehension*

1. Lisa was John's
   - ❑ a. mother.
   - ❑ b. wife.

2. Lisa thought that John
   - ❑ a. loved someone else.
   - ❑ b. worked too hard.

3. John wasn't going on a business trip. He wanted to
   - ❑ a. see another woman.
   - ❑ b. follow Lisa.

4. Lisa drove fast. She wanted to
   - ❑ a. find John's car.
   - ❑ b. catch a train.

5. At the end of the story,
   - ❑ a. John died but Lisa lived.
   - ❑ b. both John and Lisa died.

6. John and Lisa really loved each other.
   - ❑ a. Right.
   - ❑ b. Wrong.

*Vocabulary*

7. John's and Lisa's cars crashed. *Crash* means
   - ❑ a. to hit one another.
   - ❑ b. to go off the road.

*Idioms*

8. John wanted to catch up with Lisa's car. The idiom *catch up with* means
   - ❑ a. capture something and hold it.
   - ❑ b. come from behind and get near something.

9. John's and Lisa's cars crashed. Everything went black. The idiom *went black* means that
   - ❑ a. night came, and it was dark.
   - ❑ b. John and Lisa did not know what was happening around them.

10. The night was over for the doctors. The idiom *be over* means
    - ❑ a. come to an end.
    - ❑ b. start again.

How many questions did you answer correctly? Circle your score. Then fill in your score on the Score Chart on page 152.

| Number Correct | 1 | 2 | 3 | 4 | 5 | 6 | 7 | 8 | 9 | 10 |
|---|---|---|---|---|---|---|---|---|---|---|
| Score | 10 | 20 | 30 | 40 | 50 | 60 | 70 | 80 | 90 | 100 |

# EXERCISES TO HELP YOU

*Exercise A*

**Building sentences.** Make sentences by adding the correct letter.

1. John waved good-bye _____
2. John got _____
3. Lisa decided to _____
4. John stopped his car _____

  **a.** follow John.
  **b.** to his wife.
  **c.** a block from his house.
  **d.** into his car.

Now write the sentences on the lines below. Begin each sentence with a capital letter. End it with a period.

1. _____

2. _____

3. _____

4. _____

Now do numbers 5–8 the same way.

5. Lisa wanted to _____
6. Lisa and John were _____
7. Their cars _____
8. John said to tell his wife _____

  **a.** crashed.
  **b.** driving very fast.
  **c.** that he loved her.
  **d.** find John's car.

5. _____

6. _____

7. _____

8. _____

*Exercise B*

**Understanding the story.** Answer each question. Write complete sentences. Look back at the story.

1. When did John leave the house?

   *He left* _____ .

2. To whom did John wave good-bye?

   *He waved* _____ .

3. What did Lisa decide to do?

   *She decided* _____ *in her car* .

4. John saw Lisa drive by. What did John decide to do?

   *He decided to* _____ .

5. What place did they both drive through?

   *They both drove* _____ .

6. What happened to their cars?

   *Their cars* _____ .

7. Who said that she loved her husband?

   _____ .

8. What happened to John and Lisa at the end?

   *They both* _____ .

## Exercise C
**Using pronouns correctly.** Study this chart.

| Object Pronouns | |
| --- | --- |
| **Singular** | **Plural** |
| me | us |
| you | you |
| him | them |
| her | |
| it | |

Fill in the blank. Use the correct object pronoun. One is done for you.

1. John said good-bye to his wife.

   He waved to ____*her*____.

2. John got into his car.

   Lisa looked at _____ as he left.

3. "John loves someone else. He no longer loves _____," said Lisa.

4. John thought that Lisa loved someone else.

   He thought that she no longer loved _____.

5. John wanted to see where Lisa went.

   He decided to follow _____.

6. John and Lisa were in the hospital.

   The doctors tried to help _____.

7. John said, "Tell my wife that I love _____."

8. Lisa said, "Tell my husband that I love _____."

*Exercise D*

**Studying irregular past tense verbs.** Look at Unit 2, pages 18 and 19. Study the past tense verbs.

Here are more irregular verbs. Look at the story. Find the past tense of each verb. Complete the verb.

**Past Tense**

1. leave     _ _ f _
2. get     _ _ _
3. drive     _ _ _ v _
4. go     _ _ _ t
5 think     _ _ _ _ _ _ _
6. see     _ _ _

*Exercise E*

**Using past tense verbs.** Write about the story. Use past tense verbs. Some are regular, and some are irregular.

Follow this example:

John / **wave** good-bye to Lisa
John waved good-bye to Lisa.

1. John / **get** into his car.

   _____.

2. John / **drive** away.

   _____.

3. Lisa / **think,** "John loves someone else."

   _____.

4. Lisa / **decide** to follow John.

   _____.

5. Lisa and John / both **drive** very fast.

   _____.

6. They / **see** each other.

   _____.

7. Their cars / **crash** into each other.

   _____.

8. John and Lisa / **die** in the hospital.

   _____.

## Exercise F

**Adding vocabulary.** On the left are six words from the story. Complete each sentence by adding the correct word.

alley

**1.** John was going away. Lisa said, "Have a _____ trip."

crashed

**2.** Lisa wanted to find John's car. So she went through the _____.

hospital

**3.** Lisa _____ down on the car's accelerator. She wanted to go fast.

patients

**4.** John's and Lisa's cars _____.

pressed

**5.** John and Lisa were _____ in the hospital.

safe

**6.** The doctors in the _____ tried to help them.

## Exercise G

**Speaking up.** Look at the conversations. Practice them with a partner.

*Activity A*

**Making a news report.** Work in groups of three. Make a news report. Tell the story of the car crash in the story.
Here are roles you can play in the news report:
> News reporter at TV desk in TV studio
> News reporter at hospital
> One of the doctors

Answer these questions in your news report:
1. Who were the people in the crash?
2. Where did the crash take place?
3. Where were the couple when they died?
4. What did they say before they died?

*Activity B*

**Sharing ideas.** It's fun to share ideas with others. Discuss these questions with your partner or with the group. Write your answer to one of the questions.

What do you think the story teaches? Here are some ideas to talk about:
> It is good to tell your feelings to others.
> It is not good to be jealous. Jealousy is a "green-eyed monster." It can make people do foolish things.

Here are some more English idioms with colors. What do you think they mean?
> I'm excited. **My mom gave me the green light** to have a birthday party.
> I didn't feel like going out, so I told **a white lie.** I said I had a headache.
> I didn't expect to get a letter from Linda. It came **out of the blue.**

Do you know any other idioms with colors? What are they? What do they mean?

——————————————————————————

——————————————————————————

——————————————————————————

——————————————————————————

——————————————————————————

# THE GIFT

When do you give gifts?
When do you *receive* gifts?

What kinds of gifts do you like to get?
Who do you give gifts to?

# The Gift

Cassie **had on** her best dress. To tell the truth, it was her only dress. She and her mother and four brothers were new to the neighborhood. They moved to the neighborhood only two weeks ago.

5 Cassie's family had very little money. Cassie usually wore her brothers' old clothes. She was happy that she liked old, **faded T-shirts** and **jeans.**

Yesterday her mother told her about an invitation. A neighbor had invited Cassie to a birthday party. Now 10 Cassie was in her dress, standing in front of a strange door. She rang the doorbell.

"Why, hello there!," said a **blond**-haired woman. "I'm Jeannie's mother. You must be Cassie, our new neighbor. Come on in." Cassie followed the woman through the 15 house into a **crowded** room. Balloons decorated the room. Cassie knew Jeannie from school. Cassie also **recognized** two or three other faces. They also were students at her high school. But most of the **guests** were **strangers** to her. "Hi, Cassie," said Jeannie. "Let me introduce you to 20 my friends."

Soon everyone gathered around the table with the gifts. Jeannie began to open her presents.

Everyone **clapped** as Jeannie opened each gift. She opened packages with CDs of **popular** singers. She opened
25 **attractive** bottles of perfume. Then she picked up Cassie's present. Cassie felt her **cheeks** turn **red.** She felt **dizzy.** Her head was spinning around.

Cassie's gift was in a simple **brown envelope.** Cassie thought it looked **ugly** and **cheap.** "What can this be?"
30 Jeannie asked.

Cassie said nothing. She felt sick to her **stomach.** How could her present ever compare to all those **expensive** gifts?

Jeannie slowly took a thick piece of paper out of the enve-
35 lope. "Oh," she said. "Look, everyone! Isn't it beautiful?"

Jeannie smiled and looked at Cassie. She held up a draw-ing of her own **face.** Cassie had made the picture the night before. "What a wonderful present from a special new friend!" exclaimed Jeannie.

# YOU CAN ANSWER THESE QUESTIONS

Put an *x* in the box next to the correct answer.

*Reading Comprehension*

**1.** Cassie's family had
- ❑ a. a lot of money.
- ❑ b. very little money.

**2.** Cassie's family
- ❑ a. was new in the neighborhood.
- ❑ b. moved to the neighborhood two years ago.

**3.** Cassie went to the birthday party
- ❑ a. alone.
- ❑ b. with her brothers.

**4.** Jeannie received
- ❑ a. many expensive gifts.
- ❑ b. many T-shirts and jeans as gifts.

**5.** Cassie gave Jeannie
- ❑ a. an expensive gift.
- ❑ b. a gift she made herself.

**6.** Jeannie liked Cassie's gift.
- ❑ a. Right.
- ❑ b. Wrong.

*Vocabulary*

**7.** Cassie recognized only a few people at the party. The word *recognize* means
- ❑ a. know someone because you met the person before.
- ❑ b. look a lot like another person.

**8.** The room was crowded with guests. *Guests* are the people who
- ❑ a. give a party.
- ❑ b. come to a party.

**9.** The guests clapped as Jeannie opened each gift. The word *clap* means
- ❑ a. hit your hands together to show you like something.
- ❑ b. say what you think about something.

*Idioms*

**10.** Cassie *had on* her best dress. *Have on* means
- ❑ a. wear a piece of clothing.
- ❑ b. place something on top of something else.

How many questions did you answer correctly? Circle your score. Then fill in your score on the Score Chart on page 152.

| Number Correct | 1 | 2 | 3 | 4 | 5 | 6 | 7 | 8 | 9 | 10 |
|---|---|---|---|---|---|---|---|---|---|---|
| Score | 10 | 20 | 30 | 40 | 50 | 60 | 70 | 80 | 90 | 100 |

# EXERCISES TO HELP YOU

*Exercise A*

**Building sentences.** Make sentences by adding the correct letter.

1. Cassie and her family

   were _____

2. A neighbor told Cassie's

   mother _____

3. Cassie knew Jeannie _____

4. Most of the guests _____

   **a.** from school.
   **b.** were strangers.
   **c.** about a birthday party.
   **d.** new to the neighborhood.

Now write the sentences on the lines below. Begin each sentence with a capital letter. End it with a period.

1. _____

2. _____

3. _____

4. _____

Now do numbers 5–8 the same way.

5. Jeannie began _____

6. Cassie felt her

   cheeks _____

7. Jeannie slowly took _____

8. Jeannie held _____

   **a.** up a drawing of her own face.
   **b.** a piece of paper out of the envelope.
   **c.** turn red.
   **d.** to open her gifts.

5. _____

6. _____

7. _____

8. _____

*Exercise B*

**Understanding the story.** Answer each question. Write complete sentences. Look back at the story.

1. When did Cassie's family move to the neighborhood?

   *They moved there* _____.

2. What did Cassie like to wear?

   *She liked to wear* _____.

3. Cassie received an invitation to a party. What kind of party was it?

   *It was a* _____.

4. Who said hello to Cassie at the door?

   _____.

5. What gifts did Jeannie get?

   *She got* _____.

6. Jeannie picked up Cassie's present. How did Cassie feel?

   *She felt* _____.

7. What was Cassie's present?

   *Her present* _____.

8. What did Jeannie do when she saw Cassie's gift?

   *Jeannie* _____.

*Exercise C*

**Using singular and plural nouns.** Nouns in English can talk about one thing (singular) or two or more things (plural). Study this chart.

Plural nouns usually end in -*s*.

| Singular | Plural |
|----------|--------|
| one girl | two girl**s** |

Some nouns ending in *s* have plurals with -*es*.

| Singular | Plural |
|----------|--------|
| one dress | three dress**es** |

Complete each sentence. Use the singular or plural of the noun in parentheses ( ).

1. Cassie had many
   ___T-shirts___ (T-shirt).

2. Cassie had one
   _____ (dress).

3. There were many
   _____ (guest).

4. Cassie's gift was in an
   _____ (envelope).

*Exercise D*

**Adding an adjective.** Complete the sentences. Use the adjectives at the left. Read the words in dark type. They give clues to each adjective's meaning.

**crowded**

1. Cassie wore old, _____ jeans. The jeans **had lost their color.**

**dizzy**

2. The room was _____ with people. **There were many people there.**

**expensive**

3. Cassie thought that her gift looked _____. The other gifts were very attractive; her gift **did not look attractive.**

**faded**

4. Cassie saw that the other presents were _____. They **cost a lot of money.**

**ugly**

5. Cassie felt _____. **Her head was spinning.**

*Exercise E*

**Using the verb *have* correctly.** Study this chart.

| The Verb *Have* | |
|---|---|
| **Simple Present** | |
| **Singular** | **Plural** |
| I have | We have |
| You have | You have |
| He has | They have |
| She has | |
| It has | |

Fill in each blank. Use the present tense of the verb *have*. One is done for you.

1. Cassie _____*has*_____ four brothers.

2. She _____ only one dress.

3. Cassie's brothers _____ many T-shirts for her.

4. Cassie's mother said, "You _____ an invitation to a party."

5. Jeannie's mother said, "We _____ a new neighbor. Here's Cassie."

6. Jeannie _____ many friends.

7. Jeannie said, "I _____ a new friend."

8. People _____ birthdays once a year.

*Exercise F*

**Describing clothes.** Work with a partner. Look at the picture on page 41. Point to various people and tell what they have on.

Example:     He has on jeans.

             They have on T-shirts.

*Exercise G*

**Understanding vocabulary.** The story has many words for parts of the body, for colors, and for clothes. Read the words in the box. Write the words in the correct place in the chart. Some are done for you.

| blond brown cheek dress face hand jeans red stomach T-shirt |
| --- |

| **Parts of the Body** | **Colors** | **Clothes** |
| --- | --- | --- |
| cheek | blond | dress |
| | | |
| | | |
| | | |

*Exercise H*

**Using vocabulary.** Correct the sentences about the story. Use the words in the chart in Exercise G.

1. Cassie made a picture of Jeannie's ~~hand~~. *face*
2. Jeannie started to open the expensive gifts. Cassie's hands turned red.
3. Cassie's present was in a white envelope.
4. Jeannie's mother had red hair.
5. Cassie wore her jeans to the party.
6. Cassie wore dresses most of the time.

*Exercise I*

**Speaking up.** Look at the conversation. Practice it with a partner.

# SHARING WITH OTHERS

*Activity A*

**Role-playing.** Do this role-play with a partner. Each of you takes a turn.

You are Cassie. You come home from the party. Tell your mother or brothers what happened.

Use these ideas:
> Jeannie's mother met me at the door. She took me . . .
> There were many guests. I knew . . .
> Balloons decorated the room. There was a table . . .
> Jeannie opened many gifts. She opened . . .
> When Jeannie began to open my gift, I felt . . .
> When Jeannie saw my drawing, she . . .
> Now I feel . . .

*Activity B*

**Sharing hobbies.** Do you make things with your hands? What kinds of things do you make? Bring some things to class and tell about them.

*Activity C*

**Sharing ideas.** It's fun to share ideas with others. Discuss these questions with your partner or with the group. Write your answer to one of the questions.

What was the best gift you ever gave?
What was the best gift you ever received?

How do people celebrate birthdays in places you know?
Do they eat cake? Do they put candles on cake?
Do they give presents? What kind of presents do they give?

_____

_____

_____

_____

# CREATION STORIES

Every culture has a story that tells how the world began.
These stories are called creation stories.
Do you know a story about the beginning of the world?

# Sumer: How the World Began

*People in the land of Sumer told this story of how the world began. The people lived thousands of years ago in Asia.*

In the beginning, all was chaos. **Wind** and **water** were everywhere. Everything was moving. Enlil, a god, decided to create a world from the chaos.

One god wanted to protect the chaos. This god **sent** a huge dragon to fight Enlil. The dragon was named Tiamat. Tiamat came with an army of dragons to stop Enlil.

Enlil asked the winds for help. When Tiamat began to fight, she **opened** her **enormous** mouth. Enlil forced all the winds inside the dragon's mouth. Tiamat swallowed the winds. She swelled up like a big balloon. She was so big that she could not move.

Enlil took a knife and **cut** her body into two pieces. He took one piece and put it down flat. This became the Earth. Then he took the other piece and made an **arch** over the **Earth.** This became the **sky.**

Next, the gods made humans. They cut off the head of Tiamat's husband. They mixed his **blood** with clay from the Earth. This is how the first humans **came to be.**

# Finland: How the World Began

*In ancient Finland, people told this story of how the world began.*

In the beginning, there was only water. Above the water lived the goddess Air. Air had a daughter named Ilmatar.

Ilmatar liked to **explore** the waters. One day she traveled far. She decided to rest on the **surface** of the water.
5  Suddenly the wind started to blow strongly. **Waves** crashed around her. The storm lasted seven hundred years. After that, Ilmatar lived in the water.

One day Ilmatar was floating on her back. She bent one of her knees. A beautiful duck saw her knee. The duck
10  thought it was a hill and landed on it. There it laid seven **eggs.** The eggs became very hot. Ilmatar felt the heat from the eggs. She put her knee under the water to cool it. The eggs fell down to the bottom of the ocean.

Time passed. One of the eggs broke open. The **bottom** half
15  of the egg **shell** became the Earth. The **top** half of the shell became the sky. The yellow **yolk** of the egg formed the sun, and the white part became the moon and stars.

More time passed. Ilmatar had a baby named Vainamoinen. He swam in the water for seven years. He
20  then left the ocean and became the first human on Earth.

# YOU CAN ANSWER THESE QUESTIONS

Put an *x* in the box next to the correct answer.

*Reading Comprehension*

1. In Story 1, the Earth came from a dragon's
   ❏ a. body.
   ❏ b. egg.

2. In Story 1, Enlil was
   ❏ a. a god.
   ❏ b. a dragon.

3. Enlil asked for help from the
   ❏ a. waters.
   ❏ b. winds.

4. In Story 2, the Earth came from a
   ❏ a. goddess's body.
   ❏ b. duck's egg.

5. Ilmatar was
   ❏ a. a goddess's daughter.
   ❏ b. the goddess Air.

6. Ilmatar's baby was the
   ❏ a. first human.
   ❏ b. first fish.

*Vocabulary*

7. The dragon's mouth was enormous. The word *enormous* means
   ❏ a. big.
   ❏ b. ugly.

8. Ilmatar liked to explore the waters. When you *explore*, you
   ❏ a. forget where you are going.
   ❏ b. go to new places.

9. The words *top* and *bottom*
   ❏ a. are opposites.
   ❏ b. are parts of an egg.

*Idioms*

10. Creation stories tell how things came to be. *Come to be* means
    ❏ a. begin.
    ❏ b. go someplace.

How many questions did you answer correctly? Circle your score. Then fill in your score on the Score Chart on page 152.

| Number Correct | 1 | 2 | 3 | 4 | 5 | 6 | 7 | 8 | 9 | 10 |
|---|---|---|---|---|---|---|---|---|---|---|
| Score | 10 | 20 | 30 | 40 | 50 | 60 | 70 | 80 | 90 | 100 |

# EXERCISES TO HELP YOU

*Exercise A*

**Building sentences.** Make sentences by adding the correct letter.

1. Enlil decided _____

2. The dragon was _____

3. Enlil forced _____

4. Enlil cut the dragon's body _____

    **a.** into two pieces.
    **b.** named Tiamat.
    **c.** to create a world.
    **d.** the winds into the dragon's mouth.

Now write the sentences on the lines below. Begin each sentence with a capital letter. End it with a period.

1. _____

2. _____

3. _____

4. _____

Now do numbers 5–8 the same way.

5. Ilmatar liked to _____

6. A duck laid _____

7. One of the eggs _____

8. The top half of the eggshell _____

    **a.** broke open.
    **b.** explore the water.
    **c.** became the sky.
    **d.** seven eggs on her knee.

5. _____

6. _____

7. _____

8. _____

*Exercise B*

**Understanding the story.** Answer each question. Complete the sentences. Look back at the story.

*Story 1*

1. In the beginning, what was everywhere?

   *In the beginning* _____.

2. What did a god send to fight Enlil?

   *A god sent* _____.

3. What did Enlil force inside the dragon's mouth?

   *Enlil forced* _____.

4. What did Enlil cut into two pieces?

   *He cut* _____.

*Story 2*

1. After the storm, where did Ilmatar live?

   *After the storm, Ilmatar lived* _____.

2. How many eggs did the duck lay on Ilmatar's knee?

   *The duck laid* _____.

3. Where did the eggs fall?

   *The eggs fell down* _____.

4. What did the bottom half of one eggshell become?

   *The bottom half became* _____.

*Exercise C*

**Using possessive nouns correctly.** Possessive nouns in English end in *'s.* Possessive nouns tell about things that belong to someone.

Enlil's knife = Enlil has a knife; the knife belongs to Enlil

The dragon's enormous mouth = the dragon has an enormous mouth

**Complete the story.** Make a possessive noun from each word in parentheses ( ). Write the possessive in the blank.

1. The goddess Air had a daughter.

   The _____ name was Ilmatar. (daughter)

2. Ilmatar decided to stay in the water.

   The _____ home was the ocean. (woman)

3. The _____ eggs fell to the bottom of the ocean. (duck)

   One became the Earth and sky.

4. Ilmatar had a baby.

   The _____ name was Vainamoinen. (baby)

5. Vainamoinen left the sea.

   The _____ home became the Earth. (child)

*Exercise D*

**Adding prepositions.** Here is a list of some of the prepositions in the story.

| above | from | of | on | under |
|-------|------|-----|-----|-------|

Complete the sentences by adding the correct preposition.

1. The goddess Air lived _____ the water.

2. Ilmatar bent one _____ her knees.

3. A duck landed _____ her knee.

4. Ilmatar felt the heat _____ the duck's eggs.

5. Ilmatar put her knee _____ the water to cool it.

*Exercise E*

**Studying irregular past tense verbs.** Find the past tense of
these irregular verbs in the stories. Write them in the blanks.

1. send       _ _ _ _
2. cut       _ _ _
3. put       _ _ _
4. make       _ _ _ _
5. feel       _ _ _ _
6. fall       _ _ _ _
7. break       _ _ _ _ _
8. swim       _ _ _ _

Find the past tense of these verbs in the puzzle. Circle them.
Note that some are regular and some are irregular.

ask
break
cut
decide
fall
feel
like
make
open
put
send
swallow
start
swim
want

| M | A | D | E | B | P | W | M | P | V | S |
|---|---|---|---|---|---|---|---|---|---|---|
| S | E | N | T | W | U | A | L | R | Q | W |
| S | B | Z | C | U | T | N | Y | D | T | A |
| W | J | K | Y | H | P | T | F | E | L | L |
| A | S | K | E | D | M | E | C | C | B | L |
| M | R | O | S | Q | L | D | B | I | Z | O |
| X | K | D | O | P | E | N | E | D | F | W |
| B | R | O | K | E | J | K | E | E | W | E |
| J | N | S | T | A | R | T | E | D | Y | D |
| L | I | K | E | D | V | U | F | E | L | T |

*Exercise F*

**Using past tense verbs.** Write four sentences about Story 1.
Write about the dragon Tiamat. Use these verbs in the past.

| cut | open | send | swallow |
|-----|------|------|---------|

1. _____

2. _____

3. _____

4. _____

## Exercise G

**Understanding vocabulary.** Answer the riddles. Use the
words in the box. Write the correct answer in the blank.

| arch   blood   bottom   enormous   shell   surface   wave   yolk |

1.  I am the yellow part of an egg.

    What am I? _____

2.  I am the opposite of top.

    What am I? _____

3.  I am the hard, outside part of the egg.

    What am I? _____

4.  I am red and I move through your body.

    What am I? _____

5.  I mean the same as big.

    What am I? _____

6.  I am round. I am like half of a circle.

    What am I? _____

7.  I am in the ocean. I move on the surface of the water.

    What am I? _____

8.  I am the top of things like the ocean or a table.

    What am I? _____

## Exercise H

**Speaking up.** Look at the conversation. Practice it with
a partner.

# SHARING WITH OTHERS

*Activity A*

**Telling the story in pictures.** Draw three or four pictures to tell one of the creation stories. Use the stories in this book or other ones you know.

Here are some ideas:

Show what there was in the beginning.
Show how the world came to be.
Show how humans came to be.

*Activity B*

**Sharing ideas.** It's fun to share ideas with others. Discuss these questions with your partner or with the group. Write your answer to one of the questions.

What things are alike in the two stories?
What things are different?

Are these stories like other stories you know about creation? How are they different?

_____

_____

_____

_____

_____

_____

_____

_____

_____

# NAMES

How did you get your name?
Does it have a special meaning?

Was there a special *ceremony* or celebration when
you were born and named?

# Names

"Some Russian names are very long, aren't they?" said the woman in the **university** admissions office. I just smiled.

"Call me Jackie," I said suddenly. "It's easier." I had **filled out** many **forms,** and I still had many more forms
5    in front of me.

"I'm not able to fit your whole name into our computer," remarked the **clerk.** "Did you know that?"

"No, I didn't, but I am going to call myself Jackie," I said.

"Like Jackie Kennedy?" asked the clerk. "Did you pick the
10   name because of her?" An image of the dead President's wife came into my mind. She had on an expensive French suit and a little round hat. If she was from Earth, I was from the moon. No, I didn't **choose** the name Jackie because of her. Will this clerk be able to understand
15   my **choice?**

I closed my eyes and thought back to the last part of my
long, long trip. In the **waiting area** for my last **flight,** there
was an American family—a mother, a father, and their two
children. The parents were reading **newspapers.** The little
girl was trying to read a book. Her brother kept putting his
hand over the pages. Finally, the brother tried to **pull** the
book away, and the girl **pushed** him hard.

"Jackie," cried the mother. "Shame on you! Behave!" I
**expected** her to **scold** the boy, but it was to the girl that
she spoke. "Leave your brother alone!"

I smiled at the little girl. My eyes flashed the **message**
"Life isn't **fair.**"

The girl looked at me and said, "One day I am going to
do **exactly** what I want."

"I am too," I replied. "I am too."

# YOU CAN ANSWER THESE QUESTIONS

Put an *x* in the box next to the correct answer.

*Reading Comprehension*

1. Jackie is a new
   - ❏ a. student from Russia.
   - ❏ b. teacher at the university.

2. Jackie's whole name is
   - ❏ a. very hard to say.
   - ❏ b. too long to fit in the computer.

3. Jackie picked her name because of
   - ❏ a. a little girl.
   - ❏ b. Jackie Kennedy.

4. The brother in the airport was being bad. The mother scolded
   - ❏ a. him.
   - ❏ b. the sister.

5. Jackie and the girl at the airport were alike. They both wanted to make their own choices.
   - ❏ a. Right.
   - ❏ b. Wrong.

6. Jackie Kennedy was
   - ❏ a. the wife of an American president.
   - ❏ b. the mother in the airport.

*Vocabulary*

7. The mother began to scold the girl. *Scold* means
   - ❏ a. tell someone that he or she is doing something wrong.
   - ❏ b. tell someone that you don't like him or her.

8. Jackie expected the mother to scold the boy, but the mother scolded the girl. *Expect* means
   - ❏ a. think that something will happen.
   - ❏ b. forget something important.

9. Jackie tried to tell the girl that "Life isn't fair." *Fair* means
   - ❏ a. the same for everyone; right or good.
   - ❏ b. happy and pleasant; with no problems.

*Idioms*

10. Jackie is filling out forms. *Fill out a form* means
    - ❏ a. write information on a form.
    - ❏ b. make something get bigger.

How many questions did you answer correctly? Circle your score. Then fill in your score on the Score Chart on page 152.

| Number Correct | 1 | 2 | 3 | 4 | 5 | 6 | 7 | 8 | 9 | 10 |
|---|---|---|---|---|---|---|---|---|---|---|
| Score | 10 | 20 | 30 | 40 | 50 | 60 | 70 | 80 | 90 | 100 |

# EXERCISES TO HELP YOU

*Exercise A*
**Building sentences.** Make sentences by adding
the correct letter.

1. Some Russian names _____

2. Jackie had filled _____

3. The woman is going to call

   _____

4. The woman didn't choose

   her name _____

a. herself Jackie.
b. because of Jackie Kennedy.
c. are very long.
d. out many forms.

Now write the sentences on the lines below. Begin each
sentence with a capital letter. End it with a period.

1. _____
2. _____
3. _____
4. _____

Now do numbers 5–8 the same way.

5. In the waiting area, there

   was an _____

6. The parents _____

7. The mother scolded _____

8. One day I am going to _____

a. the little girl.
b. do exactly what I want.
c. American family.
d. were reading a newspaper.

5. _____
6. _____
7. _____
8. _____

*Exercise B*

**Understanding the story.** Answer each question. Complete the sentences. Look back at the story.

1. Where did the first part of the story take place?

   *It took place in* _____.

2. What did the Russian woman fill out?

   *She filled out* _____.

3. What is the Russian woman going to call herself?

   *She is going to* _____.

4. What did the woman see when she thought of Jackie Kennedy?

   *She saw* _____.

5. Who did Jackie get her name from?

   *She got her name from* _____.

6. Where did Jackie see the American family?

   *She saw* _____.

7. What was the little girl trying to do?

   *She was trying to* _____.

8. Who did the mother scold?

   *She scolded* _____.

*Exercise C*
**Using *be able to*.** *Be able to* means the same as *can*.
I *can* speak Russian. = I *am able to* speak Russian.
Study this chart.

| | |
|---|---|
| I am able to (swim). | We are able to (swim). |
| You are able to (swim). | You are able to (swim). |
| He is able to (swim). She is able to (swim). It is able to (swim). | They are able to (swim). |

Complete the sentences about Jackie. Use *be able to*. Follow the example.

Example:     speak English
            Jackie is able to speak English.

**1.** write in English

_____.

**2.** fill out forms in English

_____.

**3.** understand English

_____.

**4.** speak Russian

_____.

**5.** pick her own name

_____.

Write four things that you are able to do. Write four sentences. You can use the ideas in the box. Or you can use your own ideas.

| |
|---|
| write in English   write with a computer   name ten U.S. presidents sing well   swim   fill out forms in English |

**1.** _____

**2** _____

**3.** _____

**4.** _____

*Exercise D*

**Using *be going to.*** *Be going to* means the same as *will.*
I *will* name the baby Rita. = I *am going to* name the baby Rita.
Study this chart.

| I am going to (eat). | We are going to (eat). |
| --- | --- |
| You are going to (eat). | You are going to (eat). |
| He is going to (eat). She is going to (eat). It is going to (eat). | They are going to (eat). |

Complete the sentences about Jackie. Use *be going to.* One is done for you.

**1.** Jackie *is going to* study in the United States.

**2.** Jackie said, "I _____ call myself Jackie."

**3.** She _____ go to a big university.

**4.** Jackie _____ have classes every day.

**5.** She _____ make new friends.

**6.** Jackie said, "My friends _____ call me Jackie."

**7.** Jackie said, "We _____ do many things together."

**8.** She _____ do exactly what she wants.

*Exercise E*

**Understanding vocabulary.** Complete the crossword puzzle. Look at each clue. Find the correct word in the box. Write the word in the puzzle. One is done for you.

| choose  expect  flight  form  pull  push  scold |

**Across**
1. the opposite of *pull*
2. tell someone he or she is doing something wrong
5. a paper that you fill out with information
6. think that something will happen

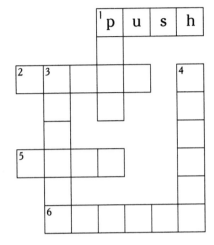

**Down**
1. the opposite of *push*
3. take one thing instead of another
4. part of an airplane trip

*Exercise F*

**Understanding vocabulary.** Answer the riddles. Use the words in the box. Write the correct answer in the blank.

| clerk  message  newspaper  university  waiting area |

1. I am a kind of school. I come after high school. What am I?

   _____

2. I am a place to sit before a flight. What am I?

   _____

3. I work in an office. I fill out forms. What am I?

   _____

4. I am information you give to a person. What am I?

   _____

5. You read me. I am new every day. What am I?

   _____

## Exercise G

**Speaking up.** Look at the conversations. Practice them with a partner.

# SHARING WITH OTHERS

## Activity A

**Name research.** Find a book about the meaning of names in English. Look up one or two names that interest you. What do they mean?
Share what you find in small groups.

Does your name have a special meaning? Share the meaning with your group.

## Activity B

**Sharing ideas.** It's fun to share ideas with others. Discuss these questions with your partner or with the group. Write your answer to one of the questions.

Why did Jackie choose her name? What did her name mean to her?

You are able to choose another name for yourself. What name do you want to choose? Why?

_____

_____

_____

_____

# ALL IN THE MIND

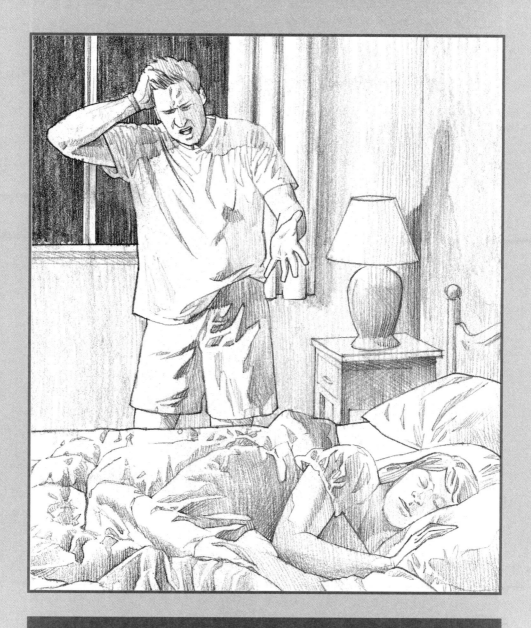

When bad things happen, do you *blame* yourself?
Or do you usually *blame* someone else?

Is it good or bad to blame someone else for things?

# All in the Mind

Gerald threw back the covers and got out of bed.

Gerald looked at his wife. Her back was to him. She was sleeping. "Can't she **hear** that **music?**" he wondered. He left the bedroom. He knew that music. His son, Danny, had played that song **over and over.** He and his son had even **argued** about it.

Now, every night for the last six months, Gerald heard that same music. Was he **going crazy?** During the day, he wasn't able to **concentrate** at work. **At night** he couldn't sleep for more than a few minutes at a time.

Gerald went to the small window in the hall. Was there a radio outside? He looked out, but there was nothing to make noise. There were no cars on the street. There were no teenagers with radios. Gerald pressed his head against the window glass. "Danny," he whispered.

Gerald closed his eyes. He could see everything happen again. It was like a video replaying the same thing over and over. The **accident** happened so quickly.

He was giving Danny a driving lesson. Danny drove too
20 fast around a **curve.** Gerald moved his foot over to the
pedals. He tried to reach the **brake,** but he pressed the
accelerator **instead.** The car went off the road and turned
over. Danny died, but Gerald lived.

Gerald remembered his wife's reaction to the news.
25 "My baby, you killed my baby. **Murderer!** I'll never **forgive**
you. Never!"

That was eight months ago. Now she looks at him with
empty eyes. She doesn't seem to hear the music.

Gerald **put on** his jeans and a T-shirt. He left the house
30 and started to walk. He closed his eyes. There was no
music now. His mind was **dark** and **quiet.** He never heard
the speeding car. He didn't see its lights. "Danny," he
cried as it hit him. "Danny," he whispered as he died.

Upstairs his wife heard the screeching **tires.** "An
35 accident," she thought. "Another family **torn apart.**" She
reached for the tiny tape player and moved it closer to
Gerald's pillow. He'd hear the music when he got back.
She'd **make sure** he'd never forget.

Put an *x* in the box next to the correct answer.

*Reading Comprehension*

1. Gerald heard music
   - ❏ a. all day long.
   - ❏ b. at night in bed.

2. Gerald's wife
   - ❏ a. heard the music.
   - ❏ b. didn't seem to hear the music.

3. Gerald's son, Danny,
   - ❏ a. died in an accident.
   - ❏ b. was in the hospital.

4. Gerald's wife called Gerald a
   - ❏ a. murderer.
   - ❏ b. bad driver.

5. At the end, Gerald
   - ❏ a. went back to bed.
   - ❏ b. died in an accident.

6. There was no music. Gerald was going crazy.
   - ❏ a. Right.
   - ❏ b. Wrong.

*Vocabulary*

7. Gerald and Danny argued about music. The word *argue* means
   - ❏ a. fight with words.
   - ❏ b. have the same ideas about.

8. Gerald was not able to concentrate at work. When you *concentrate,*
   - ❏ a. you think about what you are doing.
   - ❏ b. you forget what you are doing.

9. Gerald wanted to hit the brake, but he hit the accelerator instead. When you do something *instead,*
   - ❏ a. you do the same thing twice.
   - ❏ b. you do something different from what you first planned.

*Idioms*

10. Danny played the same song over and over. The idiom *over and over* means
    - ❏ a. many times.
    - ❏ b. one time.

How many questions did you answer correctly? Circle your score. Then fill in your score on the Score Chart on page 152.

| Number Correct | 1 | 2 | 3 | 4 | 5 | 6 | 7 | 8 | 9 | 10 |
|---|---|---|---|---|---|---|---|---|---|---|
| Score | 10 | 20 | 30 | 40 | 50 | 60 | 70 | 80 | 90 | 100 |

# Exercises to Help You

*Exercise A*

**Building sentences.** Make sentences by adding the correct letter.

1. Gerald got out of _____
2. Gerald wasn't able _____

    _____

3. Gerald heard the same

    _____

4. The accident _____

    **a.** to concentrate at work.
    **b.** bed.
    **c.** music over and over.
    **d.** happened very quickly.

Now write the sentences on the lines below. Begin each sentence with a capital letter. End it with a period.

1. _____

2. _____

3. _____

4. _____

Now do numbers 5–8 the same way.

5. Danny drove too _____
6. The car went _____
7. Gerald put on _____
8. His wife reached for _____

    **a.** the tiny tape player.
    **b.** off the road.
    **c.** fast around the curve.
    **d.** his jeans and T-shirt.

5. _____

6. _____

7. _____

8. _____

*Exercise B*

**Understanding the story.** Answer each question.
Write complete sentences. Look back at the story.

1. Who was in the bedroom?

   _____.

2. Who was Danny?

   _____.

3. What did Gerald hear at night?

   *He heard* _____.

4. What did Gerald think was happening to him?

   *He thought that he was* _____.

5. Where did Danny drive too fast?

   *Danny drove* _____.

6. What did Gerald do at the end of the story?

   *He* _____.

7. What happened to Gerald at the end?

   _____.

8. Where did the music really come from?

   *It came from* _____.

*Exercise C*
**Changing statements to questions.** To make a question from a statement with the verb *be,* put the *be* verb first.

Study these examples:
**There was** a window in the hall.
**Was there** a window in the hall?
**Gerald and his wife were** in an accident.
**Were Gerald and his wife** in an accident?

Make these sentences into questions. Put a question mark (?) at the end of each question. One is done for you.

**1.** Gerald was in bed.

*Was Gerald in bed?*

**2.** There was music in the bedroom.

*Was there*

**3.** There was a radio outside.

_____

**4.** There were cars on the street.

_____

**5.** There were teenagers on the street.

_____

**6.** Gerald was in the street at the end.

_____

**7.** There was a tape player in the bed.

_____

**8.** Gerald's wife was in bed at the end.

_____

*Exercise D*

**Work with a partner.** Take turns. Ask each other the questions in Exercise C.

Examples:
**A:** Was there a window in the hall?
**B:** Yes, there was.

**A:** Were Gerald and his wife in an accident?
**B:** No, they weren't. Gerald and Danny were in an accident.

*Exercise E*

**Adding prepositions.** These prepositions are in the story.

| about | around | at | during | for | on | out | off |
|-------|--------|----|--------|-----|----|----|----|

Complete the sentences by adding the correct prepositions. Use each preposition once.

1. Gerald got _____ of bed.

2. Gerald looked _____ his wife.

3. Gerald and his son argued _____ a song.

4. Gerald was not able to concentrate _____ the day.

5. Danny drove too fast _____ a curve.

6. The car went _____ the road.

7. Gerald put _____ his jeans and T-shirt.

8. His wife reached _____ the tape player.

*Exercise F*

**Understanding vocabulary.** Match the words that go together to make phrases. Write the correct letter in the blank.

1. drive _____       **a.** sure

2. torn _____       **b.** night

3. heard _____       **c.** crazy

4. made _____       **d.** a car

5. at _____       **e.** apart

6. go _____       **f.** music

*Exercise G*

**Using vocabulary.** Complete the sentences. They tell about the story. Use the phrases from Exercise F. Use each phrase once.

1. Danny was learning to _____.

2. Gerald _____ in bed for the last six months.

3. Gerald couldn't sleep _____ because of the music.

4. "If I hear that music again, I'll _____," thought Gerald.

5. Upstairs his wife _____ the tape player was on.

6. The family was _____ because of the accident.

*Exercise H*

**Speaking up.** Look at the conversation. Practice it with a partner.

# SHARING WITH OTHERS

*Activity A*

**Retelling the story.** Do a role-play. Be Gerald or his wife. Tell the story. Tell how you feel.

Example:
I am Gerald's wife. We had a son, Danny. We were a happy family. Then there was a car accident. My son, Danny, died. But I was angry.

*Activity B*

**Sharing reading.** What is your favorite part of the story? Read it to a partner.

*Activity C*

**Sharing ideas.** It's fun to share ideas with others. Discuss these questions with your partner or with the group. Write your answer to one of the questions.

Was Gerald a murderer? What do you think?

What did Gerald's wife do to him?
Was Gerald's wife a murderer? What do you think?

What kind of music do you like hear to over and over? What kind of music don't you like to hear over and over?

---------------------------------------------------

---------------------------------------------------

---------------------------------------------------

---------------------------------------------------

---------------------------------------------------

---------------------------------------------------

---------------------------------------------------

# AN ANCIENT GREEK HERO

What is a *hero?*
What does someone do to be a hero?

What do you know about ancient Greece?
Do you know any stories about Greek heroes?

# Perseus

Once a king named Acrisius asked a prophet about the future. The prophet said, "One day your baby grandson, Perseus, is going to kill you."

So Acrisius put Perseus and Perseus's mother, Danae, into
5   a large box. He put the box into the ocean. The waves carried the box to the island of Seriphus. There Perseus **grew up** into a **brave young** man.

Now, the king of Seriphus wanted to marry Danae. Perseus was against the marriage. So the king thought of a plan to
10   **get rid of** Perseus. The king asked Perseus to kill a **terrible** monster called Medusa. The brave Perseus accepted the king's **challenge.**

Medusa was once a beautiful woman with **long, lovely** hair. But she made the gods angry. She said that she was
15   more beautiful than the goddesses. So the gods **punished** her. They made her into a monster with **snakes** for hair. Medusa had a strange power. When anyone looked at her, that person **turned into** stone.

The gods decided to help Perseus. They gave him a **shiny**
20   shield and a sword.

After a long journey, Perseus arrived at Medusa's island. "How can I find the monster?" he asked. "I have to be careful. I can't look at her, or I will turn into stone." He **thought of** a plan. He listened for the sound of the snakes in her hair. Finally, he heard their hiss. He was near the monster!

"Now what do I do? I can't look at her to kill her." Then he noticed the sun shine off his shield. He could use the shield like a **mirror!** He could see Medusa in the shield without really looking at her. He went near the sleeping monster and cut off her head with the sword.

Perseus returned home with Medusa's head. The king of Seriphus accidentally looked at the head, and he turned into stone.

What happened to Perseus's grandfather? One day Perseus **took part in** some games. He threw a discus. The wind caught the discus. It hit an old man and killed him. The man was Acrisius.

So in the end, the prophet's words were true. We can't escape our **fate.**

# YOU CAN ANSWER THESE QUESTIONS

Put an *x* in the box next to the correct answer.

1. Acrisius was worried that
   - ❑ a. he was going to grow old.
   - ❑ b. his grandson, Perseus, was going to kill him.

2. The king of Seriphus wanted to
   - ❑ a. look at a monster.
   - ❑ b. marry Perseus's mother.

3. Medusa said that she was
   - ❑ a. stronger than the goddesses.
   - ❑ b. more beautiful than the goddesses.

4. Medusa was able to change people into
   - ❑ a. snakes.
   - ❑ b. stone.

5. Perseus used his shield
   - ❑ a. to see Medusa.
   - ❑ b. to sleep on.

6. In the end, Perseus killed his grandfather.
   - ❑ a. Right.
   - ❑ b. Wrong.

*Vocabulary*

7. The gods punished Medusa. The word *punish* means
   - ❑ a. make a person ugly.
   - ❑ b. hurt someone because the person did something wrong.

8. The brave Perseus accepted the king's challenge. The word *challenge* means
   - ❑ a. ask someone to do something hard.
   - ❑ b. ask someone to do something to make money.

9. We can't escape our fate. The word *fate* means
   - ❑ a. what is going to happen to us.
   - ❑ b. the anger of the gods.

*Idioms*

10. Perseus thought of a plan to find Medusa. When you *think of* a plan, you
    - ❑ a. get an idea.
    - ❑ b. think something is right.

How many questions did you answer correctly? Circle your score. Then fill in your score on the Score Chart on page 152.

| Number Correct | 1 | 2 | 3 | 4 | 5 | 6 | 7 | 8 | 9 | 10 |
|---|---|---|---|---|---|---|---|---|---|---|
| Score | 10 | 20 | 30 | 40 | 50 | 60 | 70 | 80 | 90 | 100 |

# EXERCISES TO HELP YOU

*Exercise A*

**Building sentences.** Make sentences by adding the correct letter.

1. The king asked a prophet

   _____

2. Perseus grew _____

3. A king asked Perseus to _____

4. The brave Perseus accepted _____

    **a.** the king's challenge.
    **b.** kill a monster.
    **c.** up into a brave young man.
    **d.** about the future.

Now write the sentences on the lines below. Begin each sentence with a capital letter. End it with a period.

1. _____

2. _____

3. _____

4. _____

Now do numbers 5–8 the same way.

5. Perseus thought _____

6. Perseus listened for

   _____

7. Perseus used his shield _____

8. We can't _____

    **a.** the sound of the snakes in Medusa's hair.
    **b.** escape our fate.
    **c.** of a plan.
    **d.** like a mirror.

5. _____

6. _____

7. _____

8. _____

*Exercise B*

**Understanding the story.** Answer each question.
Write complete sentences. Look back at the story.

1. Who was Perseus's grandfather?

   _____.

2. Where did the waves take Perseus and Danae?

   *The waves took* _____.

3. Who did the king of Seriphus want to marry?

   *He wanted to* _____.

4. What did the king ask Perseus to do?

   *He asked Perseus to* _____.

5. How did Medusa look?

   *She was* _____.

6. What power did Medusa have?

   *She turned people* _____.

7. Perseus was near Medusa. What did he hear?

   *He heard* _____.

8. How did Perseus kill Medusa?

   *He cut* _____.

*Exercise C*

**Using possessives correctly.** Study this chart.

| Possessive Adjectives | |
|---|---|
| my | our |
| your | your |
| his | their |
| her | |
| its | |

Fill in the blank. Use the correct possessive adjective. One is done for you.

1.  The king was named Acrisius.

    _____*His*_____ grandson was named Perseus.

2.  Danae had a son. _____ son was named Perseus.

3.  Danae said, "Perseus and I came to an island.

    The island became _____ home."

4.  The king told Perseus, "I want to marry

    _____ mother."

5.  Perseus said to himself, "I don't want the king to marry

    _____ mother."

6.  Medusa was once beautiful.

    She was proud of _____ hair.

7.  Perseus listened for the snakes.

    Soon he heard _____ hiss.

8.  Perseus thought of a plan.

    He thought, "I can use _____ shield as a mirror."

9.  Perseus cut off Medusa's head. He used

    _____ sword.

10. The story says that we can't escape _____ fate.

*Exercise D*

**Adding an adjective.** Complete the sentences by adding the correct adjective. Use each adjective once.

**brave**       1. King Acrisius had a _____ grandson named Perseus.

**long, lovely**  2. Perseus accepted the king's challenge. He was _____.

**shiny**       3. Medusa's hair was once _____ and _____.

**terrible**     4. Medusa became a _____ monster.

**young**       5. The gods gave Perseus a _____ shield.

*Exercise E*

**Putting words in the correct order.** Make sentences by putting the words in the correct order. Write each sentence in the blank.

1. king's / accepted / Perseus / the / challenge

   _____.

2. king / asked / monster / kill / to / The /a / Perseus

   _____.

3. decided / to / help / The / gods / Perseus

   _____.

4. snakes'/ hiss / Perseus / heard / the

   _____.

5. Perseus / home / head / Medusa's / returned / with

   _____.

*Exercise F*

**Understanding vocabulary.** Many times verbs go together with other words to make phrases. Study the verb phrases at the left. Match them with their meanings. Write the correct letter in the blank.

1. grew up _____

2. got rid of _____

3. turned into _____

4. thought of _____

5. took part in _____

a. changed from one thing into another

b. became an adult; was no longer a child

c. had a new idea

d. did something with others; joined in

e. made someone or something go away

*Exercise G*

**Using vocabulary.** Complete the sentences with the phrases from Exercise F. Use each phrase once.

1. King Acrisius _____ Perseus. The king put him in a box and put the box on the ocean.

2. Perseus _____ on the island of Seriphus. The baby Perseus became a man.

3. People looked at Medusa, and they _____ stone.

4. Perseus _____ a plan to find Medusa.

5. Perseus _____ some games. He threw the discus.

*Exercise H*

**Speaking up.** Look at the conversations. Practice them with a partner.

*Activity A*

**Putting the story in order.** Do this activity.

1. Choose five sentences from the story.
2. Write each sentence down on a separate piece of paper.
3. Work with a partner. Give your partner your sentences.
4. Put the sentences you have in order. Put the sentence that happened first in the story first. Put the sentence that happened second in the story next. Continue in this way.
5. Check your partner's sentences. Are they in the correct order?

*Activity B*

**Sharing ideas.** It's fun to share ideas with others. Discuss these questions with your partner or with the group. Write your answer to one of the questions.

Which words do you think describe Perseus?

brave
smart
stupid
foolish

Do you think that Perseus is a hero? Why or why not?

Do you think we can escape our fate? Why or why not?

_____

_____

_____

_____

_____

_____

_____

# STICKS AND STONES

There is a saying, "Sticks and stones may break my bones, but words will never hurt me."

What do you think this means?

Can words hurt people? How?

# Sticks and Stones

Charlotte felt beautiful. She knew that she had a **pretty** face. Everyone said so. "Charlotte, what big, brown eyes you have," said Mrs. Hooper, her next-door neighbor.

Charlotte had not always felt **attractive.** When she was
5   a little girl, she didn't make friends easily at school. At home, she had a **secret imaginary** friend. Her friend was named Rita. Rita looked just like Charlotte.

Charlotte and Rita were best friends. They played together. They looked through the old magazines in the
10   attic. They **dressed up** in old clothes. Sometimes they used Grandma's pans and made cookies. Charlotte and Rita liked putting their cookies into a picnic basket. Then they hid in a **closet** and ate them all.

As Charlotte grew up, Rita **disappeared** from Charlotte's
15   life. Food became Charlotte's best friend.

When Charlotte was nineteen, her doctor said, "Your **heart** is **weak.** You have to lose 100 pounds. You have to **exercise.** You need to protect your heart."

Many times, Charlotte almost gave up. She wanted to eat
20   and eat. But she didn't. She **kept up** her **diet.**

Charlotte lost 80 pounds. She began to feel pretty. She began to be interested in things around her. She liked to go to an outdoor cafe. She enjoyed watching the people. She imagined their lives.

25 Sometimes Charlotte imagined things about herself. She **enjoyed** dreaming about the future. In her dreams, she saw a **handsome** man. He stopped at her table and asked, "May I sit with you?" He and Charlotte often met at the **cafe.** They slowly **fell in love.**

30 Suddenly a noise surprised Charlotte. She looked up. Several boys and girls were standing beside her table.

"Hey, lady, give us that table," said a boy. "You've had it long enough."

"Yes, you ate too much already," said a girl.

35 Charlotte got up. She felt **embarrassed.** She imagined that everyone was looking at her. She no longer felt pretty.

Charlotte hurried away from the cafe. With every step, she felt bigger and uglier. She wanted to eat and eat. And once, she thought she saw Rita, waiting in the shadows.

# YOU CAN ANSWER THESE QUESTIONS

Put an *x* in the box next to the correct answer.

*Reading Comprehension*

1. Some of Charlotte's neighbors told her that she looked
   - ❏ a. ugly.
   - ❏ b. pretty.

2. Rita was Charlotte's
   - ❏ a. imaginary friend.
   - ❏ b. grandmother.

3. The doctor told Charlotte to
   - ❏ a. forget Rita.
   - ❏ b. lose weight.

4. After she lost weight, Charlotte began to
   - ❏ a. eat more.
   - ❏ b. be interested in the people around her.

5. The boys and girls asked Charlotte to give them
   - ❏ a. her table.
   - ❏ b. some food.

6. The boys and girls made Charlotte feel
   - ❏ a. good about herself.
   - ❏ b. bad about herself.

*Vocabulary*

7. The words *attractive* and *pretty* have
   - ❏ a. the same meaning.
   - ❏ b. different meanings.

8. When Charlotte grew up, Rita disappeared. The word *disappear* means
   - ❏ a. no longer exist.
   - ❏ b. become more important.

9. The boys and girls made Charlotte feel embarrassed. When you are *embarrassed,* you are
   - ❏ a. pleased and happy.
   - ❏ b. confused and ashamed.

*Idioms*

10. In her dreams, Charlotte and the young handsome man fall in love. *Fall in love* means
   - ❏ a. start to like someone very much.
   - ❏ b. hurt oneself by falling on the ground.

How many questions did you answer correctly? Circle your score. Then fill in your score on the Score Chart on page 152.

| Number Correct | 1 | 2 | 3 | 4 | 5 | 6 | 7 | 8 | 9 | 10 |
|---|---|---|---|---|---|---|---|---|---|---|
| Score | 10 | 20 | 30 | 40 | 50 | 60 | 70 | 80 | 90 | 100 |

# EXERCISES TO HELP YOU

*Exercise A*

**Building sentences.** Make sentences by adding the correct letter.

1. Charlotte knew that _____
2. Rita looked _____
3. Charlotte and Rita liked _____
4. The doctor told Charlotte to _____

a. just like Charlotte.
b. lose weight.
c. packing cookies into a picnic basket.
d. she had a pretty face.

Now write the sentences on the lines below. Begin each sentence with a capital letter. End it with a period.

1. _____
2. _____
3. _____
4. _____

Now do numbers 5–8 the same way.

5. Charlotte lost _____
6. She enjoyed _____
7. At the end, she no longer _____
8. Charlotte wanted to _____

a. felt pretty.
b. eat and eat.
c. 80 pounds.
d. dreaming about the future.

5. _____
6. _____
7. _____
8. _____

*Exercise B*

**Understanding the story.** Answer each question. Write complete sentences. Look back at the story.

1. At the start of the story, how did Charlotte feel?

   *She felt* _____ .

2. Who was Rita?

   *She was Charlotte's* _____ .

3. What did Charlotte and Rita do together?

   *They* _____ .

4. After Rita disappeared, what was Charlotte's best friend?

   *Her best friend* _____ .

5. Who told Charlotte to lose weight?

   _____ .

6. Who did Charlotte see in her dreams?

   *She saw* _____ .

7. What did the girl tell Charlotte?

   *She told Charlotte* _____ .

8. At the end of the story, how did Charlotte feel?

   _____ .

*Exercise C*
**Using the verb *enjoy*.** The verb *enjoy* means "like very much."
Another verb often comes after it. The second verb ends in *-ing*.

Study the verbs.

Charlotte *enjoyed eating*.
Charlotte *enjoyed watching* people.

Write sentences about Charlotte. Follow the example.

Example:
play with Rita        Charlotte enjoyed playing with Rita.

**1.** look through magazines

_____.

**2.** make cookies

_____.

**3.** eat cookies

_____.

**4.** go to an outdoor cafe

_____.

**5.** think about people's lives

_____.

**6.** think about her future

_____.

**7.** dream about a handsome man

_____.

*Exercise D*

**Using the verb *like*.** The verb *like* is often followed by another verb. Study the forms.

Charlotte *liked to eat.*          Charlotte *liked eating.*
Charlotte *liked to watch*        Charlotte *liked watching*
    people.                                  people.

Make two sentences about Charlotte using the verb *like*.

**1.** play with Rita

    **a.** _____.

    **b.** _____.

**2.** dream about her future

    **a.** _____.

    **b.** _____.

*Exercise E*

**Review of *enjoy* and *like*.** Write about things you like to do. Look in the box for ideas. Use the correct form.

| read in English   play sports   go to cafes   watch TV   run   eat cookies |
|---|

**1.** I enjoy _____.

**2.** I like to _____.

*Exercise F*

**Using the verb *have to*.** The verb *have to* tells about things you must do or need to do. The past tense of *have to* is *had to*.

Write about what Charlotte had to do. Follow the example.

Example:
lose weight          Charlotte had to lose weight.

**1.** eat less

    _____.

**2.** exercise

    _____.

**3.** make friends

    _____.

**4.** talk to people

    _____.

## Exercise G

**Understanding idioms with *up*.** Many idioms in English have the word *up*. Match the idioms with their definitions. Write the correct letter in the blank.

1. dressed up _____      **a.** stopped doing something

2. grew up _____        **b.** was no longer a child; became an adult

3. gave up _____        **c.** wore good clothes

4. kept up _____        **d.** stood up; got to one's feet

5. got up _____         **e.** continued; opposite of stopped

## Exercise H

**Using idioms with *up*.** Answer these questions about yourself.

1. Where did you grow up?

_____

2. When was the last time you dressed up?

_____

3. Did you ever promise yourself to lose weight or exercise? How long did you keep up your promise?

_____

4. Did you ever stop doing something? What did you give up?

_____

## Exercise I

**Speaking up.** Look at the conversation. Practice it with a partner.

# SHARING WITH OTHERS

*Activity A*

**Thinking of endings.** Do this activity.

1. Discuss this question in groups:
   What will happen to Charlotte next?

Share your answers.

2. Give the story a happy ending.
   Work in groups and think of a happy ending. Ideas:
   When Charlotte is running away, she meets the handsome man of her dreams.
   Rita helps Charlotte lose more weight.

Share your happy ending with other groups.

*Activity B*

**Retelling the story.** Do a role-play. Be Charlotte.
Tell how you feel.

1. Tell how you feel when are sitting at the cafe table.
   I feel pretty and attractive. I lost 80 pounds. I enjoy . . .
2. Tell how you feel when you meet the boys and girls.
   I am surprised. People in the cafe usually don't talk to me.
   The boys and girls . . .
3. Tell how you feel after you leave the cafe.
   I no longer feel . . .

*Activity C*

**Sharing ideas.** It's fun to share ideas with others. Discuss these questions with your partner or with the group. Write your answer to one of the questions.

You read about the saying "Sticks and stones may break my bones, but names will never hurt me." Is the saying true for Charlotte?

How was Charlotte hurt by words?
Why does Rita appear at the end of the story?

What health problem does Charlotte have? What other kinds of health problems do people have? How can people end these problems?

_____

_____

_____

# THE WORLD IS WRONG, NOT ME

Some people *complain* all the time. They are never happy.

Do you know someone who complains all the time?
Do you think people like this can change?

# The Complainer

Every day Calvin Rogers gets up at seven o'clock. He
makes coffee. Then he waits for the morning paper.

Yesterday Calvin was not happy. His newspaper was **late.**
"Where is that **lazy** kid?" he thought. "When I see that
5   paperboy, I'll scold him."

Calvin sat down **slowly** on the porch swing. His left leg
hurt him for the last three days. A light wind made the
spring flowers move **gently** and send **sweet** smells into the
air. The sun covered the stairs with yellow light. Calvin
10   didn't **notice.** "Fifteen minutes without my paper," Calvin
thought. "Time wasted."

Calvin went inside his house. "I'm going to call the newspaper office and complain," he decided. "That kid should
lose his job." Calvin went into the kitchen to get the phone
15   book. Then he remembered that it was upstairs. He had
used it last night to find the number of the local radio
station. He called to complain about the **loud** rock music.

Calvin was at the top of the stairs. His left leg suddenly
**gave way**, and he fell backwards. He rolled down the
20   stairs. Calvin felt pain go through his body. Then he
**blacked out.**

Calvin opened his eyes. He was at the bottom of the stairs. His leg was **bent** under him. It **hurt** terribly. "I have to call for help," he thought. "But who will hear me?"

25 Long minutes passed. Calvin saw the sunlight move into the house through the open front door. The light touched his **fingertips.** They **glowed** orange. "It's beautiful," he thought. "The color of peaches."

Suddenly a voice cried, "Mr. Rogers, what happened?"
30 Then he saw a woman's face. "Mr. Rogers, don't move."

Calvin tried to speak, but nothing came out. The woman ran into the kitchen and telephoned for help. Then she hurried back beside him. "Don't worry. Help is **on the way.**"

"Who are you?" Calvin asked weakly.

35 "I'm Timmy's mother. Timmy, your paperboy." She smiled at him. "I'm sorry I'm late. Timmy told me to be **on time.** He's at home **sick.**"

Calvin felt something turn inside him. His eyes filled with tears. "Thank you so much," he said. "You have a
40 **wonderful** boy."

Put an *x* in the box next to the correct answer.

*Reading Comprehension*

**1.** Yesterday Calvin was not happy because
   ❑  a. the newspaper was late.
   ❑  b. he lost his phone book.

**2.** Calvin likes to
   ❑  a. complain.
   ❑  b. enjoy flowers.

**3.** Calvin fell and broke
   ❑  a. his arm.
   ❑  b. his leg.

**4.** At the bottom of the stairs, Calvin began to notice
   ❑  a. the world around him.
   ❑  b. all the things wrong with his house.

**5.** The person who helped Calvin was the
   ❑  a. next-door neighbor.
   ❑  b. mother of the newspaper boy.

**6.** At the end, Calvin still wanted to complain.
   ❑  a. Right.
   ❑  b. Wrong.

*Vocabulary*

**7.** Calvin didn't notice the flowers. When you *notice* something, you,
   ❑  a. see, feel, or hear it.
   ❑  b. don't want to know about a problem.

**8.** Calvin's newspaper was late. Calvin wanted to call the newspaper office and complain. When you *complain*, you
   ❑  a. say you are not happy about something.
   ❑  b. say you are happy about something.

*Idioms*

**9.** The woman told Calvin that help was on the way. The idiom *on the way* means that something is
   ❑  a. going to happen soon.
   ❑  b. moving very fast.

**10.** The newspaper was not on time. The idiom *on time* means come
   ❑  a. before a certain time.
   ❑  b. at the right time.

How many questions did you answer correctly? Circle your score. Then fill in your score on the Score Chart on page 152.

| Number Correct | 1 | 2 | 3 | 4 | 5 | 6 | 7 | 8 | 9 | 10 |
|---|---|---|---|---|---|---|---|---|---|---|
| Score | 10 | 20 | 30 | 40 | 50 | 60 | 70 | 80 | 90 | 100 |

# EXERCISES TO HELP YOU

*Exercise A*
**Building sentences.** Make sentences by adding the correct letter.

1. Every day Calvin waits

   _____

2. Calvin was _____

3. Calvin went into the kitchen

   to _____

4. Calvin rolled _____

    **a.** down the stairs.
    **b.** going to call the newspaper office.
    **c.** for the morning paper.
    **d.** get the phone book.

Now write the sentences on the lines below. Begin each sentence with a capital letter. End it with a period.

1. _____

2. _____

3. _____

4. _____

Now do numbers 5–8 the same way.

5. Calvin's leg _____

6. The sunlight _____

7. Calvin saw _____

8. Calvin told the woman that _____

    **a.** touched his fingertips.
    **b.** hurt terribly.
    **c.** she had a wonderful boy.
    **d.** a woman's face.

5. _____

6. _____

7. _____

8. _____

*Exercise B*

**Understanding the story.** Answer each question.
Write complete sentences. Look back at the story.

1. What time does Calvin get up every day?

   *He gets up* _____ .

2. What was late yesterday?

   _____ .

3. Why was Calvin going to call the newspaper office?

   *He was going to call the newspaper office to* _____ .

4. What did Calvin complain about last night?

   *He complained* _____ .

5. Calvin rolled down the stairs. What did he feel?

   _____ .

6. Who helped Calvin?

   _____ .

7. Who was Timmy?

   _____ .

8. Where was Timmy?

   _____ .

*Exercise C*

**Using the present tense.** Study this chart.

| Simple Present Tense | |
|---|---|
| **Singular** | **Plural** |
| I run. | We run. |
| You run. | You run. |
| He runs. | They run. |
| She runs. | |
| It runs. | |

Note the *-s*.

Calvin **waits** for the newspaper every day.

Complete the sentences. Use the present tense. Use the *-s* form. One is done for you.

1. Every day Calvin ____*sleeps*____ until seven o'clock. (sleep)

2. He _____ at seven o'clock. (get up)

3. He _____ down the stairs. (walk)

4. He _____ coffee. (make)

5. He _____ eggs. (eat)

6. He _____ for the newspaper. (wait)

7. He _____ the newspaper. (read)

8. He _____ to the radio. (listen)

*Exercise D*
**Adding prepositions.** Here is a list of some of the prepositions in the story.

| about  at  for  from  inside  of  under  without |
| --- |

Complete the sentences by adding the correct prepositions. Use each preposition once.

1. Calvin gets up _____ seven o'clock.

2. He waits _____ the paper.

3. Calvin was _____ his paper for fifteen minutes.

4. Calvin went _____ his house.

5. Calvin wanted to complain _____ the paperboy.

6. Calvin fell _____ the top of the stairs.

7. His leg was bent _____ him.

8. His skin was the color _____ peaches.

*Exercise E*
**Understanding adjectives.** Match each adjective with its meaning. Write the correct letter in the blank.

1. late _____
2. lazy _____

3. sweet _____
4. loud _____
5. sick _____
6. wonderful _____

**a.** not feeling well
**b.** not on time; coming after the right time
**c.** not liking to work
**d.** very good; very nice
**e.** making a lot of noise
**f.** having a nice taste or smell

*Exercise F*

**Adding an adjective.** Complete the sentences by adding an adjective. Use the adjectives from Exercise E. Use each adjective once.

1.  At the start of the story, Calvin thought that the newspaper boy was _____.

2.  Calvin was waiting for the newspaper. It was _____.

3.  The flowers had a _____ smell. Calvin didn't notice it.

4.  Calvin complained about the _____ music.

5.  The newspaper boy was at home because he was _____.

6.  At the end of the story, Calvin thought that the newspaper boy was _____.

*Exercise G*

**Speaking up.** Look at the conversations. Practice them with a partner.

# SHARING WITH OTHERS

*Activity A*
**Word game.** Do this activity.

1.  Work with a partner. Choose five words from the story.
2.  Write a clue for each word.

Examples:
This is something people drink. You drink it from a cup.
(Answer: coffee)

This has the news. People read it every day.
(Answer: newspaper)

3.  Work with other pairs. Give them your clues.
4.  Write the words for the clues you have. How many words
    does your pair get right?

*Activity B*
**Sharing ideas.** It's fun to share ideas with others. Discuss these
questions with your partner or with the group. Write your
answer to one of the questions.

How did Calvin change at the end?
Do you think Calvin will complain in the future?

Is it good to complain? What do you think?

_____

_____

_____

_____

_____

_____

# APPLES, APPLES

Nature gives us many wonderful fruits and
vegetables to eat.
How many fruits and vegetables can you name?

What is your favorite fruit?

# Mountain Mary

*People in every country tell stories about their history. Sometimes they tell about heroes or other famous people. Here are two people who are famous in the United States.*

*Both of these people lived about 200 years ago. Both loved nature. Both lived alone. Both left a **legacy** for future generations of people.*

Her real name was Maria Jung, but everyone called her Mountain Mary. She lived in Pennsylvania. She lived alone, but everyone in the area loved her. She was kind and **generous.** She especially **cared about** animals. She
5   **refused** to hurt them. When animals ate the plants in her garden, she caught them. But she didn't kill them. She took the animals up to the hills and set them free. Mountain Mary especially loved apples. She cut off parts of two apple trees and grew the parts together. This way
10   she **created** a new kind of apple known as the Good Mary. When she died in 1819, the local preacher told the people in his church there was one less **saint** on earth.

# Johnny Appleseed

His real name was John Chapman, but people called him
Johnny Appleseed. He lived in the Ohio River valley.
He walked from place to place through the countryside.
He carried nothing but a tin **cup** and a **sack** of apple **seeds.**
5   He walked through the forests to small towns and farms.
He planted many apple seeds. This way people were able
to enjoy apples far into the future. He sometimes
**exchanged** small apple trees to get food and clothes for
himself. People in the area **treated** him with **respect.** He
10   was the man who loved apples.

Johnny Appleseed also loved animals. Once he saw that
moths were dying from the **heat** of his campfire. He didn't
want to kill them. He didn't like to hurt a living creature.
So he **put out** the fire. Because of this, he ate uncooked
15   food, and he was **cold** himself. He died in 1845, and the
kind of apple known as Johnny Weed was named for him.

# YOU CAN ANSWER THESE QUESTIONS

Put an *x* in the box next to the correct answer.

*Reading Comprehension*

1. The stories about Mountain Mary and Johnny Appleseed
   ❑ a. are true.
   ❑ b. are not true.

2. Mountain Mary and Johnny Appleseed
   ❑ a. lived in the past.
   ❑ b. live today.

3. Both Mountain Mary and Johnny Appleseed loved nature.
   ❑ a. Right.
   ❑ b. Wrong.

4. Both Mountain Mary and Johnny Appleseed created a new kind of apple.
   ❑ a. Right.
   ❑ b. Wrong.

5. Both Mountain Mary and Johnny Appleseed moved from place to place.
   ❑ a. Right.
   ❑ b. Wrong.

*Vocabulary*

6. Mountain Mary and Johnny Appleseed left a legacy for future generations. A *legacy* is
   ❑ a. something expensive.
   ❑ b. something you give to your children or to younger people.

7. The word *generous* means
   ❑ a. loving animals more than anything else.
   ❑ b. liking to share or give things to others.

8. The preacher said there was one less saint. The word *saint* means
   ❑ a. a good and holy person.
   ❑ b. a person who works on a farm.

9. People respected Johnny Appleseed. When you *respect* someone, you show that you
   ❑ a. have a good opinion about the person.
   ❑ b. think the person needs money from you.

*Idioms*

10. The idiom *care about* means
    ❑ a. like something or someone very much and want to help.
    ❑ b. help grow a plant from when it is small.

How many questions did you answer correctly? Circle your score. Then fill in your score on the Score Chart on page 152.

| Number Correct | 1 | 2 | 3 | 4 | 5 | 6 | 7 | 8 | 9 | 10 |
|---|---|---|---|---|---|---|---|---|---|---|
| Score | 10 | 20 | 30 | 40 | 50 | 60 | 70 | 80 | 90 | 100 |

# EXERCISES TO HELP YOU

*Exercise A*
**Building sentences.** Make sentences by adding the correct letter.

1. Mountain Mary _____

2. Mountain Mary cared

   _____

3. She refused _____

4. She created _____

a. a new kind of apple.
b. lived about two hundred years ago.
c. to hurt animals.
d. about animals.

Now write the sentences on the lines below. Begin each sentence with a capital letter. End it with a period.

1. _____

2. _____

3. _____

4. _____

Now do numbers 5–8 the same way.

5. Johnny Appleseed

   walked _____

6. He planted _____

7. People treated him _____

8. An apple _____

a. from place to place.
b. with respect.
c. many apple seeds.
d. was named for him.

5. _____

6. _____

7. _____

8. _____

*Exercise B*

**Understanding the story.** Answer each question. Write complete sentences. Look back at the stories.

1. When did the two people in the stories live?

   *They lived* _____.

2. Where did the two people in the stories live?

   _____.

3. What did the two people in the stories love?

   *They loved* _____.

4. What was Mountain Mary's real name?

   *Her* _____.

5. Where did Mary take the animals in her garden?

   *She took* _____.

6. Where did Johnny Appleseed walk?

   *He walked* _____.

7. What did Johnny Appleseed carry with him?

   *He carried* _____.

8. What did Johnny exchange to get food?

   *He exchanged* _____.

*Exercise C*

**Using negatives in the past tense.** Negative sentences are sentences with *not.* The contraction for *did not* is *didn't.*

Johnny Appleseed *didn't have* a house.
For verbs in the past tense, the negative uses *didn't.* The base form of the verb follows *didn't.*

| Base Verb | Past Tense | Negative in the Past Tense |
|-----------|------------|----------------------------|
| have | had | didn't have |
| live | lived | didn't live |
| eat | ate | didn't eat |

Complete the sentences with negative verbs in the past. Use the verbs in parentheses ( ). One is done for you.

1. Mountain Mary *didn't live* in New York. (live)

   She lived in Pennsylvania.

2. Mountain Mary _____ to hurt animals. (want)

   She cared about animals.

3. She caught animals in her garden.

   But she _____ the animals. (kill)

4. She _____ a new kind of vegetable. (make)

   She created a new kind of apple.

5. Johnny Appleseed _____ many things. (carry)

   He carried only a cup and a sack.

6. Johnny _____ much money. (have)

   He exchanged apple trees to get food.

7. He saw moths near his campfire.

   He _____ to kill them. (want)

8. He put out his campfire.

   He _____ his food. (cook)

**Studying past tense verbs.** Find the past tense of the verbs at the left in the puzzle. Circle the past tense. Some verbs are regular, and some verbs are irregular.

call    grow
care    have
carry   leave
catch   live
cook    love
create  refuse
die     tell
eat     want

| W | C | Q | L | E | F | T | C | P | A | C |
|---|---|---|---|---|---|---|---|---|---|---|
| C | A | R | R | I | E | D | R | X | D | A |
| A | U | G | C | O | O | K | E | D | I | R |
| L | G | R | E | W | W | L | A | O | E | E |
| L | H | B | H | A | D | O | T | M | D | D |
| E | T | N | Y | L | I | V | E | D | X | O |
| D | H | W | A | N | T | E | D | Z | P | A |
| U | S | V | T | O | L | D | M | N | Z | T |
| Q | R | E | F | U | S | E | D | F | W | E |

*Exercise E*

**Using the past tense.** Complete the sentences. Use verbs from Exercise D.

1. Both Mountain Mary and Johnny Appleseed

   _____ during the early days of the United States.

2. Both Mountain Mary and Johnny Appleseed _____

   a legacy for future generations.

3. Both Mountain Mary and Johnny Appleseed _____

   nature.

4. Some animals _____ plants in Mary's garden.

5. Mary _____ the animals in her garden, but she

   didn't kill them.

6. She _____ to hurt a living creature.

7. She _____ parts of different apple trees together.

8. She _____ a new kind of apple.

9. The preacher _____ the people that Mary was a saint.

10. His real name was John Chapman, but everyone _____

    him Johnny Appleseed.

11. He _____ only a cup and sack.

12. He _____ in 1845.

*Exercise F*

**Adding vocabulary.** On the left are six words or idioms from the story. Complete each sentence by adding the correct word or idiom.

**cared about**

1. Johnny Appleseed and Mountain Mary left a _____. They left many plants to future generations. They also showed that nature is important.

**hurt**

2. Mary liked and helped people and animals. She _____ them.

**generous**

3. Mary helped people and animals. She was kind and _____.

**legacy**

4. People thought Johnny Appleseed was a good person. They treated him with _____.

**put out**

5. Johnny didn't want to _____ the moths near his campfire.

**respect**

6. So he _____ his fire.

*Exercise* G

**Speaking up.** Look at the conversation. Practice it with a partner.

*Activity A*

**Making riddles.** Follow the directions.

**1.** Work with a partner. Write 5 statements. Each tells about Mountain Mary, Johnny Appleseed, or both.

Examples:
I lived two hundred years ago. (Both)
I lived in the Ohio River valley. (Johnny Appleseed)
I had a garden. (Mountain Mary)

**2.** Work with another pair.

Read your clues to them. How many can they guess right? Then they read their clues to you. How many can you guess right?

*Activity B*

**Sharing ideas.** It's fun to share ideas with others. Discuss these questions with your partner or with the group. Write your answer to one of the questions.

What was the legacy of Mountain Mary?
What was the legacy of Johnny Appleseed?

Who are some famous people in the history of a country you know?
Why are these people famous?
Why do other people respect them?

_____

_____

_____

_____

_____

# HARVEST TIME

The *seasons* are a part of nature.
What is your favorite season?
What makes it special?

Harvest time is the time of year when people pick
food from fields. What seasons are harvest time?

How is human life like the seasons?

# Harvest Time

Granny looked out at the fields filled with fruits and vegetables. She felt the **cool** night air through the open **kitchen** window. "It's time to start to **can,**" she thought.

In her mind, she was already able to see the kitchen
5   shelves filled with shiny **jars** of peaches, pears, and plums. She could see jars filled with tomatoes, beets, and carrots. "Harvest time is the best time of year," thought Granny.

She looked out the window up into the night sky. There were many **stars.** They seemed unusually **bright.** Several
10  stars seemed to **move** in the sky. Granny finished cleaning the kitchen. The news was on the local radio station. "People continue to disappear from our area. Two more **are missing**. . . . We're in the middle of an unusually cool period for this time of year. . . . People report seeing
15  **strange** objects in the sky."

Granny really wasn't **paying attention.** She felt a cold breeze and closed the window.

Granny lived alone. Her husband was dead. Her children and grandchildren lived in the city. She slowly climbed
20  the **stairs** to bed. She was tired. She worked all day in the fields.

That night she had a dream. She saw all her family together in their Sunday clothes. They were having a picnic.
They waved to her. "I'm happy to see you," she tried to
say. But they disappeared into a great white **light.**

Suddenly Granny woke up. She remembered her dream.
She noticed that her room was filled with a white light like
in her dream. There was a humming noise like a machine.
Her whole house was shaking.

Then she heard a loud sound above her. The **roof** of her
bedroom disappeared. She heard the nails come out of the
roof. Then a **force lifted** her up out of her bedroom. It
pulled her up into the night sky. She was pulled up like any
carrot ready for harvest, torn from its bed in the ground.

Granny **closed** her eyes tightly. Soon the noise stopped,
and she felt herself **put down.** Granny slowly opened her
eyes. She saw that she was in a kind of **container.** Through
the glasslike walls of the container, she could see out. She
saw other containers with moving **forms** in them. All were
part of the harvest.

# YOU CAN ANSWER THESE QUESTIONS

Put an *x* in the box next to the correct answer.

*Reading Comprehension*

**1.** Granny wanted to put fruits and vegetables
- ❑ a. in jars.
- ❑ b. in the refrigerator.

**2.** The radio said that
- ❑ a. people were disappearing.
- ❑ b. the harvest was bad that year.

**3.** Granny had a dream about
- ❑ a. the harvest.
- ❑ b. her family.

**4.** In her bed, Granny saw a light, and she heard
- ❑ a. a crash.
- ❑ b. a humming noise.

**5.** At the end, Granny was in a container in the sky.
- ❑ a. Right.
- ❑ b. Wrong.

**6.** What do you think happened?
- ❑ a. Creatures from another world took Granny.
- ❑ b. Someone played a trick on Granny.

*Vocabulary*

**7.** Granny could see the jars filled with tomatoes. The word *jar* means
- ❑ a. a container made of glass.
- ❑ b. something to drink from.

**8.** The force lifted Granny out of the bedroom. The word *lift* means
- ❑ a. move up.
- ❑ b. move down.

*Idioms*

**9.** Granny was not paying attention to the radio. When you *pay attention,* you
- ❑ a. listen to and think about what is said.
- ❑ b. do not listen to what is said.

**10.** People were missing from the area. The idiom *be missing* means
- ❑ a. be moving.
- ❑ b. be gone.

How many questions did you answer correctly? Circle your score. Then fill in your score on the Score Chart on page 152.

| Number Correct | 1 | 2 | 3 | 4 | 5 | 6 | 7 | 8 | 9 | 10 |
|---|---|---|---|---|---|---|---|---|---|---|
| Score | 10 | 20 | 30 | 40 | 50 | 60 | 70 | 80 | 90 | 100 |

# EXERCISES TO HELP YOU

*Exercise A*

**Building sentences.** Make sentences by adding the correct letter.

1. Granny looked _____

2. In her mind, Granny

   could _____

3. Several stars seemed to _____

4. That night Granny _____

   a. had a dream.
   b. out at the fields.
   c. move in the sky.
   d. see jars filled with fruit.

Now write the sentences on the lines below. Begin each sentence with a capital letter. End it with a period.

1. _____

2. _____

3. _____

4. _____

Now do numbers 5–8 the same way.

5. Granny's room was _____

6. The roof of Granny's

   bedroom _____

7. A force lifted _____

8. Granny was in _____

   a. disappeared.
   b. filled with a white light.
   c. a container.
   d. Granny out of her bedroom.

5. _____

6. _____

7. _____

8. _____

**Understanding the story.** Answer each question.
Write complete sentences. Look back at the story.

1. Where was Granny at the start of the story?

   _____.

2. What time of the year was it?

   *It* _____.

3. What kinds of fruits and vegetables did Granny put into jars?

   *Granny put* _____.

4. What was strange about the sky?

   *Several* _____.

5. Who did Granny see in her dream?

   _____.

6. What disappeared from Granny's bedroom?

   _____.

7. Where did the force pull Granny?

   *The force pulled Granny* _____.

8. What did Granny see from her container?

   *She saw* _____.

*Exercise C*

**Using contractions.** A contraction is a short form. In a contraction, two words are used together. Study this chart.

| Contractions with *Be* | |
|---|---|
| **Present Tense** | |
| **Singular** | **Plural** |
| I'm (= I am) | we're (= we are) |
| you're (= you are) | you're (= you are) |
| he's (= he is) | they're (= they are) |
| she's (= she is) | |
| it's (= it is) | |

Complete the sentences. Use contractions with *be*. One is done for you.

1. Granny thought, "_____*It's*_____ time for the harvest."

2. The radio said, "_____ in the middle of a cool period."

3. Granny thought, "_____ tired."

4. Granny was tired.

   She thought, "_____ time for bed."

5. Granny saw her family in a dream.

   She thought, "_____ in their Sunday clothes."

6. Granny saw her husband in a dream.

   She thought, "_____ happy to see me."

7. Granny heard the strange noise.

   "_____ scared," she thought.

8. At the end, Granny is no longer at her home.

   _____ in a container in the sky.

*Exercise D*

**Using *there was* and *there were*.** A singular noun comes after *there was*. A plural noun comes after *there were*.

Singular
*There was* a strange noise.

Plural
*There were* many stars in the sky.

Complete the sentences with *There was* or *There were*. One is done for you.

1. *There were* many vegetables in the fields.

2. _____ an old woman in the kitchen.

3. _____ shelves in the kitchen.

4. _____ many people in Granny's dream.

5. _____ a bright light in Granny's bedroom.

6. _____ a strong humming noise in Granny's bedroom.

7. _____ many containers in the sky.

8. _____ people in the other containers in the sky.

## Exercise E

**Understanding vocabulary.** Look back in the story. Find the words for each category. Complete the words.

| Fruits | Vegetables | Things in the House |
|--------|-----------|---------------------|
| p _ _ _ h e s | t _ m _ _ _ e s | k _ _ c h _ _ |
| p _ _ r s | b _ _ t s | s t _ _ _ s |
| _ l _ m s | c _ _ _ _ t s | b _ d r _ _ m |
| | | r _ _ f |

## Exercise F

**Answer the riddles.** Use the words from Exercise E. Write the correct answer in the blank.

**1.** I am red. I grow above the ground.

What am I? _____

**2.** I am the top of a house. What am I? _____

**3.** You cook and make food in me. What am I? _____

**4.** You walk up me. What am I? _____

**5.** I am orange. I grow under the ground.

What am I? _____

**6.** Sometimes my skin is green. You can eat me.

What am I? _____

## Exercise G

**Speaking up.** Look at the conversations. Practice them with a partner.

*Activity A*

**Telling the story in pictures.** Draw pictures to show the story.

1. Draw a picture of Granny at the beginning of the story.
2. Draw a picture of Granny at the end of the story.
3. Draw a picture of any other part of the story.

Talk about your pictures in small groups.

*Activity B*

**Sharing ideas.** It's fun to share ideas with others. Discuss these questions with your partner or with the group. Write your answer to one of the questions.

Who do you think took Granny into the sky?
What unusual things do you think were happening?

Do you think any part of the story was scary?
Which part? Why?

Stories about people from other planets are called science fiction. Do you know any science fiction stories? Share them.

_____

_____

_____

_____

_____

_____

_____

_____

_____

# GUILT AND GRASS

## Part 1

What kinds of *chores* do you do around your house?
Do you like to do chores?

Do you know people who always talk about others?
Why do you think people say bad things about others?

# Guilt and Grass

## Part 1

Mrs. Farley and Mrs. King spent Thursday mornings
together. They stood at the back **fence** between their
**yards.** They met there about 8:45 a.m. They waited for
Georgia Haney Graham to come out of her house in her
5   gardening clothes.

While they waited, they talked about their neighbors.
They **gossiped** about their **neighbors'** problems. They
talked about the Harrelson girl. "When are she and her
boyfriend going to get married?" they asked. They
10   remarked about Mr. Jackson's new job. "Is he going to
make enough money?" they asked. But most of all, they
wondered about Georgia Haney Graham. "Why does she
come out every Thursday to **mow** her **lawn?**" they asked.
"She is seventy-five years old!"

15   Georgia put on her old straw hat. She left the cool **interior**
of her house for the bright sun **outside.** She took the old
lawn mower from the back **shed.** She noticed her neighbors already at the back fence. "Gossips," she said to
herself. "The only thing they do is to talk about their
20   neighbors."

Georgia didn't like to be in the sun. But still she came out every Thursday to mow the lawn. She **struggled** to push the old lawn mower over the **grass.**

She knew that Mrs. Farley and Mrs. King wondered about 25  her. "They really want to know why I do this," she thought. Then she **frowned.** As she mowed, she thought back to the beginning.

It was the year the handsome young English teacher came to her high school. The usual English teacher, Mrs. Ryan, 30  had a car accident. The new teacher was going to **take her place** for the rest of the school year. All the girls wanted Mr. Wallace to notice them, and so did Georgia.

When Mr. Wallace **announced** a poetry **contest,** Georgia decided to be the winner. Every night after school, Georgia 35  tried to write a **poem.** But every night she got lost in a **daydream:** Mr. Wallace was giving her the first-place **prize,** and he looked deeply into her eyes. The days passed. Georgia had a drawer filled with crumpled papers. But she didn't have a poem. So what happened the day of the 40  contest seemed like fate.

*To be continued.*

Put an *x* in the box next to the correct answer.

*Reading Comprehension*

1. Georgia was
   - ❏ a. an old woman.
   - ❏ b. a young woman.

2. Every Thursday morning, Georgia
   - ❏ a. gossiped with her neighbors.
   - ❏ b. mowed the lawn.

3. Mrs. Farley and Mrs. King were
   - ❏ a. Georgia's friends.
   - ❏ b. Georgia's neighbors.

4. Mrs. Farley and Mrs. King wondered why Georgia
   - ❏ a. wasn't married.
   - ❏ b. mowed the lawn.

5. Georgia was
   - ❏ a. able to write a poem for the contest.
   - ❏ b. not able to write a poem for the contest.

*Vocabulary*

6. Mrs. Farley and Mrs. King gossiped about their neighbors. The word *gossip* means
   - ❏ a. talking about yourself.
   - ❏ b. talking about other people.

7. Georgia struggled to move the lawn mower over the grass. The word *struggle* means
   - ❏ a. work hard; make a big effort.
   - ❏ b. move like a snake.

8. Mr. Wallace announced a poetry contest. A *contest* is
   - ❏ a. a game or test that often has a prize.
   - ❏ b. a meeting at school where all students come.

9. Georgia daydreamed that she won the prize. The word *daydream* means
   - ❏ a. sleep during the day instead of at night.
   - ❏ b. think about some nice things that might happen.

*Idioms*

10. The idiom *take someone's place* means
   - ❏ a. do someone's job, often for a certain time.
   - ❏ b. move into someone's house for a certain time.

How many questions did you answer correctly? Circle your score. Then fill in your score on the Score Chart on page 152.

| Number Correct | 1 | 2 | 3 | 4 | 5 | 6 | 7 | 8 | 9 | 10 |
|---|---|---|---|---|---|---|---|---|---|---|
| Score | 10 | 20 | 30 | 40 | 50 | 60 | 70 | 80 | 90 | 100 |

# EXERCISES TO HELP YOU

*Exercise A*

**Building sentences.** Make sentences by adding the correct letter.

1. Mrs. Farley and

   Mrs. King _____

2. Georgia came out every

   Thursday _____

3. Georgia struggled to push _____

4. The two women wondered _____

   **a.** about Georgia.
   **b.** the lawn mower over the grass.
   **c.** to mow the lawn.
   **d.** talked about their neighbors.

Now write the sentences on the lines below. Begin each sentence with a capital letter. End it with a period.

1. _____

2. _____

3. _____

4. _____

Now do numbers 5–8 the same way.

5. The new teacher

   took _____

6. Georgia decided to _____

7. Georgia _____

8. Georgia got lost _____

   **a.** win the poetry contest.
   **b.** Mrs. Ryan's place.
   **c.** tried to write a poem.
   **d.** in a daydream.

5. _____

6. _____

7. _____

8. _____

*Exercise B*

**Understanding the story.** Answer each question.
Write complete sentences. Look back at the story.

1. Where did Mrs. Farley and Mrs. King meet?

   *They met* _____.

2. Who did they wait for?

   *They waited* _____.

3. How old was Georgia?

   _____.

4. What did Georgia do every Thursday morning?

   *She mowed* _____.

5. Who was Mr. Wallace?

   _____.

6. What did Mr. Wallace announce?

   *He announced* _____.

7. What did Georgia decide to do?

   *She decided* _____.

8. What did Georgia see in her daydream?

   *Mr. Wallace gave* _____.

*Exercise C*
**Using question words.** Study this chart.

| Who | for people: | *Who* mowed the lawn?<br>*Georgia* mowed the lawn. |
|-----|-------------|----------------------------------------------------|
| **What** | for things: | *What* did Georgia put on?<br>Georgia put on *her old hat.* |
| **When** | for time: | *When* did the women meet?<br>They met *in the morning.* |
| **Where** | for places: | *Where* was the mower?<br>It was *in the shed.* |
| **Why** | for reasons: | *Why* did Georgia wear her hat?<br>She wore it *because the sun was hot.* |

Complete each question with the correct question word.

1. _____ did Mrs. Farley and Mrs. King stand?

   They stood **at the back fence.**

2. _____ did Mrs. Farley and Mrs. King meet?

   They met **about 8:45 A.M.**

3. _____ did Mrs. Farley and Mrs. King meet?

   They met **because they wanted to gossip.**

4. _____ did they wait for?

   They waited for **Georgia.**

5. _____ did Georgia take from the shed?

   She took **the old lawn mower** from the shed.

6. _____ didn't like to be in the sun?

   **Georgia** didn't like to be in the sun.

7. _____ did Georgia mow the lawn?

   She mowed the lawn **every Thursday.**

8. _____ did Georgia push?

   She pushed **the lawn mower.**

*Exercise D*

**Putting words in the correct order.** Make sentences by putting the words in the correct order. Write each sentence in the blank. The sentences are about the story.

1.  women / talked / The / neighbors / about / their

    _____.

2.  Georgia / old / hat / put / her / on

    _____.

3.  took / mower / Georgia / from / shed / the / the

    _____.

4.  noticed / Georgia / fence / at / neighbors / the / her

    _____.

5.  like / Georgia / didn't / be / to / sun / the / in

    _____.

*Exercise E*

**Understanding vocabulary.** Match each word at the left with its meaning. Write the letter in the blank.

1.  announced _____
2.  fence _____
3.  frowned _____
4.  grass _____
5.  mowed _____
6.  prize _____
7.  shed _____
8.  yard _____

a. a small house to keep tools in
b. cut (the grass)
c. a green plant that covers a yard
d. a railing or wall, often made of wood, around a yard
e. told people news
f. area in front or in back of a house
g. looked unhappy or angry
h. something you get when you win a contest

## Exercise F

**Using vocabulary.** Complete the sentences. The sentences tell about the story. Use the words from Exercise E. Use each word once.

1. The two women stood at the _____.

2. Georgia _____ the lawn on Thursday.

3. Georgia went out into the _____ behind her house.

4. Georgia's lawn mower was in the _____.

5. It was hard to cut the _____ with the old lawn mower.

6. Georgia _____ when she thought about the past. Her face showed that her thoughts were not happy.

7. The teacher _____ a poetry contest. There was going to be a prize.

8. Georgia had a daydream. In it, she was the winner of the poetry _____.

## Exercise G

**Speaking up.** Look at the conversation. Practice them with a partner.

*Activity A*

**Guessing the end.** What will happen next? What do you think Georgia's secret is?

1. Work in small groups. Think of two secrets.
2. Share your ideas with the class.

*Activity B*

**Reading a poem.** Follow these directions.
1. Look for a poem in English. Choose a poem you like. Practice reading it.
2. Read your poem to a small group.

*Activity C*

**Sharing ideas.** It's fun to share ideas with others. Discuss these questions with your partner or with the group. Write your answer to one of the questions.

What did Mrs. Farley and Mrs. King gossip about?
What did they want to know about Georgia?

What did Georgia think about Mrs. Farley and Mrs. King? Did she like them?

Were you ever in a contest? What happened?
Did you ever win a prize? What happened?

_____

_____

_____

_____

_____

_____

_____

# GUILT AND GRASS

## Part 2

Do you think it is wrong to *cheat* at school?
Why?

Did you ever find something another person lost?
Did you try to return it? What happened?

Why do you think people *steal*?

# Guilt and Grass

## Part 2

The day of the poetry contest, Georgia didn't eat lunch.
She went to sit at her **favorite** place in the park. There she
noticed a notebook. She opened it, but there was no name
in it. The notebook was filled with drawings and poems.
5   She **got interested in** looking at the drawings in the book.
Then she read one of the poems. After that, things seemed
to happen as in a dream.

Georgia's poem won first place in the contest. The **last** day
of the school year, she walked up to the stage in front of
10   the entire school. Mr. Wallace gave her the prize. When he
handed it to her, he looked deeply into her eyes. He said
that she surprised him with her **talent.** Georgia **received**
**congratulations** from all her family and friends. But she
didn't feel **happy.**

15   Summer was always Georgia's favorite time of year. But
that year she wasn't **looking forward to** it. She **rarely**
went to the swimming pool or on picnics with her friends.
She felt a shadow over her. She seemed to **always** be
carrying a great weight.

20 One hot morning she heard the sound of the lawn mower in the yard. The heat was already **terrible.** There was a young black man mowing the lawn. His shirt was wet with **sweat** from the heat. "That's not a job I would like. I'm glad my parents **hire** someone to do it," Georgia thought.

25 The man walked by her window. Georgia **realized** that she recognized him. His face was among those in the notebook.

"Would you like a glass of water?" Georgia asked when he went by the window again.

"Why yes, ma'am, thank you," said the young man. When

30 she handed him the glass, he looked **directly** at her. He studied her face with a **serious** look. He **hesitated** for a moment. Then he spoke. "I read about your poetry prize in the newspaper. Congratulations."

"Thank you," Georgia answered.

35 "You chose one of my favorite poems," he said. With that, he gave the mower a push and walked out of her **view.**

Georgia spent the rest of the summer inside. The next summer Georgia told her parents, "I'll take care of the yard work." And she **continued** to do so for the rest of her life.

# YOU CAN ANSWER THESE QUESTIONS

Put an *x* in the box next to the correct answer.

*Reading Comprehension*

1. The day of the poetry contest, Georgia
   - ❑ a. found a notebook.
   - ❑ b. lost her notebook.

2. Mr. Wallace gave Georgia
   - ❑ a. a scolding.
   - ❑ b. the prize for the poetry contest.

3. After she won the contest, Georgia was
   - ❑ a. happy.
   - ❑ b. unhappy.

4. Georgia recognized the young man because his picture was in the
   - ❑ a. newspaper.
   - ❑ b. notebook.

5. Which is true?
   - ❑ a. The young man wrote the poem that won the contest.
   - ❑ b. Georgia wrote the poem that won the contest.

6. Why did Georgia mow the lawn?
   - ❑ a. Her parents told her to mow the lawn.
   - ❑ b. Georgia felt that she had done wrong.

*Vocabulary*

7. Georgia's talent surprised Mr. Wallace. To have *talent* means
   - ❑ a. you write many poems.
   - ❑ b. you can do something well.

8. You use the word *congratulations* to a tell a person that you are
   - ❑ a. not happy about something the person did.
   - ❑ b. happy when something good happened to the person.

9. Georgia realized that she knew the man's face. The word *realize* means
   - ❑ a. suddenly learn something.
   - ❑ b. make a drawing of something.

*Idioms*

10. The idiom *look forward to* means
    - ❑ a. get excited about what will happen in the future.
    - ❑ b. look directly ahead and not look at anything else.

How many questions did you answer correctly? Circle your score. Then fill in your score on the Score Chart on page 152.

| Number Correct | 1 | 2 | 3 | 4 | 5 | 6 | 7 | 8 | 9 | 10 |
|---|---|---|---|---|---|---|---|---|---|---|
| Score | 10 | 20 | 30 | 40 | 50 | 60 | 70 | 80 | 90 | 100 |

*Exercise A*

**Building sentences.** Make sentences by adding the correct letter.

1.  The notebook was _____

2.  Georgia's poem _____

3.  Mr. Wallace gave _____

4.  Georgia received _____

a. won first place.
b. filled with drawings and poems.
c. congratulations from her family and friends.
d. Georgia a prize.

Now write the sentences on the lines below. Begin each sentence with a capital letter. End it with a period.

1.  _____

2.  _____

3.  _____

4.  _____

Now do numbers 5–8 the same way.

5.  Georgia wasn't

    looking _____

6.  Georgia recognized _____

7.  The man said that _____

8.  Georgia spent _____

a. the young man.
b. forward to summer.
c. rest of the summer inside.
d. Georgia chose one of his favorite poems.

5.  _____

6.  _____

7.  _____

8.  _____

*Exercise B*

**Understanding the story.** Answer each question. Write complete sentences. Look back at the story.

1. Where did Georgia go for lunch the day of the contest?

   *She went* _____ .

2. Georgia found a notebook. What was the notebook filled with?

   *It was* _____ .

3. What did Georgia receive from Mr. Wallace?

   *She received* _____ .

4. What did Georgia receive from her family and friends?

   _____ .

5. Who was mowing the lawn on the hot day?

   _____ .

6. How did Georgia recognize the young man?

   *His face* _____ .

7. What did the man tell Georgia?

   *He said she chose* _____ .

8. Where did Georgia spend the rest of the summer?

   *She spent* _____ .

*Exercise C*

**Using the past tense.** Retell the story. Write complete sentences. Use the past tense form of the verbs. Some verbs are regular. Some verbs are irregular. Follow the example.

Example:
Georgia /go home
Georgia went home for lunch.

1. Georgia / go to her favorite place

   _____.

2. Georgia/ notice a notebook

   _____.

3. She / read a poem

   _____.

4. Her poem / win first place

   _____.

5. Mr. Wallace / give her the prize

   _____.

6. Georgia / receive congratulations

   _____.

7. Georgia / be sad

   _____.

8. Georgia / hear a lawn mower

   _____.

9. Georgia / hand the man a glass of water

   _____.

10. The man / speak to Georgia

    _____.

11. Georgia / choose one of his favorite poems

    _____.

12. The man / walk out of view

    _____.

*Exercise D*

**Adding an adjective.** Complete the sentences by adding the correct adjective. Use each adjective once.

favorite

**1.** Georgia went to one of her

_____ places for lunch.

happy

**2.** She got _____ in the faces in

the notebook.

interested

**3.** On the _____ day of school,

Georgia received the prize.

last

**4.** Georgia won the poetry contest, but she

wasn't _____.

serious

**5.** One day the heat was _____.

She heard the lawn mower.

terrible

**6.** The young man gave Georgia a

_____ look. He knew that she

used his favorite poem.

*Exercise E*

**Adding vocabulary.** On the left are five words and an idiom from the story. Complete each sentence by adding the correct word or words.

**congratulations** 1. Georgia won the poetry contest. Georgia's family was proud of her. Georgia received _____ from her family.

**hesitated** 2. Mr. Wallace said that Georgia's _____ surprised him. He didn't know she was so good at writing poetry.

**hired** 3. She was unhappy. She didn't _____ summer.

**look forward to** 4. Georgia's parents paid someone money to mow the lawn. They _____ someone to do the job.

**realized** 5. Georgia saw the man mowing the lawn. She _____ that his face was in the notebook.

**talent** 6. The young black man _____ and then he spoke. He offered Georgia congratulations about the poetry contest.

*Exercise F*

**Speaking up.** Look at the conversations. Practice them with a partner.

*Activity A*

**Taking a survey.** Follow the directions.

1. What are your favorite things? Look at the chart. Complete the column under "You."
2. Now work with a partner. Ask your partner questions. Complete the right side of the chart.

Ask questions like this:
What is your favorite story in this book?
Who is your favorite person in this book?

|  | You | Your Partner |
|---|---|---|
| **Favorite story in this book** |  |  |
| Favorite character in this book |  |  |
| Favorite song |  |  |
| Favorite poem |  |  |
| Favorite movie |  |  |

*Activity B*

**Sharing ideas.** It's fun to share ideas with others. Discuss these questions with your partner or with the group. Write your answer to one of the questions.

The word *guilt* means to feel sorry that you did something wrong.
Why does Georgia feel guilt?

How did the poetry contest change Georgia's life? Why does Georgia mow the lawn?

When people do something wrong, sometimes they are punished. What was Georgia's punishment? Who gave her the punishment?

How do you feel about Georgia? Do you feel sorry for her? Why or why not?

# Score Chart

This is the Score Chart for You Can Answer These Questions. Shade in your score for each unit. For example, if your score was 80 for **Hello, Good-bye,** look at the bottom of the chart for **Hello, Good-bye.** Shade in the bar up to the 80 mark. By looking at this chart, you can see how well you did on each unit.

| Score | | | | | | | | |
|---|---|---|---|---|---|---|---|---|
| 100 | | | | | | | | |
| 90 | | | | | | | | |
| 80 | | | | | | | | |
| 70 | | | | | | | | |
| 60 | | | | | | | | |
| 50 | | | | | | | | |
| 40 | | | | | | | | |
| 30 | | | | | | | | |
| 20 | | | | | | | | |
| 10 | | | | | | | | |
| Unit Title | Hello, Good-bye | Roots | Lions' Tales | The Green-Eyed Monster | The Gift | Creation Stories | Names | All in the Mind |

| | An Ancient Greek Hero | Sticks and Stones | The World is Wrong, Not Me | Apples, Apples | Harvest Time | Guilt and Grass, Part One | Guilt and Grass, Part Two |
|---|---|---|---|---|---|---|---|
| 100 | | | | | | | |
| 90 | | | | | | | |
| 80 | | | | | | | |
| 70 | | | | | | | |
| 60 | | | | | | | |
| 50 | | | | | | | |
| 40 | | | | | | | |
| 30 | | | | | | | |
| 20 | | | | | | | |
| 10 | | | | | | | |